China on the Lam

On Foot Across the People's Republic

Books by Bill Purves

Barefoot in the Boardroom – Adventure and Misadventure in the People's Republic of China

Three Chinas

China on the Lam – On Foot Across the People's Republic

Living With Landmines

China on the Lam

On Foot Across the People's Republic

Bill Purves

Asia 2000 Limited
Hong Kong

ISBN: 962-8783-08-4

Published by Asia 2000 Ltd
Fifth Floor, 31A Wyndham Street
Central, Hong Kong

http://www.asia2000.com.hk

Typeset in Goudy by Asia 2000 Ltd
Printed in Hong Kong by Editions Quaille

First Printing 2002

For

The Peasants

Contents

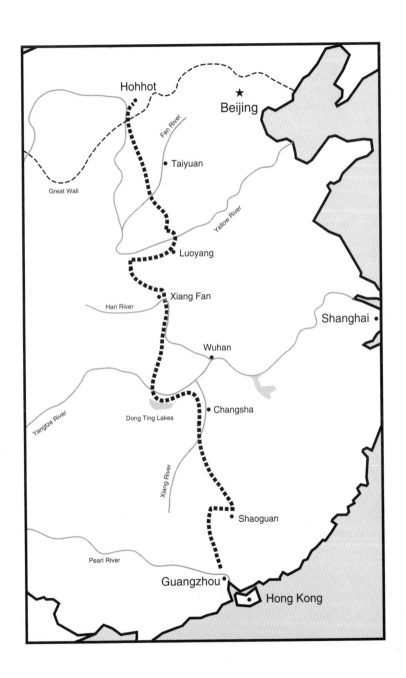

Hohhot

★
Beijing

Fen River

• Taiyuan

Great Wall

Yellow River

• Luoyang

Xiang Fan

Han River

Shanghai •

Wuhan
•

Yangtze River

Dong Ting Lakes

• Changsha

Xiang River

• Shaoguan

Pearl River

Guangzhou •

Hong Kong

Introduction

I spent the summer of 1998 walking across China. It's a country about the size of Canada, so one of the largest in the world. The journey took me more than three months, and it was quite an adventure. If you'd care to accompany me through the following pages, I'll tell you all about it. The appendix even suggests how you could organize such a trip for yourself.

For reasons which will become clear, I can't properly acknowledge the invaluable help I received from so many old and new friends in China. I can't mention them by name, but without their help and support I would never have made it. I express here my gratitude.

I must, though, mention Sheila and Lilianne Purves, Christine Delaney and Michelle Baker who helped with the preparation of this manuscript. Thanks too to Peter and Ben Bruckner of Designers' CADD Company who helped me draw the map and process the photographs. Thomas Lui helped me to convince myself that a trip like this might be possible, and then to get walking.

Most of the little towns I visited in the course of the trip were named for me in obscure Chinese dialects which have no accepted English orthography. In writing about major cities and provinces like Beijing and Hunan, I've tried to use the official spellings, but for all the small places I've created phonetic spellings which I hope will render something close to the correct name in the local dialect.

China on the Lam is actually the third in a series of descriptions of life in modern China. *Barefoot in the Boardroom – Venture and Misadventure in the People's Republic of China* (Allen & Unwin 1991) describes my experiences living and working in a traditional Chinese factory, and presents in some detail the life of the "worker" class. *Three Chinas* (NC Press 1994) discusses the life of China's "intellectuals" and compares it with the situation in Hong Kong and in Taiwan. In *China on the Lam* we are dealing with the "peasants" and, as in those previous works, I've tried to slip in among my travel adventures a few observations about life in the Chinese countryside in the last decade of the twentieth century. China has been changing so quickly in recent years that some of these observations will inevitably be out of date by the time you read them. Such errors, and indeed all others, are mine alone.

Let's get started.

1

Off on the Wrong Foot

If you were planning to walk across China, how would you begin? Most people imagine starting off in the deserts of the far west and finishing up on the east coast in, for example, Shanghai. It sounds logical, but when you look a bit closer, it turns out to be a scheme that's pretty difficult to implement. The deadly deserts of western China call for preparations worthy of an Antarctic expedition. As soon as word of those preparations got out, the Public Security Bureau (the police) would make sure that the expedition never reached its jumping off point. Foreigners are barred from almost all of western China. (Indeed, foreigners are still barred from almost every part of China.) The conventional west-to-east route is the path to loads of trouble and expense.

My trip wasn't that sort of caper. It wasn't an expedition at all. It could better be described as one guy with a small knapsack and a few bucks in his pocket wandering through the countryside.

China is a country about the size of Canada. My objectives were to sample some of China's diversity and to see for myself how the peasants are dealing with the recent upheavals in Chinese life – the disbanding of the communes and the recent growth of a market economy after a generation of striving for socialism. With those objectives in mind, and since I live in Hong Kong, I set out to cross the country on foot from south to north. Or maybe I just wanted some exercise. I forget.

So, if you were planning to walk across China from south to north, how would you begin? Someone with a romantic turn of mind might, perhaps, think immediately of starting off on a palm-fringed beach and finishing up with a toe poking through the barbed wire into Mongolia. And I must say that I thought of that too. But in fact I started in a brickworks.

Maybe I'm not very romantic, but I let myself be dissuaded from the palm-fringed beach option by a couple of practical considerations. In the first place, the barbed wire on the Mongolian end is almost surely backed up with land mines. Ah…yes. Well, now that we've compromised on the finishing point, what about the southern end of the trek? There too the dangers are not insignificant. The skyrocketing prosperity of southern China in recent years has put a large number of unreliable vehicles in the hands of learner drivers. The narrow highways are overcrowded with trucks, minibuses, motorcycles and even a few cars. Many have feeble wipers, poor alignment, uncertain steering. Their bald tires and inexperienced drivers make them a lethal stream of semi-guided missiles. So my Central Guiding Principle Number One for traveling around on foot is to get off the roads and stay off, especially in southern China. Central Guiding Principle Number One: Don't walk on any road shown on the map. Even riding around in cars and minibuses is relatively risky. From Hong Kong, positioning myself on the nearest palm-fringed launch pad would have involved a couple of days shoehorned into a minibus full of chain smokers careening along southern highways. You really have to be pretty romantic.

So I started in a brickworks.

On a blustery, showery spring evening I boarded the riverboat that runs overnight from Hong Kong to the southern city of Guangzhou. This is a relatively scenic boat trip at any time, but the night run from Hong Kong begins with a spectacular panorama of the lights of the city and the hundreds of ships moored in one of the world's busiest harbours. I settled down for the night in one of the vast bunkrooms that comprise the second class. By first light the ship was approaching Guangzhou, the hub of China's recent industrial development. The river was alive with boats, scows, launches and ferries feeding food, fuel and manpower to the city's ongoing economic boom. Though I'd experienced this boat trip many times before, I was on deck at first light in the drizzle and fog, taking it in.

Disembarkation and customs were a bit of a rugby scrum. My knapsack for a cross-country journey was a good bit smaller and more manageable than the unwieldy bundles hefted by my fellow passengers returning from Hong Kong to the relative scarcities of China. The customs hall featured a special channel for foreigners carrying passports instead of the "visiting home pass" that most Hong Kong people use. The policeman at that end of the hall was handing out the English version of the arrival form. These forms are usually distributed on the boat, but now I realized why the purser had been out of stock. In the other lines the policemen were selling the Chinese version of the form at one yuan a piece. (At the time, one yuan was worth about 13 U.S. cents.)

Despite this, the foreigners' line wasn't very busy and I was away from the pier by 7:00 for the long walk to the railway station at the other end of town. Not too bad at that hour of the morning, as many of the shops were still shuttered, not yet blocking the sidewalks with their merchandise. On the way I bought some packages of instant noodles, peanuts, candy and several bottles of (ostensibly) clean water. That brought me to the railroad station just about in time for the 9:05 train.

At that point I had a stroke of good luck. In keeping with Central Guiding Principle Number One, I had decided that rather than try to walk out of the city, I would buy a ticket to the first station up the line and figure out from there how to get onto roads heading north that are too small to be shown on the map. According to the schedules on the wall, the first station was a place called Yuan Tan, about 65km northwest of the city.

Train service is pretty good in China, but ticket selling is a mess. The standard procedure involves long waits lined up in a grotty station hall among bullyboys and roving pickpockets. With no one to help watch my gear, I'd have to strap my knapsack to my chest and shuffle slowly through the line with my hands in my pockets. Reaching the station at nine, I was expecting that by the time I'd negotiated the ticketing process I'd be catching a train about midday. Instead, I ran into a scalper with a ticket for Yuan Tan. For 13 yuan, I was in Yuan Tan by 10:45.

There were plenty of seats, but sitting in a cold, dank carriage watching the rain course down the window wasn't the happiest possible start to this sort of trip. By the time I emerged from Yuan Tan's filthy station into the muddy main square it was raining steadily. The glutinous expanse was crowded with vendors trying to keep dry and not succeeding. I bought some hard-boiled eggs. Struggling to postpone the inevitable, unwilling even to unfold my clean, dry map, I decided it was time for one last hot meal.

The meal, at least, wasn't bad. China is a rough place in many ways, but where food is concerned you can't go far wrong. Almost any little hole-in-the-wall can whip up simple fare that's tasty, fresh and well cooked. The trick is in learning to ignore the filthy floor, the grimy fingernails and the overflowing spittoon under the table. In this case the fried noodles were nicely done, and the big plate of sautéed vegetables was hot from the wok and delicious. Eight yuan for the lot. The extra tea from the pot went to top up the bottled water drunk on the train.

Okay, I admit it. Looking back now I'm sure I could have found a route to walk out of Yuan Tan and launch the trip. But my feet were already damp. I was already besieged by a mob of curious citizens crowding out of the rain to quiz me on my itinerary. I was fresh. I was green. I didn't have my slick story worked out yet. To put them off, I told them that I'd left the train here to visit a regional tourist attraction mentioned on the map: the Fei Lai gorge. As a story it worked fine, but it had the predictable result that several in the crowd offered to be my guide, my companion or my driver. I think I did pretty well to escape encumbered with nothing more than directions to the correct minibus.

In fact, directions were hardly necessary. The muddy slough in front of Yuan Tan station supplements its role as town square and market by serving as the minibus terminal as well. Decrepit vans with crude signs in their windshields were lined up on both sides of the market street, aggravating the congestion. The one with the Chau Sam sign left from almost directly in front of the little joint where I had been entertaining the masses. By the time I'd managed to finish my noodles and extricate myself from my public, the next bus was sitting there about half full. Or so I thought.

The minibus is a popular form of transportation throughout Southeast Asia, but in mainland China minibus service has really proliferated only with the liberation of the private economy in the late 1980s. A couple of families get together and buy a Japanese van. They install seats for about 18 passengers and cooperate to man trips over a 10 to 50-kilometre route of their own devising. The men take turns driving; the women serve as their conductors and touts. It's probably helpful if one of the people involved has a driver's license, but in any case they soon learn. It's a simple and lucrative business once you've raised the money for the van and squared a few local bigwigs.

When I boarded the Chau Sam bus, there were only three or four empty seats left. In good weather that's often close enough. The driver will head out expecting to pick up a few more passengers along the highway. But not today. We waited until a few more passengers arrived with their wet bundles and live chickens. All the seats were now full. The driver fired up the engine, and his assistant yelled, "Chau Sam, Chau Sam, lets go." But we didn't go. This team must have been particularly hard up for cash. Slowly, gradually more riders trickled in. Tiny stools were placed in the aisle. Bundles were piled on the engine cover. Children climbed into their mothers' laps. Still the driver didn't put the machine in gear. By the time we left, there were 28 passengers squeezed into an 18-seater. I hugged the pack in my lap and consoled myself that the shoulders forced against the loose fitting windows were pretty effective in keeping out the muddy spray and the draughts.

The move from the noodle joint out through the rain into the minibus had shaken off my original entourage, but as the passengers began to show exasperation with the driver's greed and procrastination, they began to strike up conversations. Once again, I was the centre of attention. Not imagining that I could speak Cantonese, they were wondering aloud among themselves what a foreigner could possibly be doing in this little town. I eventually broke the ice by suggesting, "He doesn't seem to be going very far in this minibus today." That surprised them, but the result was distressing. They immediately led me through the exact same catechism that had disrupted my lunch: "Where are you from? Said one. "Yes, okay, but where were you born?" said another. "How old are you?" another chimed in. "How many children do you have?" said yet a fourth. I'd uncovered a serious problem. Traversing the nation off the main roads was going to involve asking directions of almost everyone I met, all day every day. I was confident that I could count on this sort of help and support, but now, too late, I realized that I was going to have to pay a price. I had condemned myself to three months of catechism.

2

On the Tourist Trail

Rain or no rain, it was time to get off the bus, get walking and try to come to grips with what I had gotten myself into. When I'd concocted the story of intending to visit the Fei Lai gorge, my inquisitors had recommended taking the minibus about 20km West to the village of Chau Sam on the Bat Gong branch of the Pearl River. The gorge is on the Bat Gong where it flows through some hills about 15km north of Chau Sam. Rivers in this part of China are diked against flooding, and the noodle shop experts had confirmed that I could follow the dike north out of Chau Sam up the river to the gorge. That would take me off the roads and get me started.

In the event, that plan too was changed. On the bus, the old man in the seat behind me volunteered the information that if I was intending to walk through the gorge, there was indeed a trail, but it was on the other bank of the river. I could cross on a ferry about 10km north of Chau Sam, but if I intended to do that, there was no point in going all the way into town. It would be quicker and easier to get off a few kilometres before Chau Sam and walk northwest through the fields directly to the ferry crossing. He arranged it with the bus driver, and with the good wishes of my fellow passengers I stepped out into the cold drizzle at 2:30 on a gray afternoon at the gate of a disused brickworks. A grim beginning.

To the northwest, rice paddies stretched away into the mist. Behind me, steady traffic threw up dirty spray from the highway. All I could see of the brickworks was a tall chimney poking over a blank brick wall closed with a rusty gate. A lane stretched ahead along the wall. The first few metres were metalled with cinders; after that all was muddy clay. Though I was standing almost exactly on the Tropic of Cancer, the temperature was about 8 degrees centigrade with a keen southerly breeze. Standing there, I'd soon be cold as well as wet and dirty. I began to walk.

Planning the trip, of course I'd expected rain. Holing up and waiting for better weather wasn't an option because China requires visas of almost all visitors, and a Chinese tourist visa is good for only thirty days. So I was prepared to walk and camp in the rain. Although I had no tent, I had a poncho and a waterproof fly. What I hadn't realized is that I couldn't just find a piece of waste ground and set up my fly, for the same reason that I couldn't just duck into a noodle stall and wait out a shower. I was learning that my every move in China was going to be the subject of intense curiosity and investigation. Only when I was actually walking (and sometimes not even then) would I have a moment to myself. At 2:30 on a rainy afternoon, I realized that I was not only going to have to find a place to set up a dry camp for the night, I needed a decent campsite that was also away from civilization and out of sight. And once encamped I'd never be able to show a light or do anything to attract attention. Not for fear of robbers. Quite the contrary. For fear that I'd immediately be invited to the nearest village, fed, fêted and interrogated for hours about my origins, my family, my job and all my personal details.

The foreigner walking in the countryside will every day encounter a couple of hundred people who have literally never before seen a Westerner face-to-face. Their reaction seems to vary from one district to another. In some areas the men will actively initiate conversation with a stranger. Elsewhere, they wait for the visitor to stop and ask a question before trying to satisfy their curiosity. Women will always let the stranger make the first move. But once the questioning starts, it always follows the same course. Only the order of questions might vary a bit.

"Where are you going?"

"Where have you come from?"

"Where do you live?"

"What are you doing around here?"

"How old are you?"

"Are you married?"

"Where is your wife?"

"Is your wife Chinese?"

"How many children do you have?"

"What is your job?"

"What kind of work unit do you work for?"

"What is your wife's job?"

"How much do you earn in a month?"

and so on, and so on. There are perhaps 50 standard questions on the list, and how far you get with each person you meet depends only on how much time you have to stop and chat. A Chinese peasant would rarely be too busy to take time to interrogate a foreigner. Visiting a village overnight, it's easy to go through the entire list four or five times. The whole business became so repetitive that I imagined printing up handbills with all the questions answered in Chinese characters.

Clearly, this was going to be quite a trip. Sneaking across China. Three months on the lam.

The first few hundred metres was slow going, because tractors and carts had churned up the track into a muddy wallow. I tried climbing onto a berm running parallel to the track, and then I realized why the track was such a mess. The berm had been formed in digging clay for the brickworks, but it was now partly grown up with grass. Clay was no longer being excavated from the pit behind. Instead, the local villagers had gone up-market and converted the clay pit into a fish farm. The pit had been sectioned off with nets and allowed to flood, and now was no doubt turning out fish for the markets and restaurants of Guangzhou. The fish seemed to be raising themselves on this particular afternoon. There was nobody on duty.

From atop the berm it was easy to spot a firm track winding its way, not northwest exactly, but north through the paddies toward a village a kilometre or so away, just visible in the murk. I headed over there hoping to pick up a trail direct to the ferry crossing, or at least some more specific directions, but I was disappointed on both counts.

It was a typical Chinese village of about 15 houses and no streets. Each of the houses had been sited and oriented individually according to the dictates of *feng shui*, the Chinese geomancy that wards off bad luck by entrusting town planning to the spirit world. To the profane visitor the houses seem simply to have been scattered around every which way in a grove of shade trees. In fact, each was designed and oriented in consultation with a *feng shui* professional who, at considerable expense to the owner, recommended the best arrangement in light of the local topography, family history and the client's horoscope. This sort of planning has been strongly discouraged for about 40 years, but it was never fully suppressed – perhaps because the recommended alternative was barracks housing in long, straight parallel rows. That alone was enough to maintain geomancy's good name, and now it's back in fashion.

Without organized streets, you feel like a burglar wandering around in a Chinese village. There's no way to avoid cutting through what seem to be everyone's front and back yards. But in a communist society the only private property is inside the buildings themselves. The fields, the paths, the fishponds, the space between the village buildings, all is public property. Some of it has been given to particular families to use, but they don't really own it in the Western sense. Visit a few of these villages and you get over your inhibitions about walking through people's front yards soon enough.

There was no one abroad. I'd walked all the way through the village (the work of two or three minutes) before I saw a lady herding ducks at a little pond on the far side. She pointed out a line of trees on the horizon and revealed that there was a road running along under the trees that led directly to the ferry crossing. Apparently, people from the village rarely use the ferry, because there was no established trail from the village across to the road. She indicated that I should simply work my way across the intervening fields on the berms between the paddies.

Walking the little clay ridges dividing rice paddies is a nice way to travel. They're straight enough and smooth enough not to command your entire concentration, yet short and narrow enough to be interesting walking. They're usually about 25cm wide and almost always have a smooth clay trail along the top. When the paddies are fallow, missing your step results in nothing more serious than slipping down about 20cm onto the cracked mud of the paddy bottom. When they're in use, you come up muddy to the knee, but with no real harm done. It's nice steady walking, except that every few hundred metres you come to a major drainage ditch that's too wide to simply step over. Most of these are a couple of metres wide and a metre or so deep, so you have to climb down and out again. In rainy weather these ditches are full of water, but the farmers have to get to their fields, so there's always a crossing of some sort every hundred metres or so.

Winding through the deserted paddies was pleasant enough, but I was glad nevertheless to get out to the sandy lane along the tree line. I was walking in Adidas trainers with mesh ventilation in the uppers, so it didn't take long to get my feet thoroughly wet. The sandy road surface was dry underfoot and gave me a chance to really step out and get properly warmed up. Beyond the road, under the trees, was an intermittent row of houses, each with a substantial vegetable garden. None showed any sign of a driveway, so apparently the occupants commuted by bicycle either to the ferry or to Chau Sam and worked in some sort of non-agricultural employment. It looked as if they were raising vegetables on the side, which they could sell to the town dwellers at the local market. The levee along the river was visible beyond the row of houses. Twenty minutes on the road brought me to the ferry crossing without encountering a single vehicle.

Cresting the levee, I could see the ferry coming across toward me. I had just time for a quick look around before walking down to meet it. There was a small tarpaper shack perched atop the levee to sell drinks and snacks to travellers waiting to cross. Just outside the levee was another rather quiet looking factory. From my vantage point there was no way to tell what it might have been intended to produce. Factories in China are invariably surrounded by a high brick wall. At the gate they'll be identified by a very explicit nameplate along the lines of "Linfen County, Huangchuan Township, Number 2 Fertilizer Factory". In this case, though, the gate seemed to be around on the other side, so I headed off down the levee in ignorance.

Apparently the levees are not just for show. The level of the Bat Gong must vary quite a lot with the seasons, because the ferry didn't use fixed piers. Instead, old hulks were moored to each bank as floating docks that could be moved as water levels demanded. The ferry itself was an old steel barge retrofitted with a minuscule pilothouse and a one-lung diesel. The coxswain was assisted by two women to help him tie up and collect the fares. They were making a round trip about every half hour. The hold of the barge measured 2x3m, so a full load would be about 20 people and their various bicycles and bundles. I was riding in what must have been more or less the rush hour, and at 40 fen (about five U.S. cents) per person they took in 4.80 yuan for the trip. I spent the crossing running through the catechism with my fellow passengers, so I didn't get a chance to ask the crew whether this was a private enterprise, or to investigate their finances, but the three of them couldn't take in more than 100 yuan in a day. That couldn't leave them much after buying fuel. And if it's a private enterprise, they presumably must pay something to the local authorities for their concession. Still, it's easy work with a steady cash income. That's a rare boon in rural China.

On the far side, the river ran along the base of a steep bluff, and clinging to the face of the bluff was a surprising sight: a good-sized town not shown on the map. This mystery was explained within minutes of clambering off the ferry. The whole place was filthy. It was far worse than Yuan Tan, because after the rain it was covered in an inky slurry of coal dust. It wasn't a town; it was a coalmine. Publicly owned enterprises in China are responsible for the cradle-to-grave security of their employees in the classic communist way. So any mine or factory, in addition to the usual workshops, warehouses and office buildings, maintains dormitories, canteens, schools, clinics and all the infrastructure of a town to house its workers. The ferry was docking in the middle of a Chinese "work unit."

I never saw the mine itself. It couldn't have been anywhere near the ferry dock, as in that part of town there were no proper streets. The shops and houses were lined up in rows along the face of the bluff with walkways no more than 2m wide for access. Have a look at photo number 2. It was taken in a different little village, but it gives you an impression of how crowded living conditions can be. Anxious to shake off my inquisitors and get out of town before dark, I struck off along one of these narrow walkways intending to cover as quickly as possible the 200m to the edge of town. But it didn't work out that way.

I'd gone about half way when I came to a new, or perhaps newly renovated, temple. Not the usual brick. As befits a mining community, it had been built, or rebuilt, in beautiful cut stone. The roof was of shiny new green tiles, turned up at the eaves and decorated with dragons at the ends of the ridgepole. The interior was plastered and elaborately decorated with calligraphy and colourful murals. Set in the wall was a large stone carved with the names of the contributors and enumerating the amounts of their contributions. From the shreds of firecrackers everywhere, it was clear that there had recently been a grand opening. The scraps were pretty soggy, but bright red—about the only thing in town not yet black as if it had been drenched in ink. Like the minibus and the fishponds, here was another development typical of the new China.

Until 5 years ago, the employees of a government coalmine would never have been permitted to maintain a temple this way. I dropped a bit of change into the collection box and asked the gods if they couldn't consider turning off the rain.

They took their time over my request, but I was soon rewarded with another blessing just as welcome. A few more minutes in the narrow, crooked cliff-side streets and I was at the northern edge of town at the top of a flight of stone steps. Below was a narrow beach harbouring half a dozen rowboats. There was a nice view up and down the river, and to the north I could make out the southern entrance of the Fei Lai gorge. The old guy on the bus had been right about the trail. I could see the track winding up from the beach into what appeared to be a disused stone quarry.

It was almost 6 p.m. by the time I'd made it over to the quarry and determined that it was, in fact, disused. Amidst a desert of broken rock was a one-room cement building, which had once been the office. The door and windows had all been removed for recycling elsewhere (not vandalized as they would have been in any other country), but the roof was intact and the interior was dry. The townspeople must have seen me going in there, but the quarry was just far enough from the town, the trail was just rocky enough and the hour was just late enough that I could reasonably hope to spend the night dry and undisturbed. What remarkable luck.

I fired up my stove and drank a pot of tea while watching the trail out from town. Nobody followed me before it was fully dark, and after that no one could hope to do so without a light, so I had a dry and quiet campsite for the night. It was breezy, and the cement floor was as cold and hard as a miser's heart, but I was out of the rain.

The next day was my first real test—my first full day on the trail. Anticipating more showers, I climbed back into my cold, wet socks from the day before, and it's a good thing I did. The trail just about reached the other side of the quarry before it plunged into tall wet grass and thick underbrush. In minutes I was wet to the armpits. There was a monument at the edge of the quarry announcing the boundary of the gorge nature reserve, but nothing had been done to improve the trail. Indeed, it soon became clear that the trail had once been an important route, with substantial stone bridges over many of the tributary streams and a bit of cutting and grading in the more difficult sections. But these days many of the bridges were in disrepair and the trail was badly overgrown. In any other country fishermen would have kept it open, but the Chinese have little time for recreational fishing, and until recent years that kind of individual activity was severely discouraged. Solo walking leaves plenty of time for quiet contemplation, and I eventually worked out the theory that the little tributary ravines had once been inhabited, and that this trail had been their main supply route to the outside world. Forty years ago, the solitary homesteads were closed when the peasants were grouped into collectives and then communes. The area had then been declared a nature reserve, so the gorge remains deserted today and the trail goes unmaintained. In many countries the local authorities would be eager to fix up the trail as a cheap and simple tourist attraction, but here they had a different approach.

The gorge wasn't spectacular, but the scenery was certainly pleasant. The trail was wet, but just wild enough to be good, challenging walking. What made the walk memorable was the parade of passing boats on the river. The bulk of the traffic consisted of self-propelled wooden barges about 20m long with a pilothouse at the stern. Each seemed to have a crew of two men and a woman, accompanied by a child or two. Most were loaded with sand, stone or logs. Business was brisk, as there were often 20 or more in sight at any one time. These were supplemented by wooden skiffs about 5m long and very narrow, which usually carried only one man tending fish nets. It was apparent from the racket they made that both types of craft were powered by one-cylinder diesel engines. The river was only 100m wide through the gorge, and the reverberation from so many unmuffled engines made for a pretty noisy walk at times.

I wondered at first why the noise hadn't kept me awake the night before. Then I realized that the river was too shallow to be navigated at night. It was fascinating watching the boats weave back and forth across the current dodging sand bars. The current was swift, and the bigger barges in particular had to post one crewman on the prow with a pole to probe for the bottom and direct the helmsman. There was no buoyage, but the traffic was thick enough that they could pick out the channel by simply following the boat ahead. The channels were narrow, and up and down traffic had to take turns at the narrowest points. Their maneuverings sometimes brought them almost to the bank below me where we'd exchange a wave in the din.

Then, by mid-morning another class of river craft began to appear. These were passenger boats, roofed over with long glassed-in windows and modern, relatively quiet outboard motors. Apparently it was possible to take boat tours through the gorge from somewhere farther downriver. There were even a couple of modern fiberglass speedboats making the run. There had been a rash of boat thefts in Hong Kong recently. I couldn't help but wonder...

By late morning I was running out of water. I had crossed several tributary streams, which seemed to spring from the walls of the gorge. If that were truly their source, they could be clean enough for drinking. But the Chinese really do recycle human waste to fertilize their fields, so if the streams were contaminated with water flowing into the gorge off the surrounding farmland, drinking from them could be almost suicidal. I delayed as long as I could, then picked a stream which definitely seemed to come from a spring and filled one of my bottles. I added a couple of dihydrochlorazone tablets and prepared to take my chances when the other bottle ran out. It was a risk I could have avoided had I remembered to top up my water back at the mine. I was learning.

As it turned out, I never had to drink the water. Twenty minutes later I came to civilization. Well, civilization of a sort.

Maps for most parts of China are extremely hard to find, but this most southerly region is an exception. I was carrying three different maps of Guangdong province that I had found in Hong Kong, and one of them showed a cave in the gorge marked with the symbol for a tourist attraction. I hadn't given it much thought until, after a whole morning of bashing through wet underbrush, I suddenly burst onto a stone terrace outside the imposing portals of what appeared to be a large temple complex. Broad stone steps led down to a series of wooden docks accommodating many of the passenger boats I had seen over the course of the morning. So this is where they went on their boat tours. The docks and steps were lined with souvenir stalls selling the same tacky temple-visiting knick-knacks you find at every Chinese tourist stop. And several dozen surprised tourists had suddenly been presented with a new attraction not mentioned in the itinerary.

Since it wasn't raining, I took off my poncho. The clothes underneath were wet through, but even so they made me look a bit less eccentric than wandering around in a poncho. Ignoring the stares, I calmly toured the souvenir stalls until I found one where I could buy a couple of bottles of water. A vendor offered to sell me a pair of live fish joined by a vine threaded through holes punched in their dorsal fins. I contemplated the portal of the temple as if I were able to read the inscription on the lintel. I considered going in, but thought the better of it. I've toured many a Chinese temple and found them hard to appreciate without a good cultural grounding. Also, I had to keep moving pretty vigorously to keep warm. I shouldered my pack and moved on.

I didn't have to re-install the poncho. To my delight, the trail north of the temple was being maintained, and the walking was excellent. I could devote much more of my attention to the scenery and less to finding the trail. Within a few minutes my clothes were beginning to dry. Apparently a stroll starting from the temple was part of the attraction, but the trail in from the mine was left overgrown to encourage tourists to take the boats. The whole arrangement was surprising. You wouldn't expect the Chinese to have spare cash for that sort of tourism. The answer is probably that the gorge is still very close to Guangzhou, the leading city of China's recent modernization. Guangzhou residents may be about the only people in the country who can afford this sort of recreation. Sadly, the temple and its tawdry vendors may be a forerunner of what we'll soon see at scenic spots all over the nation. It was a depressing thought. But there was worse to come.

About two hours north of the temple I suddenly came across two beautiful, fat chickens foraging by the trail. A minute later I was amidst an incredible mess. On the opposite shore was a break in the gorge where a dirt road descended to a parking lot full of buses and vans. Skiffs ferried tourists across to the western shore where half a dozen restaurant barges were moored in disarray under the cliffs. Each was rafted with a second barge accommodating the kitchen (See photo number 3). Tourists arriving from downstream or crossing from the parking lot would buy fish and vegetables from vendors on the shore, then take them to one of the barges to be cooked to order. It was a reasonable concept in principle, but the whole complex had no organized waste disposal. Kitchen waste, human waste, scales, feathers, entrails, all ended up in the river. What a mess. And the water supply? Well, I didn't inquire.

Various restaurateurs encouraged me to dine, and in truth I needed a hot meal, but I moved on. A sobering sight, but I'd learned something. I codified it as Central Guiding Principle Number Two: Stay away from tourist attractions. And, of course, I'd learned something else as well. Now I knew why the lady at the temple wanted to sell me a pair of live fish.

No boat tours ran down the river from the north, so the trail beyond the restaurant barges continued smooth and easy. At one point the trail consisted of a ledge that had been chipped by hand out of a sheer rock face. It must have been weeks of work with a hammer and chisel. Clearly this had once been an important trail, for lining boats upstream against the current if nothing else. These days it was little used on a showery day in the middle of the week. I was able to stop for a picnic lunch and still reach the northern mouth of the gorge without meeting a soul.

Beyond the gorge the river was diked on both banks. The tall levee made smooth, easy and scenic walking. The villages were set well back from the river, so I met no one apart from the occasional cowherd. Fortunately, there was no need to ask directions. My various maps all agreed that I could simply follow the Bat Gong upstream to the first major tributary, then follow that to the town of Go Tin where, with luck, I could get a restaurant meal.

I walked past a couple of navigational beacons on the shore without paying them much attention until the grass dried out to the point where I could sit down near one of the beacons for a rest. It then struck me that the quaint little hats that I'd noticed covering the beacons were in fact panels of solar cells. Quite a surprise. Not at all the sort of high technology you'd expect to find out in the Chinese countryside. Each beacon was also served by a conventional power line. With the explosion of economic activity over the past 10 years, China's generating capacity is badly overstretched and power outages are frequent. Surely each beacon must run primarily off a battery, which is trickle-charged from the grid whenever power is available. How does a solar cell add to the reliability of that setup? Is it just a belt-and-braces approach to ensuring that the beacon never goes dark? Anywhere else you'd just shake your head and let it go at that, but in China you have to consider another possibility.

The old central planning system tried to control so many things that it ended up controlling nothing well. Labour, food, power, even the most basic commodities were often over or under-supplied in each market. You're tempted to guess that the planners at some point selected solar cells as the technology to keep the beacons burning in remote locations without mains supply. But they then had no reliable information on the exact reliability of supplies in different areas. Even in modern Taiwan, the departments of a Chinese government tend to operate as isolated satrapies hoarding information and avoiding inter-agency cooperation. In the absence of the necessary information, you could visualize the planners solving the problem by installing the cells on every beacon just to be sure. It's all speculation, but those little hats over the beacons certainly did look out of place.

Thus cogitating on high technology for developing countries, I came across some very low technology much closer to the hearts of the ordinary people: another quarry. But this one was in operation. Not actually in operation at the moment I walked through it, in fact there was no one around. But the place was obviously in production. Indeed, from the size of the tailings pile it seemed like a relatively new venture.

The setup was simple in the extreme. The site was unfenced. There were no permanent buildings – open lean-tos of bamboo and matting provided the only shelter. The operation consisted of a rock face about 30m back from the river, a narrow gauge rail line running down to the river's edge and just about enough little hopper cars to fill one of the river barges. A rusty old crusher sat off to one side, but apparently had not yet been installed. I was looking at one of the new rural enterprises typical of the response out in the countryside to China's recent economic liberalizations.

I'd spent the previous night in a quarry producing the same kind of rock, but that quarry was dormant. This little quarry had recently been developed, and indeed the rails, the cars and the crusher may well have been recycled from the large quarry down the river. The difference is that last night's quarry was part of an established government work unit: the coalmine. That work unit depends on central planning for all of its machinery and labour, and for "orders" (central planning directives) for its output. When the railway bureau is laying a new spur, the mine may be told that a government barge will call on a particular date and that they should load it up with a certain number of tons of stone meeting particular specifications. But in between rail spurs, the mine is not officially supposed to go out and drum up demand for the output of its quarry. Such salesmanship might even be interpreted as unauthorized diversion of the people's resources. So the mine concentrates on mining coal and the quarry sits idle most of the time. (Again, this is all just speculation in the present case, but you have plenty of time to speculate while walking alone on a Chinese levee. It's certainly typical of how Chinese industry works.)

So meanwhile, a nearby village has an undeveloped rock outcrop on its land within easy reach of the river. Someone has a relative with a barge. Someone else has a relative who's a worker at the mine. From there, all it takes is a few banquets to get everyone on board.

The mineworker sets up a deal with his manager under which he takes a leave of absence without pay but retains his status as a mine employee and access to his iron rice bowl. The villagers set up a rural enterprise which rents some of the mine's unused rail and cars. If the mine manager is an honest public servant, the rent goes into the mine's books rather than into his own pocket, but for his cooperation the mine manager almost surely is listed as one of the owners of the rural enterprise and gets a personal share of any profits. The village, of course, has lots of excess labour to actually do the quarrying and to push the cars by hand down to the river's edge. When they have a load, the relative with the barge comes by and hauls it away to sell for cash. It's small, it's simple, but it's typical of the kind of initiative that has been transforming the face of rural China in recent years.

It was getting to be late afternoon when my way was blocked by the tributary I'd been planning to follow up to Go Tin. I could see a trail along the opposite bank, but to get there I was going to have to put my life on the line. Well, perhaps not literally, but the bridge crossing the tributary was a perilous private initiative.

The stream itself was about 25m wide and, like the main river, it was diked on both sides. The crossing was spanned by a bridge about 6m high lashed up entirely from wood and bamboo without the benefit of any sort of metal fastenings. The whole thing was lashed together with vines. The 25m was broken into four 6m spans by piers lashed together on poles stuck into the sandy bottom of the stream. Each pier consisted of two vertical poles joined with cross-bracings of bamboo. The deck surface spanning the 6m between piers consisted of nothing more than three bamboo poles lashed more-or-less stably together to make a deck surface about 20cm wide. Above this, nothing. No railing. Not even a rope. Worse yet, there was no attempt to make the deck spans abut at the piers. Instead they sat side by side. On reaching the end of one span the user was obliged to step sideways onto the next span to proceed. Photo number 4 shows the process. Six metres may not sound very high, but the whole structure swayed alarmingly as you crossed. If the water in the stream hadn't been so shallow it might not have been so bad. As it was, if you fell off you'd probably hit bottom and hurt yourself. At the same time, the stream was shallow enough to open up the option of wading across and giving up the bridge entirely.

It was about an hour from the bridge upstream to Go Tin. With each kilometre, the levee gradually faded away. After seeing hardly a soul since the restaurant boats, I gradually began to encounter other travellers on the trail, and eventually the trail matured into what was apparently intended as the base for a new road. It wasn't yet complete, but it was passable by motorcycle, and that introduced me to another new private enterprise that has sprung up in China in recent years: the motorcycle taxi.

Villages of half a dozen houses each were strung out every kilometre or so up the valley. Throughout history the inhabitants had travelled from village to village on foot, crossing the stream on stepping stones and carrying their burdens on shoulder poles. It was only during the last few decades that they'd moved up to bicycles. Then, beginning about 1990, a few people realized that they could afford to buy a small motorcycle if they were to use it taxiing people back and forth to market. These days, their business is booming. I was about the only one walking. There seemed to be at least half a dozen mad motorcyclists supporting themselves on just this short run in and out of Go Tin. Their prosperity may be short-lived, as the new road will probably bring in cheaper and more comfortable minibus service. But for right now the new motorcycles have raised everyone's standard of living in an obvious and important way.

Well, everyone's except mine. My heretofore peaceful walk was now continuously noisy and, on the potholed roadbed, even slightly dangerous. Worse yet, the drivers and their passengers served as my heralds. I was undoubtedly the first foreign visitor to these villages in a very long while, and word of my progress rippled out before me, spread by those who sputtered past me on the trail. Families came out to watch me pass. Not to meet me – they couldn't imagine that we would have any common language – just to watch me pass and to show me to their children. Well, it was all friendly enough, but the zoo animal routine wears thin pretty quickly.

3

At Home with the Jaus

I had been hoping to reach Go Tin in time for a hot meal, but it was beginning to look like a lost cause. More showers were threatening overnight, so I'd have to allow enough time to find a secluded campsite and rig up my fly. Rather than rush through Go Tin and camp on the other side, I'd be wiser to find a spot before getting too close to town, then stop in the morning on the way through for a hot breakfast.

But first things first. I was low on water. I decided to approach one member of my curious audience for some boiled water to refill my bottles before leaving the trail to look for a campsite back in the hills. As I passed one of the little villages I noticed Mr. Jau standing watching me from the courtyard outside his gate. I climbed down off the new road bed and approached him, half expecting him to retreat inside. But in fact he seemed anxious to meet me, and when he heard me speak Cantonese he promptly invited me in for a cup of tea. Though I couldn't actually afford to linger, I accepted gratefully, and within 15 minutes Mr. Jau had invited me to stay for dinner and then to spend the night. He later told me that he had heard of my approach from a neighbor who had passed me on a motorcycle. He'd gone outside specifically to catch a glimpse of me, and was pleasantly surprised to have the chance to spend an evening with the first foreigner he'd ever had an opportunity to meet.

For my part, this was my first visit to a peasant's home. Let's look around.

Mr. Jau's house is one of seven in a tight cluster about a kilometre outside the town of Go Tin. For the time being, no road reaches him. When he needs to go to town he can either walk or ride a bicycle along the levee. Three of the nearby houses are owned by his relatives. As in the first village we visited, there are no streets or paths among them. They're simply built in a cluster set at odd angles. On the other hand, there are no fences either. Each family's private space ends at the door sill.

Mr. Jau's house is almost identical to the others in the village and typical of many rural houses in Guangdong province. It was erected by members of his family using traditional Chinese measurements, but I'll describe it approximately in metric units. It's built primarily of unfired mud bricks plastered over and whitewashed, though it no longer looks very white today. Only the foundation course and the doorposts were built with fired brick. The roof, though, is of tiles set on rafters of round wooden poles. You need a good roof when your walls are mud. The eaves overhang almost a metre.

The overall floor plan is about 12m wide by 7m deep. The main door is in the centre of one wall facing out to the river. There's a little false portico over this door, and next to it a little altar is set in a niche in the outside wall. On entering, you find that this door doesn't lead indoors at all, but into a courtyard. Straight ahead, at the back of the courtyard, is the actual main door to the interior. Both the outer door and this inner door are about 2m wide and have a 30cm sill.

The courtyard, open to the rain, is paved with flat stones. The other rooms have mud floors. In the centre of the courtyard a 1.5x3m sump is recessed 10cm below the level of the rest of the floors. It has a hand pump at one end and a drain at the other. Mr. Jau has indoor water supply even if he has no plumbing. In one corner of the courtyard a small cubicle has been erected from bricks to serve as a quasi-indoor toilet and bathroom. The toilet fixture is simply a bucket with a bit of water in the bottom so that the products can be recycled to fertilize the garden.

As you stand in the outer doorway, the left-hand side of the courtyard is a blank wall. Behind it is a shed that's accessed from outside. On the right, the courtyard has a half wall 1.5m high. It divides the courtyard from the semi-open shed, which is the Jau's kitchen.

Crossing to the back of the courtyard and stepping over the sill, you enter the main interior room of the house. This is 6m wide by 4m deep and has a ceiling that must be 6 or 7m high at the ridgepole. There's a chicken coop along the back wall. (Well, at least no one steals Mrs. Jau's eggs.) This main sitting room is furnished with a hard wooden bench, two wooden armchairs and a couple of chests and cabinets. There's one small table. Mr. Jau is obliged to build his own furniture, so there isn't much of it. A single light bulb dangles from the rafters. The only decoration consists of two certificates his daughter received from her primary school for active participation in the Young Pioneers. They're glued up on the wall, but not framed.

Doors lead off from each side of the main room into four bedrooms. These have ceilings of rough boards set on round poles. The space above is a loft for storage. Indeed, the reason Mr. Jau can invite me in for the night is that, although he has four children, he has no older relatives living with him occupying his bedrooms. In both of these respects his family is unusual. Typically a family like the Jaus would have at most two children and an aunt or grandparent in the household to help take care of them. As it is, he uses two of the four bedrooms for storage. The one I'm to sleep in has a pile of dry sand on the floor along with various machinery, some sweet potatoes and a pile of ginger roots.

In cool weather, the centre of activity is the Jaus' kitchen. This is in fact a shed 3m square, walled in on three sides but with a half-wall on the fourth side opening out into the courtyard. The roof is about 4m high at the ridgepole.

The stove is a sort of brick furnace about the size of a large desk but only 1.5m tall. The top surface has two holes about 50cm in diameter, each holding a giant wok. In the side wall of the stove are a couple of ports for feeding the fire. There's a separate small mud fireplace to one side. The fireplace burns wood and serves for boiling soup and rice. The woks are used only for quick frying, and for this the stove is fueled with bundles of grass and dried ferns. Cooking is a two-woman job. Mrs. Jau wields the wok while her daughter continually feeds the fire.

Huge bundles of grass and a small pile of wood take up most of the remaining floor space. There's room left only for a small table, some shelves in the corner holding a few dishes and utensils, two benches, two small bamboo stools and a baby's high chair. Mr. Jau made all of this himself. The high chair in particular is pretty impressive.

Remarkably, Mrs. Jau's kitchen lacks a chimney. The smoke from the stove or fireplace (and burning grass makes copious smoke) simply billows out into the room. It swirls up under the peaked roof where a bit seeps out between the roof tiles, but most of it accumulates until the cloud is deep enough that it can stream out under the eaves into the courtyard. At that point the bottom of the cloud is only about 1.5m off the floor, so you can see across the Jaus' tiny kitchen only while sitting down. If you're standing up, you must be on your way out the door. You'll be able to breath again once you get there. It's not clear why this design evolved. Perhaps if all the fuel were dry wood there'd be a lot less smoke, and the smoke would be hot enough and the roof porous enough that everything could escape by seeping between the tiles. These days, very few peasants have access to that sort of fuel supply, but the design hasn't evolved. Everything in the room above the 1.5m level is coated with a thick layer of tar and soot. It must, at least, discourage the mosquitoes.

The Jaus are Hakkas – a subgroup of Chinese who do much of the farming in Guangdong province and are heavily represented among Chinese in Hong Kong, Taiwan and overseas. The Hakkas are one of China's many officially recognized minority groups, but to the foreigner they seem indistinguishable from the Han, the majority Chinese culture. The distinctions are cultural rather than racial. In European terms, they'd be analogous to the Basques rather than the Lapps. The young children speak Hakka, Mr. and Mrs. Jau speak Cantonese, and their school-age daughter also speaks Mandarin, the official national language used in all the schools.

The house belonged to Mr. Jau's father, and three of his brothers and a sister live in the adjoining dwellings. But despite all that, Mr. Jau lives here illegally. He, like many others, was displaced during China's upheavals of the past few decades. During the last residence registration exercise he was registered on Hainan Island, now a separate province, hundreds of kilometres to the Southwest. Despite his family background, the residence registration system says that he's not supposed to be living around here. Now he's worried that if there were another crackdown he might have trouble, not only over his illegal residence, but over his four children as well. One child is encouraged, two are usually allowed in the countryside, but four is really carrying things a bit too far.

In fact, most of the troublesome features of China's communist system – the one-child policy, residence control, party membership, corruption, cracks in the system of benefits known as the "iron rice bowl" – are all academic to most Chinese most of the time. The communist system aspires to organize all citizens to serve society under scientific central control, but in China communism never got that far. Leninist controls were imposed on the city dwellers, the army and what communists call the "worker class." But in China that's only about 15 percent of the population. The remaining 85 percent are referred to as peasants. Like Mr. Jau, they live in the countryside cut off from most of the benefits, but protected from most of the impositions of a communist society. The government has made various attempts, some of them very vigorous, to bring the peasants under communist control. But each of the collectivizations led eventually to a drop in food production, something no Chinese government can ever afford.

So Mr. Jau survives pretty successfully as an outlaw. A couple of years ago, he lost all his identity papers in a highway robbery. He's never bothered to replace them. He has enough local contacts to get his kids into the school. He doesn't earn enough cash income to attract the attention of the taxman. Rather than regularize his status, he prefers simply to keep his head low.

As with most peasant families, Mr. Jau's biggest problem is money. He has no land. His father's land passed to his brother, who has set aside a plot where Mrs. Jau grows the family's vegetables. The Jaus help this older brother with planting and harvesting, and thus earn the family's staple rice for the year. Because they have no land, they're not liable for taxes. Mrs. Jau and her daughter collect their fuel on the communal hillsides. The family doesn't own so much as a bicycle. Apart from a bit of salt, oil, tea and soy sauce, their main expenses are medical and school fees. Mr. Jau earns these by collecting snakes, turtles and wild mushrooms and selling them in a city about an hour away by bus.

It's a quiet life out in the country. The highlight of an evening with the Jaus is when his brother comes around with a bottle of liquor and some hot sweet potatoes. He too is anxious to talk with his first foreigner, but equally anxious, it seems, to have a fresh audience for the well-worn tales of his years in the army. It was the only time in his life when he travelled more than 50km from his birthplace. No doubt my brief and unexpected visit qualifies as a fresh adventure that he'll now be able to recount for years to come. I know I will.

Although I took a warm water sponge bath and put on dry clothes before dinner, I actually spent quite a chilly evening. Dinner consisted of rice with three large woks of stir fried vegetables, one of which was supplemented with chicken or duck meat, which Mrs. Jau had apparently borrowed from one of her neighbors. We ate it at the table in the kitchen shed, Mr. Jau and I eating while his wife carried on cooking and the kids sat and listened. I found it chilly and draughty despite the smoke, but the toddler kept kicking off his sandals to play barefoot with a scrap of foam packing material that he was pushing around the floor in imitation of a railway train.

I mounted the flash on my camera and took a few pictures in the kitchen and in the courtyard, and I then asked Mr. Jau to write out his address so that I could send him the prints. This prompted him to show me their family photos – six or eight shots taken at the time of their wedding. Mine would be the first pictures of their children. The knowledge made me feel a bit less guilty about imposing empty-handed on their hospitality.

So in the end I never had my restaurant meal in Go Tin. Mrs. Jau warmed up the leftover stir fry for breakfast, and they sent me on the road with several warm sweet potatoes in the top of my knapsack. I did, though, stop on the way through town to buy a packet of cookies and some oranges. In the process, I learned that a 100 yuan note can be difficult to break in these country towns. Coins are very durable, but minting them involves the government in a big initial investment, so coins only work well in an economy with low inflation. Like many other countries around the world, China relies mostly on paper currency. This can load your pocket with a big wad of low-value scrip, but travelling in the countryside you're more likely to face the opposite problem: finding a merchant who can break a large bill.

Changing foreign currency or travelers cheques in China involves a fair bit of paper work. As a result, there's a tendency to change a large sum each time. This will yield several hundred yuan in Chinese currency. One hundred is the largest common note, and these are quite widely used in the cities, so a foreign exchange teller won't hesitate to pay out most of your sum in hundreds. But out in the countryside a 100-yuan note is rare. Some merchants have trouble with a ten. I had no choice but to carry the bulk of my funds in hundreds. Cheques and credit cards are completely useless out in the countryside. The only solution was to take every opportunity to break a couple of hundreds. Normally, this meant keeping an eye peeled for rural banks and credit unions. When I found one, at first they would invariably try to turn me away. One look at my Western face and they'd assume I was seeking foreign exchange, for which they aren't licensed. But they do have lots of tens in the till, and when they found out that I could speak a bit of Chinese and simply wanted to break a large bill, they were usually very happy to serve their first-ever foreign customer. So before leaving Go Tin I spent a few extra minutes waiting for the bank to open and took the opportunity break some of my stash into tens.

The first half hour after Go Tin was a bit of a chore. I followed a gravel road out of town, and for half an hour was never out of sight or sound of a motorcycle taxi. There was no other traffic. The road was wide enough that the motorcycles weren't dangerous, but the noise was a letdown after the quiet beauty of the rivers the day before.

I spent my time studying the village houses and comparing them with Mr. Jau's. In overall layout they seemed identical. It was probably cultural. Mr. Jau had said that most of the families around here were Hakkas. Back downriver, almost everything had been constructed of fired brick, but here mud brick was common, particularly for sheds and outbuildings. Every village had electricity, but not every house had a television aerial. And in most of the villages there was not a sign of a glazed window. Mr. Jaus' had been closed only with wooden bars, so they were either open to the breeze or shuttered up completely. That may well be where the people in Hong Kong got their tradition of barring all their windows with aluminum grilles and their door with an iron gate.

At the first junction north of Go Tin I pulled out my compass. Most of the motorcycles were heading west. The road north was smaller and quieter, so there was no real question which to choose. I asked the first person I saw whether the road north led to Yu Jeui, a name from the map.

"What's that?" he said.

"Yu Jeui. Is this the road to Yu Jeui?"

"I don't speak English."

"Excuse me. My Cantonese isn't much good. I just want to know whether this road will take me to Yu Jeui."

"Waah! You speak Cantonese. Where are you from?"

And with that we were off and running with the catechism. He didn't seem to understand my question, and I certainly couldn't decipher much of his answer. The road climbed gently for a couple of hours, following a stream. Traffic petered out to nothing and it began to drizzle. The sides of the valley narrowed to what might almost be called a gorge.

At a narrow point, down a steep bank below the road, the stream had been dammed for a mini-hydroelectric plant, now apparently out of commission. The access track hadn't been used recently, and the powerhouse looked as if all its doors and windows had been recycled elsewhere. These small hydro plants are quite common all over China. It leads you to suspect that at some point central planning decided that the nation could be electrified quickly by encouraging decentralized power generation through hydro plants built and maintained by the local communes. You can visualize how the enthusiasm for electrification would have led local authorities to approve projects on streams like this one – so small that the tiny amount of power generated couldn't justify the maintenance. On the other hand, the project got the entire valley hooked up to the national grid. The generating project may be dead, but that benefit lives on.

Only a few kilometres farther up the valley I came across the remains of another little initiative that had come to a bad end. Tyre tracks led to a section of the road embankment that had given way. Down below, trees were bent and broken. At the bottom, a five-tonne truck had apparently completed four or five rolls and was now lying upside down in what might well prove to be its last resting place. It was a recent calamity – from the previous weekend, perhaps. Someone had been paying more attention to the scenery than to his driving. He strayed too close to the edge and the embankment gave way beneath him. This wasn't a road to attract much heavy truck traffic. Someone may have been learning to drive. For many years, driving licenses weren't issued to the general public, so learning is now all the rage. Out in the countryside, there are no driving schools and no one owns private vehicles, so someone may well have borrowed a truck from his work unit to give it a try. Alternatively, there could have been a professional driver at the wheel. Many of them aren't very good. In that case he'd probably grown up in this valley and had misappropriated a vehicle from his work unit to do some sort of service for his family. Either way, someone was in deep trouble. Thank God for the iron rice bowl. They can't fire him, and they won't get far trying to dock his pay. He wouldn't earn enough in a lifetime.

The road dwindled for another couple of hours, then ended suddenly in the woods. It was the classic road to nowhere. I noticed a trail heading off into the bush, and after following it for only a few metres I realized what was happening. I had just crested a ridge, which marks the county line. A traditional walking trail had always linked Go Tin and Yu Jeui, but it was now being upgraded into a road. One county had finished its part, but the other hadn't yet started, or perhaps was starting from the other end.

Despite the misty drizzle, the walking north of the saddle was much better than it had been on the road. Pack animals are little used in South China. Until very recent times, goods were transported by men with shoulder poles. All the villages were laced together by a network of expertly graded walking trails, complete with bridges over the streams or stepping stones at the fords. Photo number 7 shows a typical section. Steep hill sections were paved with flags that had been hauled up on shoulder poles and carefully placed to form a paved track for better footing and to prevent erosion. Between major towns some of these ancient trails have gradually been upgraded into roads. In recent years the trend has accelerated. But there are still many of the ancient trails in use, still maintained by the local villages. This was the network of trails that I planned to use to cross China, and this example on my third day out was a very hopeful sign.

The trail gradually descended out of the mist. When I first reached the highest fields in the new county, I decided I had better take my lunch break before reaching civilization. Once I reached the first village, I wouldn't be able to stop without attracting a crowd.

I sat by a traditional stone bridge decorated with a big slate on which were carved the names of all those who had contributed to the bridge's latest rebuilding sometime in the 19th century. (The actual date was expressed in the old form: such-and-such year of the reign of the emperor so-and-so.) Most of the families listed contributed one yuan, but a few of the real big shots of the day had kicked in as much as fifty. Back at the mine, their new temple also had a plaque, and the standard contribution there had been 10 yuan, with sums up to 250 yuan for the plutocrats. A hundred years of inflation, collapse, colonization and war have driven the value of the yuan through incredible gyrations, but the value today in buying terms is not that different from what it was at the beginning of the 20th century. The gap between the rich and the average has been cut in half, but it's not clear whether that's an economic or a social change.

I'd been back on the trail for only a few minutes after lunch when I came to a sign setting out regulations for collecting firewood. The wording suggested that in the '70s this area must have been administered by one of the communes. The communes supported a whole layer of rural administrators who were trained in a bit of bookkeeping and that sort of thing. When the communes were dissolved, these cadres had nowhere to go and no work to do. Then Beijing adopted the four modernizations policy and opened up opportunities, which gave these ex-managers a new lease on life.

For the record, the original four were the modernization of agriculture, industry, science-and-technology and defense. They were originally announced by Zhou Enlai in 1975, but there wasn't much action until Deng Xiaoping had consolidated his power at the end of 1978. After that, the term was invoked as justification for any sort of change to the old communist system, including new soft drink factories and karaoke bars. These days it seems as if the phrase "four modernizations" has become not much more than a slogan.

The reason the slogan can be invoked to justify just about anything new is that many of the original modernization initiative were extremely popular. In the countryside the old system communes, brigades and teams was dismantled and each family allowed to farm a particular plot of land year after year, subjec to delivering a pre-set quota of grain to the state. This was really a return to the old imperial tax farming system, but it allowed the individual families to shift production to more lucrative crops, and also freed the surplus family labour to migrate to the cities and work for cash. The resulting rural boom continues today.

The old commune managers, now leaders without an organization, are the people who've been running around trying to start little industries out in the countryside. Not many succeed, but in some cases they've taken some useful initiatives. The sign about the firewood suggested that the local bunch was hoping to develop some sort of forest industry. It might be a pretty good idea. China is tremendously short of wood and paper, though you wouldn't immediately guess it walking in the woods all day. The Chinese decimated their forests during the great leap forward period of the late 1950s, and now they're paying the price. A woodlot employs a lot of people and should have no trouble selling its output.

A few hours later I was in Yu Jeui – hardly a major milestone, but important because I'd managed to find my way from Go Tin over trails not marked on the map, simply by asking the way of everyone I'd met. Better yet, I'd confirmed that many of the old traditional pack trails had not yet been upgraded into roads, were still in use and made excellent scenic walking. It was promising to be quite a trip.

4

Through the Sunny South

The topography is one of the joys of central Guangdong. It's a jumble of low but rugged and wooded hills. As a child, my image of China had always been of vast rice paddies, but now I was spending my days climbing up and down forested ridges. The rice paddies were small and contorted, moulded into the bottoms of the narrow valleys. The public way either wound along a stream bed, crossing back and forth on stepping stones as required, or hugged the edge of the forest a metre or two above the level of the adjacent fields.

Route finding in country like this consisted of deciding how far to stick with the current valley before striking off on a trail over the bounding ridge. At each ridge top there was likely to be a junction of several trails marked by a clearing with a little shrine. Picking the wrong trail at that point would bring you down in the wrong valley, far off your planned course. Fortunately, there were usually plenty of woodsmen, travellers or firewood collectors around to set you straight. In the worst case each climb and descent amounted to only a half-hour's walking. In the absolutely worst case, my planned route could always be changed.

The typical valley shelters a string of villages – each a cluster of half a dozen adobe houses, usually occupied by members of the same family and with no commercial establishments at all. Once or twice a day my route took me through a small town. These named towns were my signposts – the places whose names I could read from the map and refer to in asking directions on the road. They were also my only reliable opportunities to get a hot meal.

You can literally spot a town in Guangdong province a mile away. I emphasize the word town as opposed to village. In contrast with the peaked tile roofs of the villages, most town buildings are cast concrete creations with flat roofs and whitewashed exteriors. It's the white wash which is so unusual in the countryside and so strikes the eye from the nearby hillsides. Newer towns and villages, built by the communes since 1949, have straight streets and buildings lined up like army barracks. Yuh Jeui was typical of many older ones, with a warren of narrow streets intersecting at odd angles.

Town buildings in Guangdong are mostly built to a common plan. There's a smooth concrete pavement about 2m wide across the front of the building, raised about 35cm above the level of the roadway. Since the buildings abut each other all down the street, this could form a sort of sidewalk, except that each building will have built its pavement to a slightly different height. Walking along, you're repeatedly forced to step up or down each three or four paces. In decent weather, most pedestrians ignore the sidewalk and walk in the road. There are very few vehicles in the smaller towns. But on a rainy day the streets will be deep in mud. They have a roadbed of cobbles underneath, but it becomes covered with a layer of rural clay that makes a smoother surface, and so is preferred when the weather is dry.

The buildings normally have two storeys. The bottom storey is one large room with a high ceiling. The wall facing the street is wide open, closed only with a set of removable boards. Shops remove them all during the day; private residences remove just two or three to let in some light and ventilation. The second storey is reached by stairs at the back. It overhangs the pavement right out to the street line, so the pavement is sheltered from the sun and the rain. The ceiling of this second storey is a more normal 2.5m high. The flat concrete ceiling is the underside of the roof. It must make the upper storey pretty warm in the summer sun. The second storey is ventilated by a long window across the front, grilled with wooden bars so it can be left open at night.

Town buildings are electrified, though it doesn't always work. Most have glazed windows at the back. Water is usually piped in, but the piping system doesn't come from any sort of purification plant. Everything must still be boiled before drinking. Toilet facilities consist of a public block of latrines at the edge of town. These too are built to a standard plan – holes in a concrete slab separated by low, conversation-friendly partitions. There's a men's side and a women's side feeding a common pit. This can be emptied through manholes at the back so that the products can be sold to the local farmers. Presumably most homes must supplement this service with a bucket in the corner, and presumably few bother to carry this bucket out to the edge of town when it needs emptying.

Schools, the municipal offices and the occasional small factory have their own standard architectural styles. The other standard edifice in these towns is the public market. This is just a pitched tile roof supported on brick or cast concrete pillars without walls. It shelters rows of long concrete tables where the vendors display their wares. The floor is usually cobbled, though it may be cast concrete. It doesn't matter that it may be rough. There are no carts or trolleys in a Guangdong market. Everything is transported on shoulder poles or, at best, by bicycle.

Towns are further distinguished from villages by invariably having vehicular road access. The road may be rough and muddy, but it's always good enough for a truck or van. As a result, there's some sort of bus service to the nearest city. If the town is at the end of the road, this may be no more than a single van leaving early in the morning and returning at supper time. But usually there's a road passing through, and this allows more frequent unscheduled services by buses and vans stopping on their way through from elsewhere.

I'm happy to report that in the new climate of economic liberalization, restaurants have quickly established themselves as one of the most popular forms of private enterprise. The fittings and sanitation in these establishments vary widely. In the prosperous south, I've seen shed-roofed joints equipped with karaoke machines. At the other extreme, I met one proprietor who may not have offered karaoke, but she brought a metal basin of hot coals and placed it under my table. I found it a far more welcome amenity at the time, as I had stumbled in cold, hungry and wet. Whatever the standard of decor, the food and service in these little private places were always good – a real boon to the weary traveller.

With all the rainy weather, finding snug places to camp was a constant worry. I was invited to stay in village homes about every other night, but I remained reluctant to accept. In most cases it was because the invitation came too early in the day, but I also felt guilty about accepting hospitality from families in such obvious poverty and, after a long day on the trail, I was also put off by the prospect of spending the whole evening rehashing the same aspects of my personal history. So I usually declined.

On one occasion I spotted on a hillside a very ramshackle hut half-roofed with corrugated sheeting. It proved to be a faggot store – a community project that buys up bundles of grass and ferns from rural women and sells them to the town dwellers for firewood. The shed was piled high with bundles of dried grass that made an excellent mattress. It was a pleasure to awake on a chilly night and hear rain drumming on the tin roof, then snuggle deeper into my makeshift bedding and drift back to sleep without a care. Camping out this way was often a nerve-wracking experience, particularly during the early evening and early morning hours. There was nothing illegal about my spending the night in a communal shed – it's everyone's property in a socialist state – but had someone come along, the discovery that I'd slept out rather than accepting local hospitality would have led to embarrassment all around.

Unfortunately, on that occasion heavy showers continued into the following morning. I once again felt forced to set off in the rain. By donning shorts I could keep most of my clothing dry at the expense of only temporary discomfort, but in this case the climb up the next ridge had been "improved" by upgrading the traditional trail into a road suitable for tractors. Worse, a great many tractors had attempted to use it in the rain and had chewed the amateur grading into a quagmire. Within half an hour I was muddy to the knees. The track must have been upgraded to serve some sort of mining initiative, because at the top of the first ridge the last few metres of climbing had been eliminated with a short tunnel. It was the first I'd seen and quite a surprise, but a welcome spot to stop and re-organize out of the rain.

I spent about an hour and a half there hoping to wait out the showers. In that time I met three family groups. In each case the man was walking ahead leading or carrying the child through the mud. The mother came along behind carrying all their belongings on a shoulder pole. Confucian etiquette.

The showers eventually won. There was a nasty breeze through the tunnel that dried my clothes but chilled me to the bone in the process. At a moment when the showers had perhaps let up a bit, I launched myself back out into the rain and mud. The rain persisted off and on all day, but I escaped the mud pretty quickly, as I was able to fork off the amateur road effort onto a traditional trail paved with giant flags.

In this complicated, hilly country many of the trails were marked by signposts chiselled into slabs of stone erected like tombstones at the junctions. Marking the junctions on the ridge tops must have involved a lot of work hauling the stones up by hand. The signs had been erected more than 30 years ago, before the communist era, because the carver had used traditional Chinese characters, not the new simplified sort invented under the communists. I saw scores of these direction stones over the next week or so, but was rarely able to make any use of them. In most cases they gave directions to local villages too small to be shown on my maps.

Another feature of this hilly country that I never saw farther north was the use of small home generators (See photo number 8). All the watercourses were fully tamed and channelled to flood the rice paddies. In the steep and narrow valleys the paddies were usually only a few metres square with a drop of a metre or so from one to the next all down the valley. In some places the villagers had led some of the flow off into contoured irrigation ditches just a few centimetres wide, which held the flow at a high level until it reached a point on the slope of the valley just above the village. Then they'd drop it down through a penstock into a set of little packaged generators each not more than 15cm in diameter. No turbine could generate enough power to run much more than a couple of light bulbs, but those first couple of light bulbs must have seemed pretty important when the alternative was going to bed at sunset. Sadly, it seemed a rather temporary expedient. The bearings in many of the units didn't sound healthy. China lacks any sense of organized distribution for its products, so parts were probably impossible to get.

Forest industries seemed to be the economic backbone of the part of central Guangdong I traversed over the next few days. Houses, which farther South would have been roofed with tiles, here were roofed with bark. People stood hardwood poles under their eaves to dry for firewood. Fences which had previously been constructed by mounting "pickets" of dried ferns between two longitudinal strips of split bamboo could now be made entirely of sawmill off-cuts. The trails crossed hillsides which had been clear cut and replanted in conifer or bamboo monoculture. At one point, I stopped to ask directions of a cowherd whose cow wore a bell carved completely from wood. Not very melodic, but its three clappers made a distinct clack-clack.

I made the mistake of asking this same fellow why his kids were playing by the trail and not in school. He politely pointed out that it was Sunday. I'd completely lost track of time. It's interesting that the Chinese have adopted the custom of resting on Sunday. It has no religious basis in their culture. He told me that he pays school fees of 1800 yuan per year for each of his two children. He's basically a farmer, but he can't generate that sum in cash through farming, so he's forced to do a bit of forest work as well. A tough life.

One township had apparently decided that there was money to be made in farming bamboo. The current economic liberalizations have unleashed a building boom all across the country, and in the cities construction work is always swathed in scaffolding lashed up from bamboo poles. Although it's remarkably strong, bamboo is actually a type of grass and correspondingly quick and easy to grow. This particular township had cleared its forests over several ranges of hills and valleys and replanted with bamboo.

These plantations were still immature, so there was no harvesting going on. The traditional trails had been maintained, but I could walk for hours without meeting a soul. At one point, on a spur with a spectacular view, I came across a deserted camp constructed by the woodsmen. It was in the form of a level platform lashed up from poles using lengths of vine and enclosed with mosquito netting to soothe their afternoon nap. The view over the surrounding plantations was great, but I found the rubbish tip just as interesting. The main component was orange peels. There were a few liquor bottles, but no other glass. There were wrappers from packages of instant noodles and a few bits of foil from cigarette packs and the spices that come with the noodles. But no paper. Paper had all been recycled into the latrine a few metres off the trail. Toilet paper is a luxury in China. Cigarette packets are carefully saved along with any wrappers, newspapers, anything made of even the coarsest paper.

My own purchases showed the same pattern. I was trying as much as possible to live off the land and not carry any more than emergency rations. Most villages had no shop at all, but in the towns I would always take the opportunity to stock up with whatever was available. Hardboiled eggs were a good bet. I could often find them for 50 fen each. I could get 6 apples for 2 yuan or 4 oranges for 1.5 yuan. Rather poor instant noodles were 50 fen a package. They're light enough to carry, but have to be eaten pretty quickly. They take up a lot of room, and once they're broken they're a pain to eat with chopsticks. So I too didn't have much garbage to bury on my travels. But by the same token, it didn't leave me much in the way of toilet paper.

I wish I could have spoken more with the old women I met on the trail. I'd have asked them about their clothing. The younger women usually wore an ordinary long-sleeved blouse with work trousers, but many of the older women went around in what seemed a rather impractical traditional costume. They wore a black tunic buttoned up to the neck and trousers covered with a black apron down to their knees. They covered their heads with what seemed to be a folded piece of heavy black linen held in place with a colourful embroidered headband. In good weather the whole getup must be pretty hot and uncomfortable, and the red clay in the fields must quickly soil the black colour scheme. In some countries widows wear black, but black doesn't signify mourning in Chinese culture. I found it all a bit puzzling.

Central Guangdong is bisected by a belt of karst formations. The whole region was once covered by an ancient sea, which deposited a bed of limestone. In one region, a string of lava eruptions intruded up through the limestone. The sea level receded, the limestone was eventually eroded away and a string of spectacular pitted lava pillars was left standing above the surrounding terrain. Today these pillars support a mining and quarrying industry in a string of towns all across the province, and at Guilin in neighboring Guangxi province they form one of the nation's premier tourist attractions.

My own visit to the karst belt lasted no more than an hour and a half. It began unexpectedly when, just north of an isolated town called Sa Ba, after days in the woods, I was directed through a field of what appeared to be tailings from a mine. Inquiring, I was told that it was a sulfur mine, and I later saw some of the product piled waiting for shipment. Within minutes, the trail was paved with what appeared to be cinders, but in fact proved to be crushed lava. It wound in and out among sheer-sided pillars of pitted black lava 10 to 20 metres in diameter and each about 30m tall. In the subtropical climate the mysterious pillars were crowned with foliage and draped with brilliant green vines and moss. The cindery soil between the pillars was apparently unsuitable for cultivation, and the whole area stood deserted and silent. An impressive sight. Photo number 9 doesn't really do it justice.

I climbed a long stairway of lava blocks to a higher level and stopped among the pillars for a quiet rest and a shave by a tiny stream with the colour of orange juice and the taste of rust. Twenty minutes and another flight of lava stairs later, I was back down to the level of the surrounding agricultural land on the outskirts of a village. I'd enjoyed beautiful green vistas every day of the trip so far, but that brief hour was the first moment of real spectacle.

A few hours north of the karst belt I was faced with crossing the Lin River, a major tributary of my old friend the Bat Gong. I wasn't far from the major town of Sai Ngau, so I decided to cut through town and use the road bridge rather than hunt for a ferry. It was the biggest town I'd seen so far and, as I expected, the area around the bridge offered a wide variety of choices for a hot restaurant meal. In fact, the strip of highway approaching the bridge serves as a sort of caravanserai for inter-city buses. Enough strangers pass through that I was able to enjoy an inexpensive bowl of noodles and a plate of vegetables in relative peace. Normally I would no sooner sit down than several hangers-on would invite themselves to sit at my table and question me while watching me eat. But at Sai Ngau I was able to chat peacefully with the proprietor without attracting any other participants.

I avoided approaching the town along the main highway. In fact, I had expected to be able to get all the way to the bridge along trails through the fields. But just at the outskirts I came upon a new bypass not shown on any of my maps. It was open, but not heavily used. At one point the bypass had been driven through a little knoll forming a cutting. The cutting had exposed some tiny seams of coal in the bank, each about 80cm wide, and the townspeople were busily mining them. Peering into one of these narrow slots you could hear the sounds of digging in the pitch darkness a few metres into the hillside. On the road outside each of these enterprises was a small pile of coal. Though I didn't disturb them at their labours, it's safe to guess that the miners were townspeople nominally employed by Sai Ngau's government work units – banks, shops and so on – who were skipping work to get a share of the free coal before it was all gone.

Despite the showery weather, water in the Lin was pretty low. I could see from the bridge that the river was buoyed for navigation, but it was also clear that all the boat owners had beached their craft along the banks and were busy with repairs waiting for navigable soundings. To stay off the noisy and dangerous highway, I took the first opportunity to clamber down the bridge abutment on the far side and stroll along the bank watching the refit work. It was an interesting end to an interesting day. Better yet, the skies were clearer than before, and for the first time I felt justified in trying to camp without rigging up my poncho as a tent.

I discovered the next morning that the Lin still marks a distinct boundary between ethnic groups. Forced to ask directions about every 15 minutes in the maze of country trails, I was immediately aware that the clans north of the river spoke a different dialect from the peasants farther south. They were much more reticent in replying to my enquiries, but also less intrusive in questioning me.

The Chinese are quite proud of their imperial heritage, and the People's Republic we know today takes in most of the area ruled by their ancient emperors at the height of their powers. Much of this vast territory has a history of only intermittent Chinese control, and much of that not very well organized. As a result, the PRC of today has inherited a patchwork of minority groups who have managed to preserve a certain sense of their own identities. Mr. Jau's Hakkas are one example.

The minorities are the inspiration for the five stars of the Chinese flag. The big star represents the united country dominated by the Han group, the overwhelming majority in the country as a whole. The smaller stars surrounding it represent the Manchurians, the Mongolians, the Tibetans and the Moslems. Among them, these groups take in all but a few of the population, but in terms of diversity this list barely scratches the surface. More than 50 ethnic groups have official minority status. Members of these groups enjoy certain privileges, the most valued of which is partial relaxation of the birth control regulations. Minority women dancing in colourful traditional dress are a staple of Chinese tourism publicity, but in real life most members of the minorities are so thoroughly assimilated that a tourist could never notice any distinction. Often even a Han could spot them only by their speech. Language is the best-preserved remnant of most minority cultures.

The first day or two north of the Lin was through less rugged terrain – a long, broad valley heading due north. Where previously the farmers had been supplementing their incomes through forestry, here fish farming was in vogue. The clay soil retains water well, so digging out ponds even 150 or 200m across was simply a matter of hiring a bulldozer for a few days. The berms between the ponds made good walking with a view out over the surrounding paddy fields. At intervals along the berms were tiny lean-tos thatched with reeds for guarding the ponds against fish rustlers, but it must have been early in the growing cycle. All the hutches were empty.

What with the ponds and the paddies, the entire valley had been deforested. With the exception of one very old, large and twisted tree by the side of a tiny brook flowing through the centre of the valley. Not surprisingly, all the trails converged there, and it was clearly a popular rest stop for travellers in hot sunny weather. The day I passed, there was a keen northwest wind blowing and I was wearing a windbreaker over a T-shirt and sweatshirt, but I stopped anyway. Because around the tree, nestled in the twisted roots, were three separate shrines, each just a few sticks of incense and an offering or two of oranges, tea or rice liquor. Animism lives. I pondered whether each clan in the area maintained a separate shrine, or whether each shrine represented a different creed or ritual. They all looked much the same to me, and there was no one around to ask. Perhaps I should have left an offering. Later that day the strong wind brought in heavy rain and I finished the day pretty wet and cold.

Still, the rain had its brighter side. My route crossed a busy highway, and from there I found that the traditional trail had been upgraded into a road over a stretch of about 13km. I had no real alternative but to follow the new road, which would have been a dusty business but for the rain. Then, at dusk, I was lucky to find that the road crossed a minor stream on a four span viaduct far longer than necessary. I took the opportunity to knock off early and jumped down under one of the dry spans for a snug, weather-proof camp.

If sleeping out under bridges sounds a bit austere, let me explain that most Chinese towns (as opposed to villages) do indeed have at least one public place to stay. This may sound encouraging to the foreign visitor, but in fact it's of little help. In an effort to earn foreign exchange through tourism, the government has opened many new areas of the country to foreign visitors, but at the same time it has maintained a restrictive system of hotel licensing. Most hotels are not allowed to accept foreign tourists. The licensed hotels are concentrated in the major cities and at popular tourist destinations. Those in the small towns are useless to the foreigner.

The visitor's best hope lies in the emerging private economy. In many towns, private individuals are redeveloping their residences into guesthouses. These don't offer many amenities, but on average they seem at least as clean and well maintained as the city hotels. These private establishments can be hard to find because, as in English, they go under a variety of names. (Think of guesthouse, bed and breakfast, inn, motel.) To find one, look first near the bus station and watch for touts carrying signs or a book of photos. If you approach them gently you may be able to convince them that your lack of language skills won't cause too much of a problem.

Even in the private sector you're not home and dry. These private setups usually have no license to accommodate anybody. Officially, a traveller, Western or Chinese, is supposed to register with the police each night. One way or another, the police will have been convinced to overlook this requirement as it applies to the unlicensed guest house, but many illegal operators might feel that taking in a foreigner could be pushing the authorities a bit too far. It's worth a try, but don't count on it.

As it turned out, I was fortunate to enjoy my dry night under the bridge. The next day I was back into hilly terrain. The rain was heavier than it had been before, and the conditions were altogether wetter. I spent the morning climbing through a whole series of hanging valleys. Within each valley the paddies were, of course, terraced dead level so that they can be flooded to nurture the rice crop. You walk and walk, stepping up just a little from one terrace to another until the terracing process becomes impractical – the terrace level is too far below the natural level of the valley floor and requires too much cutting. At that point there's a major slope up to the next set of terraces, and on that slope the villagers have built their houses crowded along narrow cobbled streets. In this particular valley the villages were about 800 metres apart, and each had a panoramic view back down the entire cascade.

After a morning of steady climbing in the rain, I began to see evidence of something that's unusual in the settled, eastern part of China: abandoned land. The terraced fields gave way to pasture and then to woods that showed no sign of forestry management. My informants continued to point out established trails leading north, but at one point I came across a creek in a deep, narrow ditch bridged by a stone slab. The slab had slipped off its abutments and fallen into the ditch and not been repaired. It would have been a day's work for several men to raise it again, but nothing had been organized, perhaps because the villages were becoming sparse and there was none nearby. A hour or so later I came to a ghost town.

In the old cowboy movies ghost towns always consisted of dilapidated wooden buildings. It must be easier for the set designers to build them that way, but I suspect that most real ghost towns must be like this one – built all in stone. If I'd looked around awhile, I'd probably have found an abandoned mine somewhere nearby. There was no place to grow rice among the surrounding hills, so when the mine gave out everyone had to leave. Standing in the deserted central square was more like visiting a European castle than a cowboy ghost town. Most of the roofs had fallen in, but the rest of the place appeared ready to last forever. In fact, the slate-paved alleys and courtyards were a lot more pleasant on a rainy day than the alleys deep in mud of the towns I'd been visiting recently. I was inclined to poke around at length but thought the better of it. Travelling alone, I couldn't afford to get snake bitten.

North of the ghost town I found myself following what must have been its main access route. The trail had been painstakingly graded and paved with flags, with impressive arched stone bridges over each stream. It was rough country, and for four hours in heavy rain I met no one. The town and its mine had apparently been maintained entirely by trains of human porters. Finally, the beautiful old trail climbed to a pass through a sea of wet grass and at the top merged with a new vehicular road under construction. The whole business would have been an excellent day's walk in better weather.

The road crews were taking the day off, probably at home out of the rain. You could see, though, that they'd adapted ancient methods to building modern roads. In the old days, each village was obliged to contribute so many man-days a year to maintaining the roads and bridges in its area. The people cut back the brush and repaired any washouts or loose stones in the pavement. These days when they're making a new road they cut the grade with a bulldozer and a roller, but they still rely on local crews for the finishing. In this case it appeared that the people were bringing in basket-loads of broken rocks and placing them one by one on the sub-base to make a metalled surface, just like laying flags in the old days. Each worker (they're probably local women) has an assigned section about 4m long and the full width of the road. She squats under an umbrella with a basket of broken rocks and places them side-by-side to cover her whole patch. She's probably paid piece-work and in cash. Afterward, they probably go over the whole thing again with the roller and dump another layer of clay on top to make a smooth surface.

It's hard to imagine why they choose to use such a labour-intensive system. Surely, if they just broke the rocks up a little smaller they could spread them with a shovel instead of placing them by hand, one by one. Perhaps the larger rocks make a more stable base. But I suspect a more important point is that the hand-built system allows them to continue paying the workers in the ancient way, and this may be central to recruiting them from their clans. If that sounds implausible, let me mention another occasion when I watched a similar crew laying out the white lines on a newly paved road. Surely in that case you would expect them to drive along with a paint sprayer, even if the sprayer were operated by hand. Instead they were heating up the fresh tar and pressing in bits of broken white pottery they'd salvaged from a porcelain factory. The pieces all had blue designs on them, and you could walk along trying to guess which had come from broken cups, which from plates and which from saucers. It was an incredibly labour-intensive way to paint a road. At least, you might suppose, such lines would never wear off. In fact, in hot summer weather the tar would creep on the curves and the lines would all sag out of shape. They were then almost impossible to repair. The only reason I can imagine for doing it that way is the need to maintain each clan's annual labour quota and to pay for it in something like the ancient way.

I'd reviewed several kilometres of this deserted construction site when the new road-to-be unexpectedly approached the lip of a spectacular gorge. It must have been 500m deep. It wasn't the Grand Canyon, but it was breathtakingly big. And not mentioned at all on any of my maps. In any other country it would be a major tourist attraction. Fortunately, the rain had abated and visibility had improved. I took a long break, brewed a cup of tea and contemplated how far I'd climbed during the day.

5

The Social Whirl

I found out a bit more about the gorge when I reached a village near the town of Dai Bo late in the afternoon. With the bad weather and the wild country, I'd seen hardly a soul all day. I was thoroughly damp and in need of a hot meal. So I was in a receptive mood when I noticed a teenage girl who seemed to be beckoning to me from the village and calling out: "Come! Come!" Her name proved to be Miss Chan.

The Chans are Hakkas, and the family is not originally from Dai Bo. Dai Bo is considered a "mountain area" with potential for hydroelectric power generation. In the late 1950s the government selected it as the site for a pioneering commune, so when Mr. Chan left the army he was sent here as a sort of involuntary frontiersman. In fact, he came from a poor farming family and the commune system promised him better living conditions and a less uncertain existence than traditional farming in a one-family village. Happily, that's pretty well how it has worked out.

The Chans live about a kilometre outside the former commune headquarters of Dai Bo in a satellite village. Unlike traditional villages, these commune buildings are arranged in long parallel ranks like military barracks. Rather than being long and empty like real barracks, they're divided into a series of identical 4m rooms. Each room has its own door leading out into the alley between the rows, but there are no interior connecting doors. The narrow alleys between the buildings are paved with flat stones. A stone-lined open drain runs down the middle carrying a fast, cleansing flow of water most of the year.

Mr. Chan, his brother, their parents and their children live together in an extended family of 16. They occupy four adjoining rooms on each side of the alley. Each brother has his own living room, but their families share one kitchen and the work of food preparation. The other rooms are used as bedrooms and for storage.

The commune system is now defunct, but for many years Mr. Chan was a rural cadre. The term cadre doesn't mean he was a member of the Communist Party, simply that he was one of the local leaders. He got extra work points and ration tickets for helping with the management of the commune. These days the commune's original mining enterprises don't bring in much cash. The hydroelectric works at the huge gorge south of town has ample head, but at most times of year it hasn't enough water to run as designed. So Mr. Chan and his brother rely on farming just like the other peasants in the region. This high, dry land isn't very productive, but the family has been allocated a large area and taxes on poor land are very low. So they've been getting by.

Things have been looking up over the past few months, as Mr. Chan's eldest daughter (the one who invited me in) has finally become old enough to get a job in the nearest small city. She works in a textile factory, lives in their factory dormitory and sends money home. She's happier too. There are many more things to see, do and buy in the city than in this small and isolated place.

Like many country people, Mr. Chan has never been too concerned with the one child policy. Apart from his 17-year-old daughter, he has another set of twin daughters, 11, and now a young son of 6. Now that he has a son, he's content. His daughters will all marry into other families, but his son will carry on the family line and maintain the Chan family shrine with the ancestral record including, of course, the memory of Mr. Chan himself.

In the early days, life was tough in this isolated place. An outside visitor would say that it's still tough today. But Mr. Chan and his family notice primarily the improvements. With the hydro works, they've always had electric lights, though the voltage is pretty erratic in the dry season. Now they have television, though the one station they can pull in with decent reception broadcasts only in the evening, and at that time of day the voltage is often too low to get a picture. In the mornings the voltage is much higher and they have a radio cassette player, which works very well.

School fees remain a problem, but his eldest daughter's recent conversion from scholar to wage earner makes a big difference. By the time she reaches the government's official marrying age, the twins will be through school as well. In theory any of the kids could qualify to go on to college, but in fact rural schools don't give adequate preparation. The fields, the cows, the geese and chickens, the pigs; with these resources, and working long and hard, they get by.

The biggest problem is, in fact, firewood. The planners built a commune that's actually too big for this valley to support in terms of fuel. Over the years the firewood supply has been pretty well cleaned out. Weeds and grasses are available, but for wood fuel they have to make some pretty elaborate all-day excursions into the surrounding hills.

It's not often that strangers come wandering up this valley. It gives Mr. Chan a chance to brush up his Mandarin. He sometimes had occasion to use it when he was a commune manager, but most of that administrative work wasn't really very productive. These days it has pretty much fallen away. My visit also gives the children a chance to speak something other than Hakka around the house and to see and hear someone they haven't known all their lives. And it's a good excuse to kill a chicken, dig up a few potatoes and bring out the bottle of rice liquor for a special dinner.

Peasants may not have a lot of money but, to a much greater extent than city dwellers, they're their own masters. If Mr. Chan wants to invite in a wandering visitor to spend the night, there are no forms to fill out, and there's no neighbourhood committee to come around asking questions. Let's party!

Cigarettes are often suggested as good gifts to bring along when visiting China. I was glad I hadn't. Non-smokers are rare in China, and after offering a gift of cigarettes you'd have a job convincing anyone that in declining a cigarette you weren't just being polite. As it was, I let Mr. Chan and his brother do the smoking, but we all enjoyed plenty of rice liquor. They even brought it out again in the morning for breakfast. With no refrigeration it makes sense to finish up the leftovers the next morning, but the Chan brothers were ready to extend that to the liquor as well. I managed to get away with just a couple of thimbles full at breakfast, but even that little bit saps your determination faced with climbing a steep rocky ridge first thing in the morning.

As luck would have it, I was back into the beer again at lunch. The other side of the ridge was wooded with a developing lumber industry. The woodland trails gradually broadened into a jeep track, and as I approached the first village I fell in with a father and his son who invited me in for lunch.

I had expected potluck, but instead the whole family mobilized to whip up a pot of dumplings. This was something I had always considered more of a northern custom. When you visit someone up in Hubei Province, they'll very often ask you to sit down and help them make a few dozen dumplings, then boil them up and tuck in. Indeed, I suppose the well-travelled visitor should have developed the knack of stuffing them, but I hadn't. It seemed, though, as if my hosts made them often. They had a couple of beer bottles set aside as rolling pins, and a stuffing dexterity almost as impressive as their ability to roll cigarettes one-handed.

These people too were Hakkas. Within minutes of our arrival, my host and I found ourselves sitting and drinking beer with the family patriarch while 30 curious neighbours tried to squeeze into the tiny room. Everyone seemed able to speak Cantonese, but among themselves they preferred Hakka, perhaps because they knew I wouldn't understand it.

In conversation, it developed that this was another of the pioneering communes, this one specialized from the outset in forestry. As at Mr. Chan's place, the village had been built in stone and laid out, not as separate houses, but rather in housing cubicles built in long rows like barracks (See photo number 6). This has the distinct advantage that the smoky kitchen is separated from the sitting room, but it doesn't leave a growing family any scope for expanding its living space. Mr. Chan's kitchen had been across the alley. Here they were using the unit next door and had punched a hole through the wall as a serving port.

This architectural innovation allowed the revival of an interesting old-fashioned convention. Once the dumplings were ready, they chased all the little boys out into the alley to peer in through the window. The women and girls retired into the kitchen, and I dined in the exclusive company of the grown men of the clan. The women seemed to be holding up more than their half of the sky by regularly shoving fresh bowls of dumplings through the serving port. This is old-fashioned Confucian etiquette. I hadn't seen it before.

Beer at lunch is pleasant while you're drinking it, but it sure saps your enthusiasm for walking in the afternoon. It was all I could do to decline their suggestion that I join them in their traditional siesta. But after three hot meals in a row I was feeling guilty. I left them to it.

The old commune had set a pretty good standard in conserving the forest in this area. The trees were large by Chinese standards, and the stream I was following ran clear and free of mud. Farther down was a small hydroelectric project, which seemed to run a bit better than some of the others I'd seen. Just as well, as my hosts had been obliged to burn their electric lights all through lunch. Their housing had apparently been built to a standard commune design more suitable for the north of China with its cold winters. The windows weren't big enough to light the rooms, and the whole place must have been terribly hot during the tropical summers.

Following the directions I'd received at lunch, at the town which had been the headquarters of the old commune I crossed the stream and set off on a jeep road climbing out of the valley over the next ridge. I fell in with a man and his son. The son insisted on carrying my pack for the better part of an hour up a long steady climb. Although he wanted no thanks, I took his picture in all my gear and wearing my hat, with a promise to send it to him later from Hong Kong.

Meanwhile, his father explained that the old commune leadership, now ostensibly out of a job, still did a lot for the community. It was responsible for the orchards we were walking through. Apples, cherries, pears, lichees, tea; he pointed out each in turn. They were all still young trees, but in principle it sounded like a winning enterprise for a community in such a remote location. They were exploiting the land, the know-how, the government connections and all the old roads and buildings left from the former commune. If they could get the business established, expansion would be just a question of labour, and there's never any shortage of that. And in any case, the threshold of success isn't high. Just a little bit of cash makes a big difference in these remote rural areas.

Unusually, the boy and his family lived in an isolated house at the top of the valley. Though there was only a single isolated building, it still housed an extended family. It was another stone barracks divided into four units without connecting doors. Here again, the standard layout left little scope for home improvements. In this case all the units were devoted to bedrooms and cooking was done over an open fire under a shelter in the front yard. That must be fun on a winter morning. It must be nippy for bathing, too. But in contrast with village life, the isolation provided a clean, quiet environment. Clean water, clean air (except for those doing the cooking) and a great view.

Once I got started on taking the son's picture, of course everyone wanted to be included, so I took quite a few. They assured me that they could receive mail at the post office in town, and they got the son to write out the address in my notebook. They had no envelopes. Indeed, they had to go find some sort· of official document to look up the postal code. While all that was going on, the women of the family lit a fire and boiled up some water for tea. My trans-national walk was turning into a series of social occasions.

Indeed, I could have enjoyed another night indoors with yet another hot meal that evening. As I was getting ready to hit the trail, they sent me off with a woman who, I thought, had been delegated to show me the correct trail to the top of the tea plantations. In fact, she too was travelling over the ridge to her home in the next valley. I declined her invitation to stop in for a visit, in part because I was feeling guilty about doing too much socializing and not enough walking, but primarily because she spent the whole trip over the ridge complaining to me about her husband. I couldn't make out half of what she was on about, but she never quit. She'd be really grim company for someone who'd already heard all her complaints a hundred times before. I can't imagine she has many friends.

By the time we'd reached her village there wasn't much left of the day, but I excused myself and pressed right on regardless. The weather had cleared, my feet were dry and I was looking forward to a bowl of my own instant noodles with a hard boiled egg. It was only a kilometre or two before I found a quiet grove of pines behind a ruined temple. The Chinese have a lot of superstitions about ghosts, so the old temple made it the kind of spot where I could count on a quiet night.

6

Among the Yao

Late the next morning I crossed the major highway that runs west from the northern Guangdong city of Shaoguan. From the directions I was getting, I never did figure out whether I was crossing at a village called Lung Gwai or at the crossroads where you turn off for a village called Lung Gwai. That's typical of the confusion involved in wandering around trying to ask directions in some common language of people who normally speak an obscure dialect. Whatever the name, it was a pretty scruffy excuse for a village. Nevertheless, I took the opportunity for a hot lunch in one of the noodle stalls along the highway. Just as well. It was my last restaurant meal for a while.

Faithful to guiding principle number one, I didn't try to follow the highway but set off up a rough track heading away to the north. I quickly discovered why the track was rough. Within a kilometre I came upon a small rural iron foundry. Unlike a regular government work unit, this factory had no wall around it, and it was interesting to stand for a few minutes and watch the proceedings. They apparently purchased their raw material as crude iron pigs, remelted it in a single small furnace and recast it in sand moulds formed on a flat area of casting floor. It was all done by hand. Particularly spectacular was the sight of two men carrying a crucible of molten iron shod only in rubber sandals.

I couldn't stand watching for more than a few minutes, as I was quickly drawing a crowd. I pushed on up the incredibly rutted and muddy track and within fifteen minutes came upon another alarming example of industrial development. The foundry had apparently been organized because the hillside above it supported extensive amateur coal mining. The whole hillside was peppered with small pits each worked by one or two men without benefit of any obvious mechanization. There were tailings piles everywhere. Every few minutes as I picked my way up the muddy track, explosions rumbled from here and there across the hillside. The casualty statistics must be depressing. The rural and township enterprises are said to be about the most vibrant section of the economy, but you hear less about their real costs.

Some of the mine tailings could profitably have been applied to the trail. On top of the ridge it deteriorated to the point where it was literally knee deep in mud and water. There was a village up there, but the residents had widened the trail so much in trying to detour around the bog that there was no dry route left. So my feet, which had now been dry for more than a day, were once again back into it.

On the way into the village I noticed a set of stairs leading down into a cave next to the trail. Apparently that was why the trail had been routed this way, because four or five metres down the stairs was a ledge by an underground stream. This was where the residents drew their drinking water. It would be a cool place to spend the afternoon in hot weather, but on a chilly spring day it was deserted.

The villagers tried to convince me that there was no trail out of the village leading north. They would have succeeded had the trail in from the south not been such a slime pit. As it was, I wasn't taking no for an answer, and kept asking until I found someone who was willing to describe how I might find the start of a trail over into the next valley. Though he warned me it wasn't very easy walking.

He was right. The descent off the north side of the ridge was very steep, and the soil was clay rather than the rocky terrain I'd climbed through coming up. At some point, someone had cut hundreds of steps down the steepest part of the descent, but they hadn't been maintained. With rain and the passage of herds of animals, the stairs had been almost completely worn away into a slick clay chute. The decent would have been easier with a walking stick, but of course sticks are usually rather hard to come by in the Chinese countryside where everyone cooks over wood fires. I eventually got down without breaking a wrist or getting too dirty, but it involved hours of nerve-wracking maneuvering. Once I got past the steepest part I was glad to camp for the night in a very scenic location with a panoramic view over the valley, backed by the sobering spectacle of an even more forbidding ridge ahead of me on the other side.

My maps didn't give me much guidance on how to proceed. They showed a couple of isolated towns off to the north, but no roads, rivers or any other hint how I might reach them. I used the names of the towns to inquire about a route the next morning down in the valley, but those inquiries too got me nowhere. It was difficult to find anyone who had even heard of them. The steep ridges were apparently a pretty effective bar to north-south travel.

In the end I decided to head up a steep ravine cut into the north side of the valley, the only notch in the steep north slope that I'd been able to spot from my camp the night before. It was only when I was already following a track by the side of a stream pouring down out of the ravine that I met someone who could tell me that there was a route up through the ravine and on to the north.

My informant was a schoolteacher, which set him apart because he could speak clear Cantonese. Cantonese is the unofficial lingua franca of Guangdong province, but in the country areas many people spend so much of their life speaking their native dialects that their Cantonese can be pretty hard for an amateur like myself to understand. This fellow explained that he was a Yao – a member of another minority like the Hakkas. The Yao lived up in the hills and didn't mix much with the inhabitants of this valley. That was why I'd had such difficulty getting directions. The teacher assured me that once I was up the ravine and among the Yaos I'd have no trouble getting directions and I'd find the people very hospitable. Much reassured, I set off up the steep winding track.

Once I got started I found it a spectacular walk. The gorge had been dammed for a hydroelectric generating plant and a wide and well-graded track had been cut into the walls of the gorge for the construction, but it was now pretty well deserted. After an hour or two of climbing I came across what was apparently the site of a market. From the rubbish scattered about, some chopping blocks and a lot of feathers, it was clear that on certain days the Yaos and the valley dwellers met there to buy and sell their various products. When I passed it was deserted.

A few kilometres later, just past the most spectacular of many waterfalls cascading down from above, the trail suddenly ended in a landslide. All through the climb I had seen from time to time tiny trails scaling the walls and disappearing into the brush, but none since the marketplace had been large enough to tempt me to leave the wide and well-graded main trail. I could see a few footprints crossing the landslide, so now I decided that rather than backtrack and look for an alternate route I'd try to push on across the landslide and pick up the trail again on the other side, even though few others seemed to do it that way.

It worked out all right in the end, but it was tough going. The temporary track descended to the stream bed and proceeded to follow that, crossing back and forth several times through cold and fairly deep water. I was gingerly picking my way across one of these fords when an old man suddenly appeared, overtaking me from downstream. His vision was probably a bit feeble, as he didn't seem to realize that I was a stranger. He knew every pebble of the fords, and with a wave quickly pushed past me. That relieved me of the need to hunt around for the trail and I scrambled to follow him. Sure enough, a few hundred metres farther on he clawed his way up a steep muddy track and at the top I found we were back on the original trail above the landslide. I stopped to dry off and put on some socks, and my guide quickly disappeared without our having spoken a word.

There was now less than an hour of steady walking left before the gorge widened out into a pleasant, cultivated valley, but this part of the trail was much busier than farther down. Groups of porters were carrying down rough wooden beams, three or four pieces at a time. Each person must have been carrying close to 50kg balanced on his (or her) shoulder with no special padding or equipment. The trail twisted back and forth, and I had to keep my eyes open, as they were in no position to stop or even to change direction suddenly. On the other hand, neither were they able to stop and quiz me. I just stepped off the trail and greeted them as they passed. Here was clearly one product of the Yaos' dominions. China is very short of decent wood and these beams would fetch a price to justify all the back-breaking labour.

I didn't spend long in the hidden valleys at the top of the gorge, but they struck me as a real Shangri-la. The scenery was beautiful, the people were friendly, the whole ambience was clean and quiet. I would have liked to have visited on a sunnier day, or on a snowy day in winter. The valley had a bit of a Swiss look to it with the steep hills all around. I suppose it doesn't seem so idyllic when you have to spend your life carrying 3-metre beams and live without access to so much as a bottle of store-bought beer.

The few people I met who could speak Cantonese had heard of the towns on my map and gave me some explicit directions, but as soon as I headed off into the woods the trail began forking every few hundred metres. I was soon lost. Where are the beam carriers when you need them? I stopped for lunch hoping someone would come along, but no luck. I then spent most of the afternoon trying one trail after another, only to have each peter out in a deserted clearing. Finally, on what was definitely not the trail I was seeking, I heard voices from the woods above me. I persisted scrambling up an extremely steep and slippery rock fall and eventually came upon a party of woodsmen skinning logs.

It's no exaggeration to say that they were dumbfounded to see me, the first foreigner they had ever encountered, emerging from the woods in the middle of nowhere. It was a classic moment. These guys were Yao people as well, but not from this valley. Rather than coming up by one of the ways I'd come, they had come over the top. They assured me that if I pushed on upward another few hundred metres I'd come to a summit trail. The slope was almost vertical and very muddy, but having climbed so far I had no inclination to head back down. At first they let me go, but then decided I was so interesting that they couldn't just let me get away. So they chased after me and showed me the best way up. We paused at the top and shared some of my store-bought cookies.

The walk down the other side reminded me even more strongly of Switzerland. There were no snowy peaks in the background, but the pastures extended far up the steep green hillsides, and the valley bottoms were dotted with individual farms, themselves a rarity in China. From far above, the whole scene gave the impression of Swiss cleanliness and neatness. The trail descended vaguely northward as dry, as clear and as steadily graded as any you'll find in the Alps. The long, gradual descent was a beautiful conclusion to a rough afternoon.

Once the trail had dropped off the ridge it began to run along the banks of a stream, and the topography fell into a pleasing pattern. There would be a kilometre or two of cultivated valley and pasture. The stream and trail ran along almost level. Then there would be a few hundred metres where both stream and trail would descend steeply to a new level through a narrow, rocky gorge. I was getting tired, but the alternating open valleys and intricate gorges kept me fascinated.

I hadn't seen any sort of vehicle, not even a bicycle, all day long, when I was startled by the sound of someone trying to start a truck. It proved to be, not a truck, but a hand-cranked generator in very dodgy repair. I had come upon two men fishing in the rushing stream. One was cranking the generator and the other held a pair of electrodes with which he was trying to stun the fish. Screened by the racket from the generator and the roar of the current, I was able to watch them for a while unobserved, but I didn't see them catch any.

Finally, in late afternoon, one more dip in the cold water. The trail and stream ended at a larger river, and on the other bank was a gravel road. There was no bridge, and it was too deep for stepping stones. After wading across I was faced with the choice of turning up or downstream. In search of advice I headed for a small sawmill a few hundred yards along the road, and that's where I met Mr. Yam.

Mr. Yam was 27. He lived, and no doubt still lives today, in an extended family of seven with his wife, his two children, his mother and mother-in-law and his unmarried younger sister. His house is the last one at the top of a steep valley, 30 minutes hard climbing from the nearest road where he works as a labourer in the mini-sawmill. He walks up and down daily, but in fact the nearest village, where his children will go to school when they're old enough, is over the top of the ridge in the next valley, a shorter and easier walk from his high-altitude abode.

When I showed him my map and asked directions, Mr. Yam not only recognized the names of the towns I'd been heading for, he suggested that the most direct route led right past his front door. He immediately offered to show me the way and to put me up at his home overnight.

His house is a rather impressive two-storey structure of mud brick with a tile roof (See photo number 11). The ground floor consists of three 3metre-square rooms set side by side. Each of the two end rooms has a front door to the outside and an interior connecting door to the room in the centre. There are no back doors, because the house is set on a terrace cut into the steep hillside. Indeed, except for what he has levelled himself, Mr. Yam doesn't actually own any level land. A path 150cm wide, the main path from his valley over the ridge to the town, runs along the front wall of the house taking up the rest of the terrace and forming Mr.

Yam's front yard. The outer edge of this path is stabilized by a stone wall about 250cm high dropping down to another 20x5 metre ribbon of terrace, and this in turn drops off to a third. Mr. Yam, or rather his mother and mother-in-law, cultivate on these terraces the rice which Mr. Yam uses to pay his taxes.

From the path outside his door Mr. Yam can look down on a whole cascade of such houses perched on the steep sides of the valley. All are of similar design and construction. The ones nearby are mostly occupied by various other members of the Yam clan— close or more distant relatives. When the weather is decent, Mr. Yam and his family spend most of their time out on the path in front of their door. That's because the interior of the house is dim and uninviting. Despite the excellent view, each of the three rooms has only one small window. It's cold up there in winter, and glass is expensive and loses a lot of heat. For most of the year the windows are left wide open, closed only with wooden bars. In winter they're shuttered up entirely.

The two end rooms, the rooms with doors to the outside, function primarily as storerooms. The room in the middle has the stove and functions as the family's kitchen, living and dining room. A ladder in one of the end rooms leads to the second floor where Mr. Yam and his wife sleep with their infant son and pre-school daughter. The rest of the family sleeps in an outbuilding strung along the terrace with the cowshed and pig sty. This annex is at such a narrow point on the terrace that the path passes behind the building and the building itself is built on silts out over a steep drop.

Mrs. Yam is fortunate in having a system of running water almost into her kitchen. Mr. Yam has hollowed out some lengths of bamboo and led a small spring from farther up the hill down to the back of this house. It's only a trickle, but a large mud cistern assures that there is always enough on hand for the family's needs.

The stove too is made of mud, fired into a sort of brick through daily use. The firebox is about 2m long and 90cm high with two large holes in the top surface to hold two woks, and another smaller opening for heating a kettle. With no shortage of firewood, Mr. Yam doesn't have to devote a lot of space to storing dried grass or a lot of time to collecting it. He can cook entirely with wood, which makes less smoke and requires less constant attention. Nevertheless, there's no chimney. The inside of Mr. Yam's house is as black as Mr. Jau's. The ceiling, the walls and everything inside is black down to about 150cm off the floor.

And unlike Mr. Jau, Mr. Yam must light with wood as well. He and his clansmen strung up some amateur electricity lines a few years ago, but they haven't been able to keep the system in repair. If they want to stay up after dark, Mr. Yam hangs a small wire basket from the ceiling about 2m off the floor. He has a pre-cut supply of 5cm pine splints, which are resinous enough to light easily and burn brightly. By gradually feeding splints to the basket, lighting each off the last like a chain smoker, it's possible to see well enough for cooking or bathing the kids. Don't think of reading, though.

With his cash income from the sawmill, his garden, his pig, his chickens, Mr. Yam feels his life is going pretty well. He rarely gets out to a town with vehicle access. He rarely eats store-bought food except for soy sauce and tea. But his mother-in-law always has a vat of home brew on the go to celebrate special occasions. As a member of an official minority he has no trouble about having two children. He has his own home and about all he can imagine aspiring to in life. He's content.

My visit was considered enough of an occasion to warrant dipping into the home brew, and we spent a dark but convivial evening around the stove. With Mr. Yam's unlimited water supply I was even able to heat up some water for a hot sponge bath. His mother, meanwhile, cauterized her athlete's foot with burning splints. A tough lady. I'd have liked to ask her about this strange medical ritual, but it was the same old story: only Mr. Yam, his wife and his younger sister could speak Cantonese. The old ladies and the kids spoke only Yau dialect.

The next morning, an even stranger ritual. I got up at dawn, but by the time I got myself into the main room I found it already occupied by an itinerant mystic, hard at work. Apparently the Yams had decided that this would be a good opportunity to call in a professional to say a few prayers for their ancestors. These guys have to be fed after working, and the Yams were already planning to fry up a big breakfast to send me on my way. Might as well kill two birds with one stone.

I missed the start of proceedings, but the part I saw involved first folding up a hundred or so little papers with prayers written on them and burning them in a pile in the middle of the floor. I think the smoke is supposed to carry the prayers up to heaven. Then they set off quite a few pretty powerful firecrackers. That was followed by some lengthy chanting over several pieces of smoked meat and cups of wine. At the conclusion, we sat down and ate the offering with some big plates of rice and stir-fried vegetables. I must say that I felt a bit uncomfortable about breaking bread with the deceased. I could only hope that the consecration of my breakfast would help keep me on the right trail during the day.

I had noticed that the Yao people follow certain dress codes. In Mr. Yam's family everyone except himself, his wife and his younger sister goes around wearing some sort of head covering. The old ladies wear a towel or some other sort of headscarf all day. They keep the two children in colourful embroidered skullcaps. The baby's had little bells on it. We arranged that before leaving I would take a few family pictures and mail them back from Hong Kong. When we were ready for the photo session, Mr. Yam and his wife too put on jerkins similar to the ones the old ladies wear all the time (except bright blue instead of black) and Mr. Yam tied a scarf around his head in a special pattern.

True to Mr. Yam's directions, soon after leaving his house I crossed the saddle at the head of his valley and arrived at the town which had once been the headquarters of the local commune. This housed the head office of the local woods industry, so it supervised the sawmill down by the road employing Mr. Yam. This town had no vehicular access at all. All its wood products were shipped by hand. As far as I could make out from the handwritten Chinese characters on the blackboard outside the office, the enterprise was offering 75 fen for sawn timber. For that price people were hauling them in on their shoulders over the mountain trails. The women not only haul their share of the timbers, but often were carrying the family lunch box as well.

For all that, it was a beautiful working environment. I was again in a long series of agricultural valleys separated by short gorges, just like the day before. The area was so isolated that everything possible was homemade from wood. I saw many hollowed-out logs like the one shown in photo number 12, serving as pipes to bring water to the fields. At one point there was a series of hammer mills along the stream with homemade wooden water wheels on open wooden bearings lubricated by a trickle of water. The shaft drove the hammers using a system rather like a music box or a player piano. The hammers were stone, the walls of the building were stone, but everything else was made of wood, including the roof shingled in bark rather than tile. Quite a feat of engineering.

Some of the gorges, though small, were quite spectacular. The walls had eroded into contorted rock spires. At some point the people had managed to climb some of the spires and install little shrines on top. The shapes were so fanciful that studying them you could understand a bit about the roots of animism.

Unfortunately, all this scenic interest had distracted me from the fact that I was on the wrong trail. I'd set out with such clear directions from Mr. Yam that I'd failed to follow my usual practice of asking directions of just about everyone I meet. When I did finally stop to chat with someone, I found that I'd missed my turning an hour earlier and I was on a track descending a valley far from the one I intended. It was going to take me on a loop far back to the southeast, but by that time it was too late to turn back. I could only solicit some new directions and press on glumly.

In asking directions of a Chinese, you'll often find them using in their reply the term "public road" in a way that would seem unusual in any other context. They seem to be implying that only a few of the main arteries are truly public roads, leaving the visitor to suppose that all the rest of the road network is in some way private. In a communist country? It seems very odd.

The distinction seems to depend on how a particular route is maintained. The Chinese use the term "road" to refer to routes which in other places would be more precisely described as trails, tracks, routes, lanes, highways, superhighways, almost anything. China's great attraction as a country for walking is that most villages are still joined only by "roads" no larger than a cart track, and walking is still an important mode of travel for the general public. The small tracks and trails between villages, their cuttings, bridges, fords and stepping stones are usually maintained by a *corvée* system. Each family is expected to contribute a certain number of hours each year to public works labour. The village leader organizes work parties to keep the temple, the drains, the wells and the roads in good shape. In recent decades this network of privately maintained routes has been supplemented by roads which are maintained by public employees paid through taxes. It's these government roads which are referred to as "public roads". But that doesn't imply that the village roads are in any way private. What it means for the walker is just the opposite. Anything referred to as a "public road" will be graded and routed to a higher standard that will make it less interesting and far less safe for walking. If it's called a public road, the wise pedestrian will do his best to avoid it.

About noon my scenic mountain trail deteriorated into a public road. Apparently I was making this walk just in time, because work had started on eventually extending vehicular access all the way up the valley to the commune headquarters. This road, though, public though it may be, was still pretty benign. It dead-ended at the bottom of one of the steep gorges, and even below that point there were no villages and no cultivated fields along the roadside. The hillsides were quiet and bare. The only signs of civilization were substantial concrete dikes to contain the stream during the flood season and, here and there, tunnels with stone portals cut into the sides of the valley and sealed with iron doors.

I eventually ran into someone coming up the valley and asked him what was going on. His Cantonese was hard to understand, but he told me a story apparently involving a major figure in recent Chinese history, General Lin Biao. Remember him? He was one of the most important generals in the People's Liberation Army, beginning with their days as a guerrilla force trying to overthrow the Nationalists. After the Communists came to power, he was one of the senior military leaders, and eventually became identified as Mao's right hand man and heir apparent by the time of the cultural revolution. He was then deposed amid charges that he was plotting a coup, and is said to have died in a plane crash while attempting to flee the country.

According to my informant, during the 1950s this valley was converted to a vast secret arsenal where tanks and artillery were stockpiled to defend the south in case of any invasion via Hong Kong. The tunnels were constructed to shield the armaments from air attack. The water works were built to protect the valley from flooding during heavy rains. It seems plausible. The mountains I'd been crossing during the previous week would make a pretty good line of defense.

With the valley still barren today, it occurred to me to wonder how long ago it had been abandoned. The tunnels were all bricked up, but was it still a military area? As I followed the wide paved road down the valley, would it eventually lead me into the middle of an active military camp? I decided I'd be well advised to abandon the road and follow instead an aqueduct that was snaking along the wall of the valley at a higher level. Once I'd climbed up there, I found that some sections were being used as a route between villages, but in other stretches the aqueduct wall was uncomfortably narrow, and it took a lot of attention to avoid falling a long way down a very rocky slope. I never saw any army camp, but the view alone was worth the extra effort.

7

Railroad Days

Arsenal valley and its aqueduct led me back in a long arc to the southeast, away from Mongolia and back into the valley of my old friend the Bat Gong. By late afternoon my aqueduct merged with another, larger irrigation canal high up on an escarpment running north and south parallel to the Bat Gong. Looking East from the junction I could see the river in the distance and the important river town of Gwai Tau. This new aqueduct featured a much wider bank that was smooth, easy walking and led (within the limits of following a level contour) due north. I set off, but didn't in fact get far before dark fell and I was forced to call it a day (a rather misguided day) and camp on the scenic hillside.

The valley of the Bat Gong provides the most important route through the range of hills that bisects Guangdong Province and at one time isolated the south coast from the rest of the empire. These days the valley carries river traffic, plus the main north-south highway and rail line. Up on the slopes overlooking the valley I found myself following another national artery: a line of poles carrying telephone cables. Dangling from the wires were little metal signs pointing out that these were telephone rather than power lines. Apparently the peasants are prone to tap into power lines and steal free power. Putting the telephone trunk so far up the hill and clearly labelling it was probably intended to minimize disruption from misguided power thieves.

Heading north, I was walking against the flow of the irrigation canal. Farmers were drawing off all along the way, so by late the next morning the substantial canal had faded to no more than a faint, dry ditch. The banks were overgrown with bushes. It was time to find another route. Little hope of a rural farm track, as I was approaching a city. A city large enough to be shown even on many national maps of China. On English maps it's labelled "Lechang," though anyone who lives there knows it by a Cantonese name that should be spelled in English more along the lines of "Lok Cheung."

As in most developing countries, the Chinese, peasants and city dwellers alike, universally are convinced that the city is where it's all happening. The peasants aspire to move to the city and earn some cash, while those already authorized to live in a city would do anything to avoid a work assignment in the countryside. For my part, I'd made avoiding the cities my Central Guiding Principle Number Three. This was partly because I had previously spent quite a bit of time in various Chinese cities and was now trying to tour the countryside. It was also because the cities tend to be full of footloose peasants looking to make their fortune and not above stooping to petty crime. But the most important consideration is that the police, like everyone else, prefer to spend all their time in the cities. They'll visit the villages only when strictly necessary in the line of duty. In Guangdong province I had nothing to fear from the police, as the entire province is open to foreign visitors, but in the rest of China most of the countryside is supposed to be off limits. For most of the trip it would be important to escape the notice of the police, and the single most effective step to that end would be to stay out in the countryside away from the cities. Hence, Principle Three: Never go through any town larger than the smallest dot on the map.

In search of a route to bypass Lok Cheung I dropped down off the irrigation canal into a small village, which seemed deserted in the midday sun. When I eventually found someone to ask, I discovered that he wasn't from that village at all. He was an itinerant tinker travelling with two partners. They invited me along.

The three of them lived in Lok Cheung and had an established round in the surrounding countryside. They travel for eight to 10 days at a stretch, which brings them back to each village about once a month. It takes them about 15 minutes to walk between villages, then they stop and set up shop for a half-hour or so until all the jobs have been handled. Their traditional work is to fix leaky pots, and when they reach a village they wander around beating on a pot and crying out for business. But on the day I travelled with them the bulk of their income came from repairing broken umbrellas. A typical repair earned them 2 yuan. They carried all their tools and spare parts, all their personal gear and some little stools and workbenches in baskets slung from shoulder poles.

Speaking of shoulder poles. Ever tried walking a kilometre or two carrying an outboard motor? The Chinese have the perfect answer. They carry buckets of water and baskets of coal every day and do it in comfort with the help of a shoulder pole.

The Chinese pole is less a pole than a lath. They take a piece of bamboo about 130cm long and about as thick as your wrist and they split it to get a curved sector of the outer tube about 4cm wide. A strip this wide is about as thick as the wall of a coffee cup and is not quite flat. It retains a bit of the circular shape of the bamboo stem. The curved outer surface sits well on the shoulder. The cupped inner surface retains a little bit of each of the cross sections that interrupted the original tube. These strengthen the lath and keep it in its rounded shape. It's the rounded form that's the key to the pole's amazing strength. On it, the owner can carry loads that would immediately snap a flat board of similar dimensions.

The ends of the pole are carved down to an arrowhead shape, which makes it easy to tie on the loads. The pole's great limitation, of course, is that it only works with a load on each end. It's far better at carrying two outboard motors than one. But users adapt to this without a second thought. They carry two buckets to the well, two baskets to the field and two small bags to the bus stop instead of one larger one. The loads needn't be exactly equal. It's easy to vary the position of the pole on the shoulder to balance them.

Snobbish city people disdain to resort to the shoulder pole, but they have no better replacement. They can only hire a porter with a pole to follow them through the streets carrying their bags to the bus station.

The tinkers invited me to share their lunch. They avoid carrying very much by bartering repairs for food when mealtime approaches. All they carry with them is some pickled cabbage and some hot peppers. All land is public property, so they think nothing of settling down and lighting up a fire to brew some tea right among the houses of a village. I couldn't sense whether the locals respected them as tradesmen or regarded them as shady characters wandering into these insular little places.

Like most Chinese, these tinkers were walking around in five layers of clothing on a warm spring day. Among the farmers you could partly understand it. They were preparing their fields to plant rice, so were standing around barefoot up their knees in mud and water much of the time. But the tinkers were walking in the sun. It was hard to believe.

I was making very slow progress with the tinkers, so in mid-afternoon I bid them good-by and set off on my own again, armed with their directions for avoiding Lok Cheung and hitting the Bat Gong north of town. It wasn't long, however, before I fell in with an old man who was wallowing his water buffalo and who invited me in for a cup of tea. The tea was good, but what I really appreciated was his stash of fresh water chestnuts. He pulled them down from the loft of his house and we sat there peeling and eating them while I recited my catechism. It was the first time I'd eaten them this way, and they made a sweet and refreshing snack.

The chestnuts, in fact, saved me a few minutes later from the temptation of an ice cream bar. As a sure sign that I was approaching the city, I came across a wayside shop with a freezer full of ice cream bars on display in the dusty courtyard outside the door. It was the first ice cream I'd seen for weeks, and a dangerous temptation. I ate many an ice cream bar on my way across the country, and the taste was always welcome. But my enjoyment was heightened by the Russian-roulette aspect of never being quite sure whether the manufacturer was using boiled water in his product.

One of the nice features of walking in Switzerland is that on reaching the top of a mountain or the crest of a difficult pass, you'll often find a little restaurant serving a glass of wine complemented by an excellent view. No hope of that in the Chinese countryside. On the other hand, economic liberalization over the past few years has led to ambitious individuals setting up small shops in almost every village and even at some rural crossroads. The hiker in China rarely has to carry very much in the way of provisions.

In most regions these shops remain basic in the extreme. The building itself may be just a tarpaper shack protected against burglary only by the fact that the proprietor sleeps on the counter at night. In many of these little places it's difficult to distinguish the items on display because they're illuminated only by the dim light coming through the open door. If the shop is on a vehicular road, everything is likely to be covered in dust. But after you've visited a couple of these private shops, none of this poses a problem. You'll already know what they have in stock before setting foot inside. Within a given region, every one is the same.

Cigarettes, rice liquor and beer are the basics. The brands vary from county to county, but in every private shop these are the backbone of the trade. There are usually basic school supplies, as well as penny candies for the children and one or two types of cookies. There will be some form of soft drink, but it might be very small cans of fruit juice, bottles of cheap and nasty local soda pop or, if you're lucky, larger bottles of one of the nationally distributed brands. China produces a lot of sugar, but for some reason Chinese soda is always artificially sweetened.

Beyond the basics, shops stock an unpredictable assortment of goods more or less useful to the traveller. Instant noodles are often available. There are usually matches or cheap gas lighters. If you're brave you might pick up a can of meat or an imitation-meat sausage. There are often various bottled fruits in syrup or jars of (very nice) vacuum-packed salted peanuts. If you need a sun hat, a needle and thread or new socks, you won't find them in every store, but you won't have to search for weeks either.

What you should not expect to find for sale in these village shops are staple foodstuffs. Rice, vegetables, cooking oil, fresh meat and that sort of thing are available only in the major towns (normally places to avoid) or on market days. Carry vitamin pills. If you stick to the country places you'll be eating lots of cookies and artificially sweetened soda.

Following directions, I managed to avoid the worst of Lok Cheung and skirted around the outskirts to a point where I could see the river and the route north. From there I could confirm that, as everyone had been telling me but contrary to my map, the main rail line had been relocated from the east to the west bank of the river. On the east shore it used to follow the river through a gorge, the mouth of which I could see opening north of town. The new line seemed to cut through the hills in a tunnel. That gave me the idea that the old disused rail line might be an easy, scenic route north along the river. The only problem was that it was on the other side, and there was no bridge without detouring back through the centre of Lok Cheung. I cut northeast across the fields toward the river bank without much hope.

In fact, luck was with me. Just before the river I crossed the new main line of the railroad, and from the top of the embankment I could see that the Bat Gong had been dammed at the mouth of the gorge and almost all the water had been diverted into a large irrigation canal. The canal had a bridge over it, and the riverbed beyond was almost dry. As I scrambled down to avoid an approaching train, I got a glimpse of a man pushing a bicycle across the rocky river bed. I grabbed a stick and took off my shoes.

On the east bank the rails weren't completely rusty, but the stations and all the switching gear had been gutted. Obviously the old line was little used. I was in business.

In fact, it proved to be a beautiful walk. The river and the gorge were continuously interesting. In case of rain, there were numerous abandoned buildings along the way. Only one little self-propelled car came by during the day or so I spent following the line, and even pedestrians were few and far between. A couple of boats dredging sand down in the river were the only intrusion on the sylvan scene.

I spent the night in one of the old station buildings, and the next morning continued up the line. Walking a rail line is always hard work, but the scenery was fine. The gorge was steep and narrow with the rushing river not far below. A difficulty I hadn't counted on was that the terrain from time to time forced the line into tunnels. Walking in the dark over railroad sleepers is no picnic, but in fact none of the tunnels was long enough to be completely dark, and at least they all were well drained.

There were a couple of villages squeezed into the gorge next to the tracks. I was enjoying the freedom from having to ask directions and recite my catechism every fifteen minutes, so I didn't stop to visit, but I did notice that the villages were constructed almost entirely of fired brick. Apparently the rocky gorge didn't provide many sources of good adobe, and shipping in real brick by the railroad was relatively cheap and easy. Up until then I hadn't seen much real brick construction outside the main towns.

My peaceful isolation eventually developed into something of a problem. The river and rail line were bending around to the west and it was important that I find a way out of the gorge and a trail continuing to the north. My map showed the old line and all of the old stations. At each station I expected to find a major trail, which folks from the surrounding area had used to descend into the gorge to catch the trains. The old stations were still there, still marked with their names, but search as I might I couldn't find any promising trails up over the rim. I began asking everyone I could find, but there weren't many around, and those I did come across posed two problems. First, I was getting down to my last few days in Guangdong province, and this close to Hunan many of the people I met didn't speak much Cantonese, the Guangdong dialect. Then, it's likely that if I were up on top looking for a way down everyone would know how to help me, but gorge dwellers took the train anywhere they wanted to go and never thought of climbing up to the surrounding farming villages. So they really didn't know much about trails I could use.

Finally I ran into a teenager who lived in a village up on top and volunteered to guide me there. It was a killing climb, but you had to admire the work of the old time settlers who had laid out a steady progression of switchbacks up the grade. We stopped at the kid's house for a cup of tea, then he guided me on to the edge of the village and set me on a trail heading north through open, hilly country.

There wasn't much woodland in those northern reaches of the province, but quite a few prosperous looking orchards. Most of the fields had a few big, black boulders scattered here and there, and the adobe houses were built on stone foundations. It was beautiful and interesting country for walking, but there were few farmers out in the fields to tell me the way. Fortunately, I'd learned by then that when the trail forks, you can often tell which is the main track because the trails were usually used as boundaries when the land was divided up among the various families under the household responsibility system. If one branch had a field of peanuts on one hand and a tree plantation on the other that was a fair indication it was the permanent, traditional trail.

The next morning I came upon a school, which had been built out in the fields midway between the villages it serves. In the rolling terrain I heard it before I saw it. It sounded as if the inmates were rioting. Chinese teaching emphasizes having the kids memorize things and then recite them in unison in class. This school had started out as a single brick building, but had now been expanded with two wings of mud brick. There must have been six or eight classes in all, each reciting its lessons aloud. It made quite a din.

Everyone I'd spoken with at length had commented on the difficulty of generating cash for school fees. Most of the peasants are largely self-sufficient and live to a large extent outside the cash economy, but school fees and medical fees must be paid in cash, and it takes a bit of ingenuity to find temporary sources of income for these occasional payments.

That got me thinking about consumer goods. When they have a bit of cash to spare, what do the peasants spend it on? I thought back over the people I'd met – Mr. Yam, for example. No one in his family had a watch, but in their living room they had a battery clock so coated in soot that its face was hard to read. But it chimed the hours. The other families I'd visited had electricity at least some of the time. They were thinking about TV. The family of the fellow who guided me up out of the gorge had both a TV and an electric kettle. A kettle uses a lot of power, but it can be really handy when you have to boil all your water over an open fire and gather all your firewood. The city people are thinking about karaoke machines, but most Chinese families seem to have struggled up the scale of consumer avarice about to the level of the electric kettle.

I eventually crossed the last highway before the provincial border not far from the town of Ching Yuen. For several hours I'd been seeing strange developments. The trail had gradually evolved into a wide but deserted cement thoroughfare. Some of the fields had been left fallow, and in other places there were extensive tracts covered with tea bushes. None of this was normal in a land of tiny plots, intensively farmed. It was all a bit reminiscent of... Ah, yes. The Secret Arsenal. Then, as I approached the highway, I saw the unmistakable walls of a prison. All of Guangdong province is supposed to be open to foreigners, but the grounds of a prison farm are very likely to be an exception. I kept walking steadily, avoiding eye contact. Fortunately, it was about lunchtime and there weren't too many people about.

I don't think Chinese prisoners get visitors, but out on the highway was a bus stop with a shop and a noodle stall. Safely off prison property, I stopped for my first restaurant meal in several days. As usual, I was immediately the centre of attention. As I was answering questions, I selected a pair of chopsticks from the rusty can in the middle of my table and began re-washing them with my tea as Chinese restaurant patrons always do. But the other patrons wouldn't let me. "Whoa, let me help you," one insisted.

"No, really, I'll be okay. I do this all the time."

"That tea isn't hot enough. Here let me . . ."

Eventually, the owner produced a brand new set, fresh from the factory in a plastic wrapper, and they washed those.

Really elegant chopsticks are made from elephant ivory. City restaurants use white plastic imitations, but out in the countryside ordinary restaurant chopsticks are bamboo. They're about 20 percent longer than a fork, square at the handle end and round at the end that goes in your mouth. In ordinary restaurants they're stored in canisters on the tables with the handle ends down. The waiter brings a pot of tea before the meal, and at that time each diner pulls a few chopsticks from the can trying to assemble a pair that are straight and about the same length. You'd hope that in pulling sticks from the can they'd be careful to grasp them half way down and not paw over the eating ends, but of course you can never be sure. So your first task is to re-wash your selected pair in hot tea and then throw the used tea out the door, on the floor or into the spittoon under the table. (Yes, there often is, and if it's there it's probably overflowing.)

I was usually the first foreigner these restaurants had ever served, and so they quite often brought me out new, virgin disposable chopsticks. It's clear that they're new, because in shaping them from the wood they'll have been left joined at one end. You're meant to pull them apart, guaranteeing that you're the first ever to eat with them. In this case, in addition to washing them in the usual way, you have to check for splinters.

Some people suggest that using wooden chopsticks is bad for the rainforest. In view of the prevalence of hepatitis in China, I have no compunctions. Tropical softwoods are an eminently renewable resource. You can finesse both health risks and ecoconciousness by carrying a pair of your own bamboo chopsticks around with you. (Bamboo is a type of grass.) Hong Kong tourists often carry their own, but then they prefer ivory.

8

Hunan in the Rain

North of the highway I was entering a new phase of the trip. Most importantly, Cantonese would no longer be everyone's second dialect. I'd have to fall back on Mandarin, the official national language. It's used in all the schools, so many people can speak it, but in the countryside they often speak with a heavy local accent. My own Mandarin comprehension is weak at the best of times, so asking directions was going to be a much bigger problem.

Equally important, outside Guangdong and Fujian provinces most of China is closed to foreigners. The major cities and tourist destinations are open, and most places along the rail lines are okay, but I wasn't really allowed to just wander around the countryside at will. I'd have to stick to my principles: no roads that appear on the map and no towns larger than the smallest dot. The police stick to their cars and their offices, so the principles offered a pretty good defense. Apart from the police, not many Chinese are aware that the closed-area policy still exists.

As I struck off for the provincial boundary, it didn't take long to notice some more tangible differences as well. I was following a valley served by a vehicular road, but the road hadn't replaced the traditional trail. Indeed, what should have been a disused trail was tarted up with amenities such as I'd rarely seen. It was easy to follow because it passed under a series of venerable trees that had apparently been left to shade travellers. Seeing one of these ahead up the valley, you could be sure that the trail would pass underneath it. Then, parts of the way were paved with big stone flags. And the stream crossings were no mere stepping stones, but elaborate arched stone bridges such as you'd expect to see in Scotland.

Indeed, stone carving seemed to be a major local industry. The trail passed several stone temples, which were now disused but had been built too solidly to be demolished during the cultural revolution. And in the villages quite ordinary houses with no glass in the windows sported elaborately carved stone lintels. Some of the villages had impressive monuments to the local ancestors erected in the main square. And of course there was a return to sign-posting the trail junctions with engraved stone slabs. I hadn't seen that in weeks.

I folded up my dog-eared Guangdong maps for the last time late one afternoon and celebrated by detouring into a town for a hot meal. Right away I was in language trouble. Pointing to the menu was no use; everything I asked for was off. I tried generic discussion and ended up with some sort of soup of the day (I knew not what), a plate of braised green vegetables (species unclear), and that old standby, fried rice. He certainly had lots of other stuff, but I just couldn't communicate with him. I was, however, able to convince him that I didn't want too many red peppers. Hunan is famous for spicy food. And I was able to get a beer.

Sadly, like most Chinese restaurateurs, this fellow kept his meat in the cooler and served his beer warm.

While waiting for my mystery meal I spent some time studying my fellow patrons. For once they were leaving me alone. They had bigger fish to fry. As far as I could make out, the skinny guy wearing the vest was a truck driver. A few days ago he had knocked down the old man in the corner with his truck. He was going to have to pay compensation, and this meeting was to negotiate how much. There was a guy running around passing out cigarettes who was apparently the driver's boss. This is the usual way these things are handled in China. People, especially out in the countryside, will go to almost any lengths to avoid having anything to do with the police and courts. Disputes are settled through this sort of private negotiation.

I was also interested to note that the restaurant had a sort of telephone. It was an old crank gadget hung on the wall. That suggests that this town was once the headquarters of a commune, and the commune had its own internal telephone system. It may or may not still work, but clearly it doesn't connect to the outside world or it wouldn't have sat idle all the while I was eating. Most country towns have some sort of electricity service these days, but telephones remain a city amenity. This place wasn't big enough.

By the time I paid my bill, dusk was falling. No time to observe the outcome of the negotiations, I had to find a campsite before dark. The track out of town was lined with houses for almost an hour, but then my route struck off up a steep ridge, and I was alone on an empty hillside with a great view. The stars were so spectacular it was hard to sleep.

But the next morning I was up early with the sound of thunder in the distance. After a deliberate start, I just about made it to the top of the ridge before it started to rain. I couldn't hole up for the day at 7 in the morning. There was nothing for it but to pull out my poncho and keep plugging. Beside, it was misty up there, a bit windy and chilly if you stopped.

The cold, damp weather drove most people indoors, so I had few opportunities to ask directions. At trail junctions I mostly used my compass to pick the trail heading more nearly north, and it worked out pretty well for most of the morning.

I passed more amateur coalmines. Some of these looked as if they had been reinforced with old-fashioned wooden pit props, but they couldn't have been very deep, as there was no forced ventilation or mechanical drainage. I would have liked to explore one or two of the shafts as an alternative to walking in the rain, but I wasn't carrying a flashlight. As camping out on the sly as was my practice, a flashlight would have been of little use. Rural China has very few artificial lights at night, so a strange light out on the hillside would be likely to attract immediate notice. These mine shafts were one of the few occasions when a flashlight would have come in handy.

In late morning my compass navigation finally let me down. I blundered my way out of a small stone village to find that it was perched on the lip of an enormous canyon barring my way north. Backtracking, I found an old man sitting under a shelter minding some ducks and, with some difficulty, eventually understood that I would have to strike off on a track around the head of the gorge and up to the far rim. This proved to be quite a climb. The descent was wide and well graded, because it led to a stream crossing where the village draws its water. After that, there was a much longer and steeper climb up the other side, which seemed to be used only for taking sheep or goats to pasture. (I never figured out which, because there were no animals out on that day and most Chinese use the same word to signify sheep or goats.) As I was getting near the top, and near the point of exhaustion, I saw a squall sweeping across the gorge with high winds, heavy rain and, as it turned out, nasty hail. Just then, I rounded a spur and saw there above me a trailside shelter. I made it just in time.

Not many regions of China improve their walking trails to the point of erecting trailside shelters, but southern Hunan Province has a network of shelters that are as architecturally pleasing as they are welcome on a rainy day. Approaching along the trail, a Chinese shelter looks a lot like a covered bridge (See photo number 15). Except it's not a bridge. It's just a sort of barn covering an area about 10 by 5 metres with a big doorway at each end and the trail going through the middle. The inside is empty except for stone benches built into the two long walls. These structures seem to have been built for no other purpose than to provide travellers with a place to sit down in the shade. What a nice idea. The names of the contributors may be cut into a stone plaque on the wall. The contributions seem to average about 5 yuan per family. In one corner there's often a bit of a shrine where, presumably, the traveller prays for a safe journey. In the centre may be the ashes of an open fire and some left-over firewood to help the next visitors sheltering from a shower on a cold day. These halts differ in size, design and construction, but they're always worth a stop and a look around for their intrinsic interest as well as for a few minutes in the shade.

Fortunately, the squall lasted only long enough for me to grab a bite of lunch. I was soaked in sweat, and this particular shelter offered little protection against the chilly breeze. I pushed on as soon as it had let up, and eventually even had an hour or two when I was able to take off the poncho and dry out a bit. Fortunately there were few trail junctions, as I was in high, wild country and never saw a soul for most of the afternoon. Finally the trail expanded into a jeep track and began to descend. It descended into a cloud bank and I was back in my poncho sheltering from misty rain.

Dusk came early and I was worried about a dry place to spend the night. I'd passed through one damp and dreary town that had all the earmarks of a former commune headquarters. The one store didn't have so much as a bottle of soda. I had to assume it was a mining commune, as there were few cultivated fields around, and there wasn't much sign of forestry work either. The road, though, was firm and not muddy, so the people had access to a good supply of crushed stone and knew how to use it.

Finally, it was getting pretty dark when my road merged with another at a junction in the middle of the woods. Facing down the way I was going was a sign informing me that I had just visited the Da Kui Shang tourist area. According to the illustration, its main attraction must be hunting. I checked both ways from the intersection before finally discovering a cement blockhouse which had apparently been erected as a vehicle checkpoint but was now disused. It was just the shelter I needed, and I lost no time in getting out of my wet clothes and boiling up a pot of instant noodles. I spent 11 hours there and heard one truck pass after dark.

The next morning began with the long, gradual and scenic descent into a north-tending valley, which led me to realize how the economy works in this area. At the bottom was a really large mining and smelting complex. This was a real old-style state industry.

I came first to the mine site with its housing area. The workers were trudging up a long flight of steps from their housing units at the bottom of the valley to the mine entrance up at the road level. They were eating some sort of fried cakes as they walked, so I promptly turned down the steps in search of a hot breakfast. No luck. They were bringing their fritters out of the factory canteen. Disappointed, I picked up the walking trail that followed the floor of the valley through the housing area and along the stream. As at most state work units, the housing area included stores, a library, a clinic, a kindergarten and, down at the lower end of town where there was better road access, a public market. In the market was a private entrepreneur selling her version of the same deep-fried snacks I'd sought earlier. I can describe them only as some sort of savory dough containing onion pieces and laced with hot peppers. A rough sort of breakfast but, craving fat, I ate three.

By walking through the housing area I'd avoided the heavy trucks, which now plagued the road. I was beginning to get the picture. Yesterday's commune had no visible means of support and no decent shops because everyone works down here in the mine and smelter. The ore was being hauled from the mine to the smelter in big trucks, which require a good road, and that road had been extended up the valley to the "tourist area," but in fact that end of it was little used. The minerals complex employed thousands, and the housing areas at the mine and at the smelter a few kilometres down the valley each amounted to a small city, but none of this was shown on the map. This may at one time have been considered a matter for secrecy in the interests of national security, but on the other hand, I had to admit that a mine isn't really the kind of political entity that maps usually show. It looks like a city to the Western visitor, but it's really just a work unit housing its workers in the communist way. Be that as it may, it was all a surprise to me.

An hour or two back on the road brought me to the turnoff for the smelter, and from the sign I learned that the work unit was a mine and smelter for non-ferrous metals. According to the usual Chinese naming scheme, the fact that the name didn't begin with

"Hunan Province, Chenzhou County..." signified that this was an important work unit directly under the control of the non-ferrous metals potentates in Beijing. So, although technically I wasn't violating my principle about avoiding towns shown on the map, this was the kind of place likely to have a police presence and especially likely to be a place not open to foreigners. I kept moving and took my first opportunity to strike out across the fields in search of the Li river, which my map showed to be just a couple of hours' walk to the north.

It was a slow business. The terrain was hilly, the streams were high and everything was pretty wet. The showers returned on and off. I made some progress. Eventually, I crossed a rail line, which my map showed to be only a few kilometres from the river. But a couple of hours later I was still plunging up hill and down dale with no sign of a trail going in my direction. Finally, in a tea plantation, I came across a lone old man trimming bushes who tried to convey the famous, "You can't get there from here" in some little-known dialect. As an alternative, he offered to lead me back to his village for the night.

The old man still referred to the place as his "commune." It wasn't very far when you knew the way. Once we got there he turned me over to the boss, Mr. Lee, who, along with a crowd of others, was of course curious to know how I had come to be walking around a remote tea plantation at dusk soaking wet. Fortunately, he realized after a few minutes that I was cold and miserable and adjourned the meeting to his parlor.

Mr. Lee turned out to be the Assistant General Manager of one of the old communes, which has renamed itself a "rural enterprise" but kept everything else pretty much the same. Its basic product is tea, with wood and cement as worthwhile sidelines. They were in the process of developing some orchards. As one of the senior managers, Mr. Lee presumably had about the best of their accommodation. It was livable, but I wouldn't describe it as a setup most people would want to devote their life to attaining.

Like most commune and factory housing, this estate was arranged in parallel rows like military barracks. Mr. Lee and his wife had the end unit in a row of six, a unit bigger than the rest. It seems Mr. Lee rates his rather large sitting room because he's expected to receive callers in the evening. They come to discuss business matters, but equally any of the many social arrangements that continue to be part of the enterprise's responsibility toward its employees. The whole farm with its hundreds of workers probably has at most one telephone. So when an employee has something on his mind he can't be expected to call for an appointment. He has no alternative but to drop in and discuss it in person. Mr. Lee's daughter is away at school all week, so there's only he and his wife at home. But most evenings the two sofas and the three chairs in his sitting room are occupied by applicants for special favours, or just people dropping in to watch Mr. Lee's television set.

Apart from this semi-public room, the Lee family has arranged two bedrooms. They originally had a private bedroom next to the sitting room with a kitchen at the back. By building a lean-to addition onto the back of the building and moving the kitchen out there, they've been able to convert the back room into a bedroom for their daughter. She surely appreciates having her own room, but there must be a lot of traffic through it back and forth to the kitchen in the lean-to.

Like many ex-communes, this one has rigged up a water tower and indoor running water for at least some of its residents. But toilet facilities are still out the back – a 2x2m hut of mud bricks with a shallow pit in the floor bridged by three or four logs. Users are expected to position their feet securely on the logs, squat down in the conventional Chinese posture and aim for the gaps. Mr. Lee and his wife share this facility with the other occupants of their row of housing units. Unlike many such arrangements, they and their neighbors have developed the convention of using it only one at a time. The enterprise no doubt has a well-organized system for collecting the yield from all of its latrines and using it for fertilizer.

Mr. Lee's house is electrified, but if the night I visited is at all typical, the supply isn't very reliable. Mr. Lee keeps candles at the ready, and while I was there he needed them twice in the course of about two and a half hours.

A night in front of Mrs. Lee's stove dried my clothes somewhat, but the next morning it didn't last long. It was again raining lightly when we set off. At first Mr. Lee attempted to guide me up the hill to a trail that would take me to the river, but the way was so muddy that he quickly changed his mind and we set off in another direction. In a few minutes we came to a swollen creek where a crude dock had been constructed by mooring some derelict barges. The commune (I might as well continue to call it that, everyone else did.) was apparently doing some construction work. They were buying sand, which was being brought in by ferrying it up the creek in the barges shown in photo number 16, best described as sort of self-propelled pontoons. They were about 20m long and a couple of metres wide, with a diesel engine mounted on deck aft coupled to a propeller shaft hung over the stern. There was no cabin. The coxswain simply stood by the engine holding the tiller.

Mr. Lee spoke briefly with one of the operators. It wasn't clear whether they were commune employees or independent contractors, but he arranged for me a ride down the creek to the river with the next pontoon going to fetch a load. Normally, that wouldn't involve much of a wait. They had a crew of eight shovelling the sand off the pontoons into trucks. But each load was about a metre deep, and they'd organized it so that four of the shovellers unloaded the sand onto the shore where three more threw it up into a truck for the eighth to distribute. At that rate it would take them three hours or more of steady work to unload a pontoon. But the work wasn't steady. Each time a shower hit they all took cover under the truck. I eventually got away before noon.

Cruising down the river on the empty pontoon, I could see that I would have had a tough walk. There was surely a trail along the bank somewhere, but the creek was over its banks in places. And once we hit the main river there were giant sandstone bluffs rising sheer out of the water. The boatman very kindly dropped me on the far bank where a sandy track came down to a ferry crossing. There was a shack there serving lunch, so I took the opportunity for another hot meal.

My intention at this point was to follow the Li River northward as I had the Bat Gong in the first days of the trip. I anticipated finding levees along the shores that would lead me north for a few days, avoiding towns and major roads. In that expectation I was disappointed, but I did find a trail following the river bank which, for one afternoon at least, led me through some very scenic country around, over and through the giant sandstone formations I'd seen from the boat. There was no need for levees, as I often found myself looking down on the river from atop steep banks and neighboring hills.

At first there was a clear riverside trail, though it wasn't very busy. At one point, I found myself overtaking a man in a traditional peasant raincoat, and I slowed down to study it as I approached from behind. It was a cape fastened around the neck and extending just below the hips woven entirely of some sort of fibre. It looked like horsehair, but in that part of the country it was more likely to come from palm or perhaps the hair of the water buffalo. The fibre was quilted with a kind of thread or string. Apparently, it is so oily that it sheds rain. A wide-brimmed straw hat (woven from reeds, actually) protected the man's head, and he wore shorts and rubber flip-flop sandals. It seemed a pretty effective costume, a lot more durable than a modern raincoat, though very heavy. In fact these capes must be very time-consuming to make and are now rare. Most peasants go to the fields caped in a sheet of polyethylene these days, and the city folk wouldn't be seen dead in such rustic garb.

As the giant bluffs gave way to smaller jumbled hills, my route became less clear. In my poor Mandarin I couldn't convey the idea that I was simply following the river. When I asked directions people would usually send me off on a trail leading down to the river's edge where local boat sharks would try to rent me a boat for a trip downriver to the next town. Apparently this stretch of the river was always deep enough that people could travel by boat, and there was no established riverside trail up and down all the complicated hills. Finally, near dusk, I felt I had to cross on one of the ferries because as I approached the bank someone had seen me coming and already called the boatman back from half way across the river to get me. The ferry was just a flat-bottomed wooden skiff with a diesel on the stern. I was the only passenger, so I took the opportunity to revert to my previous practice and ask directions to a particular town instead of trying to speak in terms of following the river. I immediately got complete directions including the locations of all the trailside shelters. It was obviously a common journey; it just didn't follow the banks of the river.

By the time the boatman had drawn me a map in the sand on the far bank and I'd copied it into my damp notebook, it was getting dark. I set off on the trail, but immediately cut back to the riverbank to investigate a possible campsite I'd seen from the boat. It was a sort of tree house in the middle of an orchard. It was just about large enough for two workers to take a nap with headroom enough for four to sit up and play cards. It was thatched with straw and branches on a wooden frame, but carpeted with a straw mat. And the roof was sealed with a sheet of polyethylene under the thatch. What luck. The perfect campsite for a rainy night.

I later realized that you can find such structures wherever valuable crops are grown. Apparently, during the harvest season when the crop is nearly ripe, these hutches are occupied day and night guarding the fields against thieves. The rest of the year they stand empty except during the noontime siesta hour.

The boatman's trail was scenic, but pretty muddy in the continuing rain. There were shelters evenly spaced every half hour, and I took advantage of most of them to shake out my poncho and dry my glasses. Unfortunately, late in the morning the trail became a road and that joined a highway about six kilometres from the major town of Yong Sing. I had to re-cross the swollen river on the Yong Sing bridge, so I was forced to violate two of my cardinal principles. Still, apart from getting pretty dirty with spray from passing trucks, I got through without difficulty.

In asking the way out of Yong Sing I learned that there was a passenger boat service on the river below this point. Nevertheless, I was assured that there was a trail following the river at least as far as the town of Tang Mun Kou several hours away. The problem was finding it. I was directed down a rough road that proved to lead to a coal mine. From the mine itself I was directed into the housing area. My informants kept directing me down smaller and smaller alleys among the barracks. I was waiting for someone to lead me through his living room and out the back door.

Then, suddenly, I broke out of the warren of accommodation units and found myself on a cliff side trail overlooking the swirling river and face-to-face with a large cathedral. It wasn't a cathedral, of course, but it certainly resembled the facade of a Christian cathedral set into the cliff wall above the river. In fact, I'd seen something like that somewhere before. It looked remarkably like the facade of the ruined St. Paul's cathedral in Macau. In this case, it was fronting a temple to the Chinese goddess Kwan Yin set in a grotto in the cliff. Apparently, the coal miners had enjoyed access to lots of labour and equipment and, over the years, had gradually diverted some of it into improving the grotto into an enormous shrine in the style of a European cathedral. It certainly appeared that they'd been inspired by pictures of Macau. It would have been interesting to know when the improvements were done and how the place fared during the cultural revolution, but on a rainy afternoon there was no-one around to ask.

Beyond the temple the trail was much easier to find because there were obvious preparations to upgrade it into a road. It was another example of a trail I was walking on just in time before it disappears. And this was a particularly scenic one, especially with the river so high.

It was Saturday afternoon, and I fell in with two schoolgirls walking home to Tang Mun Kou after a week at school. It was a lot less stressful walking with reliable guides, and they saved me some unnecessary detours, but at the same time I realized that asking the way every few minutes gave me a chance to meet a variety of local people and to stop and look around. With the girls it was just straight walking.

I suppose the girls think of Tang Mun Kou with affection, but I couldn't bring myself to agree. It was another coal mine with another rabbit warren of a housing area squeezed under the cliff above the river. The alleys were so narrow that people's rain awnings from each side overlapped in the centre to form an arcade, and runoff from the awnings poured into a drain down the centre of the alley. With the rain everything was inky black.

The alleys were deserted, and at the far side of town I found out why. A creek flowed down from the hills and into the river. Normally there was probably about enough water in the creek to do the laundry, but today they were able to bring barges up from the river to a bridge near the coal yards. Every vehicle in town had been mobilized to bring all the stockpiles down to the bridge and dump them over into the barges. Most of the vehicles were nothing more than garden tractors pulling a little trailer, but there were a few proper dump trucks, so the town had to be served by a road of some sort. I set out to find it.

By dusk I was well away from the Li and trying to find my way along a muddy track among a confusing jumble of hills. My track intersected a larger road just as a bus came along and discharged Mr. Chow and half a dozen of his extended family. I took the opportunity to ask directions, and he informed me that not only had I missed my turning, but they were going my way. As a result, I fell in with his group and, after almost two hours walking, ended up spending the night at his house.

Mr. Chow's village was another barracks-style setup, and his home was another standard housing unit, a bit smaller than Mr. Lee's in floor plan but with the advantage of a second storey. The family could sleep up there and leave the entire ground floor free. Their front door entered into their sitting room, from which you could go through to a room at the back or into another off to the side. They used the room at the back as a storeroom, but it had a spare bed, which they turned over to me. The room at the side was a pantry where they did most of the food preparation, but the cooking was done in the sitting room itself over an interesting form of stove.

The entire sitting room had been converted into a sort of window nook. In the middle of the room a briquette cooker was set into the floor. They'd arranged benches around it in a U-shaped arrangement to form an alcove in front of the window, so that in winter the whole family could sit around with their feet to the cooker, perhaps with a table over it and then a blanket over the table to hold in the heat. It wasn't winter, but I found it a nice treat after several days in damp clothes.

A word here about China's ubiquitous coal briquette. Coal is China's national fuel. The nation is short of electricity, oil, gas and firewood, but it has plenty of coal. And coal remains the dominant fuel for domestic heating. In the mining regions you'll see people pedaling around with 30kg chunks of coal strapped to the carriers of their bicycles, but in most parts of the country real coal like this is hard to get and too expensive for domestic use. Instead the people burn coal dust.

Coal dust is almost a by-product of the coal industry. It's cheap because in an ordinary boiler, furnace or railroad engine the draught in the firebox immediately picks up any dust in the coal and blows it out the stack to coat the surrounding countryside. These big industrial users burn only lump coal from which the fines have already been screened out. The fines are thus cheap enough for home use. But a heap of coal powder would be difficult to light and wouldn't burn properly without some sort of forced draught. To get around this problem the powder is formed into cylindrical briquettes.

The standard Chinese coal briquette is 10cm in diameter and 10cm high, pierced by a pattern of 12 holes parallel to the axis, each hole 1cm in diameter. So the finished briquette looks a bit like a cylindrical piece of honeycomb. Large city work units buy their coal dust by the truckload and form briquettes for their members in motor-driven presses. In the countryside, making briquettes is a hand operation using a mould on the end of a long handle. Water and a bit of clay are first added to the coal dust to make a large lump of sticky paste. The briquette maker fills the mould by pushing it into the lump of paste, then carries it to a flat piece of ground before pushing on a handle which forces a plunger into the mould and expels the briquette onto the ground, where it's left to dry. After drying, the briquettes are strong enough to be piled four or five high and to be carried around without too much breakage.

Homes in China have stoves and space heaters especially designed to burn these standard briquettes, and it was one of these that Mr. Chow had built into his sitting room floor. They can be lit with scraps of kindling and a charge of two or three briquettes will burn for a few hours depending on the draught adjustment. When burnt out, the residue is a matrix of ash and fired clay still strong enough to be extracted from the stove and disposed of in briquette form. With some grades of coal the ash fuses into a sort of clinker, and in those parts of the country the burned-out briquettes are to be seen everywhere as one of China's very few forms of solid waste pollution.

During the evening, Mr. Chow's relatives of course came over from the adjoining houses to hear me recite my catechism. At some point, as often happens, someone asked to see my passport. I usually try to play dumb in these situations, but when someone pulled out his identity card to demonstrate what he was talking about, I was forced to reciprocate to the extent of producing my Hong Kong identity card for inspection. I carried that in my pocket, whereas my passport was in a money belt, which I was loath to reveal.

While they pored over my Hong Kong ID card, I had an opportunity to study theirs. It shouldn't be a surprise that China's citizens are supposed to carry an ID card wherever they go. Many countries around the world, including Hong Kong, impose the same requirement. In fact, the format of the Chinese ID card seems to have been copied from the cards which the British imposed on the residents of Hong Kong. (Imposed, I should point out, despite fierce resistance when anyone proposes applying the concept at home in the British Isles.)

The Chinese card is a 6x9cm form laminated in plastic. It has a photo of the holder in the top left corner. Next to it on the right are the holder's name and sex, and an indication whether or not he or she is a member of an official minority. Birth date is also recorded, but most of the space on the front of the card is taken up recording the holder's address. In most countries it would be impractical to record someone's address on a card laminated in plastic, but in the traditional communist system this was no problem. Each person was considered a unit of the national labour supply to be deployed (in theory) through central planning. The individual labour quantum might theoretically be redeployed by central fiat, but could never change residence on his or her own volition. This system has now broken down, and the citizens can move about much more freely. Eventually the card system will have to be revised. Perhaps the address will be kept only in a computer file. There's already a fifteen-digit identification number across the bottom of the card, which would facilitate setting up such a system. So far this number seems completely unused. The card is intended to be good for 20 years before renewal. It will be an expensive exercise when the first wave hits. The issue and expiry dates are recorded along with the identity number.

The back of the card is an anti-forgery motif saying "PRC Citizen ID Card" over a complicated background of security printing. This feature is considered very important on the Hong Kong government's cards because so many people would like to evade immigration controls to settle there and work. The colony's free trade principles don't extend to labour, and the identity cards are one of the primary mechanisms used to control unwanted immigration. The mainland has copied the security printing, but of course they have no such difficulties.

The address on Mr. Chow's relative's card showed another difficulty the central planners had to overcome. Around the county, their village is probably known as the Chow Family Village, Grandpa Chow's Family Village or even Long-Eared Chow's Family Village. There are probably Chow Family Villages in most of the counties of China, and many counties no doubt have several. Central planners need a more definitive scheme, so Mr. Chow's official address reads "Hunan Province, Chen Zhou County, Yong Xing Number 29 Village." They simply went through each county giving the towns Mandarin names and then numbering the dependant villages. Ah, the romance of socialism.

As usual, I arranged to take pictures of Mr. Chow and his family as a sort of recompense for their hospitality. In the morning I did take a couple of shots with his family in front of their home, but Mr. Chow seemed more interested in getting a shot with his old school teacher. The teacher lived at the school, which was, in any case, on the trail to the next town. So Mr. Chow guided me there personally and roused the teacher to put on his best clothes for a Sunday morning picture. Chinese culture prescribes a special pupil-teacher loyalty, but this particular relationship must have involved some exceptional bond that perhaps was explained to me in vocabulary that I couldn't understand. Anyway, I happily took a couple of shots and the address and later mailed them back.

The rain continued, including some violent showers during the morning. About lunch time, I hit the coal mining town of Da Yi, where the local creek had burst its banks and flooded one end of the main street. The local coal mine had sent down a crew of ladies with a truckload of tailings but, unable to do much to stem the flood, they were using the fill instead to fill ruts in the unflooded portion of the street. I watched proceedings from a nearby noodle stall where I enjoyed a steaming bowl in anticipation of a couple of days out in the fields.

So far my route had relied heavily on China's maze of unmarked walking trails, supplemented by the levees along the banks of some of the major rivers. But I'd undertaken the trip with the idea of relying as well on one more variety of common cross-country route. China has an extensive network of irrigation works channelling water hundreds of kilometres to the agricultural regions. Only the largest of these irrigation canals are shown on the maps, but I was expecting to find one such during the afternoon. According to the map, it would give me a couple of days' walking almost due north without having to ask the way every 15 minutes over uncharted trails.

I had only a line on the map to go on, but in fact I had no trouble finding my canal. After lunch, I had no sooner left town than I could see ahead of me a giant aqueduct crossing the valley. It must have been almost a kilometre long, and in the middle of the valley it would have been 30 or 40 metres high. It was built in brick and cast concrete, and building it would have involved an enormous amount of labour. But then labour is one thing that's never in short supply in China. Anyway, the finished product was pretty impressive. They'd even built a sort of grand staircase down the valley wall at one end, and I climbed it with a suitable sense of appreciation.

The canal itself was about 8m wide, probably 2 or 3 metres deep and, with all the rain, was carrying a nasty current. The walls were sheer concrete, so if you ever fell in with a knapsack on, you'd be lucky to get out alive. Fortunately there were wide grassy verges on both sides, and one side had been worn down into a muddy track by people using the canal bank as a route to their fields and pastures. There was some sort of bridge every few hundred metres.

As I'd expected, I had a very quiet walk the rest of the day. The canal meandered back and forth following the contours in a northerly general direction. For much of the way, I had a good view out over the adjoining farm land. I crossed a couple of valleys on high aqueducts, and was glad to be away from the flooding down below. The rain continued.

Another reason I had a great view was that the surrounding hills had been denuded. One of the aqueducts displayed a giant sign in rusty steel letters saying: "Long Live Chairman Mao." The whole setup looked like a relic of the 1950s great leap forward campaign, when they tried to modernize the entire economy in one brief building frenzy. I could visualize armies of peasants digging the canal and building the aqueducts while all the trees were cut down to make charcoal for smelting iron. Coal was cheap enough in that district that people didn't bother with firewood, so they'd never bothered to reforest the hillsides. I was lucky, just at dusk, to come upon an isolated grove of pines where I could easily string up my shelter for the night. For lunch the next day the only shelter I could find from the continuing rain was under one of the aqueducts on the slope of a valley.

By the time I left the irrigation canal I was seeing a different sort of terrain. Rather than wandering in the hills, my route could better be described as walking through farmland with hills all around. It was still coal mining country, as evidenced by the continuing lack of trees and also some signs of prosperity. In most of the farming villages, not only were the buildings made of fired brick, but they were often decorated with a few tile ornaments – a false balcony rail, decorations at the ends of the ridge pole, or just a tile set over the door as in Holland. The peasants were taking advantage of the flooding to prepare their rice paddies. Watching them work, I could see the cash they earned in the mines applied to an intriguing bit of mechanization.

Because rice paddies are such an important feature of Chinese agriculture, the water buffalo is the principal agricultural draught animal over much of the country. The buffalo is big and strong and can work in dry fields as well, but it's particularly valued for ploughing and harrowing paddies 50cm or more deep in sticky mud. There are various types of small tractors for sale in China, which can replace the water buffalo in its other duties, but conventional tractors are no use in the deep, soft mud ideal for planting rice. On the other hand, a water buffalo requires daily care and feeding. In areas where it's possible, many landowners have taken salaried jobs and only raise enough rice to pay their taxes. In these regions, some farmers have taken to using a form of mechanical water buffalo.

The mechanical water buffalo is a small tractor useful for tilling rice paddies but for nothing else. The frame looks like a child's tricycle. The large front wheel isn't a wheel at all, but rather a contraption like the paddle wheel on a paddle wheel steamboat. It's about 50cm in diameter and has 12 paddles about 10cm wide and 15cm long. As it turns, the paddles dig into the mud and propel the tractor forward. The rear wheels of the tricycle are replaced by a plough blade or, when not ploughing, by a flat shoe about 40cm square which rides over the surface of the mud. The driver sits on a seat over the plough blade or shoe and steers with handle bars as on a tricycle. To provide stability, another shoe on the end of a 1.5m side arm rides over the mud as a sort of outrigger, a bit like a tricycle with a sidecar.

The mechanical buffalo is powered by a small diesel engine mounted in front of the handlebars over the paddle wheel. This ensures that the contraption can work only in the mud, because even a small diesel is very heavy, and on a hard surface the paddles would immediately buckle under the weight of the engine. The engine and the frame are carried to the site separately on shoulder poles and assembled in the mud. Presumably, the engine serves some other purpose for the rest of the year.

Another sign of the prosperity in this coal-producing region was the state of the trails. In this level country it was apparently possible to take a bicycle or a bus most anywhere, and many trails had fallen into disrepair. With no forest cover, the hills were badly eroded. In many places all the clay had been washed away leaving a coarse soil bright maroon in colour. Stone steps were loose or askew. Trailside shelters remained only at the ferry crossings. The rocky, eroded landscape made camping uncomfortable, as there was no way to clear all the rocks from my bed. All I could do was put down everything I owned for padding. And by day, the rain continued.

It was interesting to observe how these communist economies work. In this region, with coal going cheap, almost every little village had a homemade brick kiln. It was just an underground oven shaped like a beehive, about 15m in diameter and about the same height. Each village constructs one to make its own bricks, and thereafter all construction in the village uses brick. This amateur brick industry thrives wherever coal is cheap and easily available. Back in Guangdong, on the other hand, there isn't much coal, so most of the buildings were made of adobe. Guangdong has brick kilns, but they're official work units, properly designed with tall stacks that you can see for miles. A tall stack gives a much hotter oven and much better bricks. But government work units of all kinds distribute their products only through the official distribution system. They don't sell on the open market. So in Guangdong only government facilities are built of brick, but the quality is good. Where amateur brick-making thrives everything is built with brick, but the quality, for the most part, is terrible.

With all the rain, people were taking the opportunity to plant, or in fact to transplant, one of their two or three annual rice crops. Transplanting is one of the busiest times of the agricultural year, and over the next couple of weeks I was in the unusual position of walking through an almost continuous crowd of people all day long as I passed through the fields. Not only was the entire family out working, but sons and daughters employed in city industries or studying at distant institutions had returned to supplement the family labour pool for a few days. There were so many people out working that as I walked along I could hear the news of my presence being passed along from one field to the next like the sound of the wind in the leaves. In each paddy, in turn, the family would take a break from its labours to stand for a moment and study me silently as I passed. If I gave a brief greeting, only the head of the household would answer. On the other hand, the villages were empty. Market days seemed to be suspended for the duration. If I could find a noodle shop to buy a hot lunch out of the rain, I could sit there for an hour with only the proprietor to grill me.

Walking from district to district at different elevations, it was possible for me to watch almost simultaneously all the various steps in the complicated process of transplanting rice. Rice is grown in paddies rarely larger that 200 square metres, and sometimes as small as a table top. Since rice is grown in standing water, the paddies must be absolutely level and surrounded by a berm at least 20cm high. China's heavy clay soil makes these terraces easy to construct, even in hilly country.

During the winter the paddies are left as dry plots of stubble, and human and animal waste is dumped there as fertilizer. As the planting season begins, this fertilizer is spread and the fields are flooded, preferably through some sort of gravity irrigation scheme. Tiny irrigation schemes are a Chinese specialty, and figuring them out is one of the fascinations of walking through the Chinese countryside. Once the clay mud is good and wet the heavy work of ploughing begins. The mud is turned over and the fertilizer worked in and harrowed until the whole plot is a pit of smooth muddy slime. The surface is then re-levelled with a board. Some chemical fertilizer is spread and allowed to dissolve, then the transplanting begins.

The rice seedlings are raised in special plots, often started early under plastic sheeting. These are just like miniature rice paddies, except that the seedlings can be started in very dense array. When they reach about 20cm tall they're carefully uprooted, separated and bundled into bunches of about 50 to 100 seedlings bound with a few stalks of grass. These are then carried out to the fields in baskets and thrown out into the paddies spaced a few metres apart. The whole family then takes off its shoes, rolls up its trousers and spends three or four days setting out the individual plants one by one in well organized rows.

This transplanting process is excruciating work. It involves spending the entire day bent over double, up to the knees and elbows in mud and leeches. There's no shade and no possibility of sitting down or even changing position. The children are let off from school, and for a few days the entire village is in the fields from dawn until nightfall suffering together. It must be enormously effective in building village and clan solidarity. There's no one at home all day, and by nightfall everyone is exhausted. It's not a time for the visiting walker to expect any hospitality.

Chairman Mao came from this part of the country, and there were plenty of little indications that during his famous campaigns – the great leap forward and the cultural revolution – this area participated enthusiastically. In rainy weather, one of the least flattering reminders was to happen upon the crude earthen dams, which had been constructed across some of the valleys. In several places I came across dams which must have involved thousands of hours of unskilled labour, but which now, even after more than a week of rain, held almost no water. In the building process, all the labour had been contributed by the local peasants. The planners had done a fine job of mobilizing the masses, but completely miscalculated where the water was going to come from. What a waste.

Meanwhile, all the rivers and streams were very high. Where a trail normally crossed on stepping stones, I was often forced to make a detour to find a bridge or a place where it was narrow enough to jump across. At the larger rivers, the ferry operators were making money, as many people were heading home for the planting season but the rivers were too high to wade. I occasionally came across ferrymen who tried to ask me for exorbitant fares, though I'm happy to say that this sort of extortion is unusual out in the countryside. Ferry service usually costs 20 to 50 fen but I occasionally had ferrymen ask for as much as 20 yuan. I learned to keep this larceny within limits by always waiting to approach the crossing until I could see that there were others waiting to cross. This worked even though in most cases the local people didn't seem to pay anything at all. Perhaps their families supplied the ferryman with some sort of produce or service on a bulk basis. They'd all lived together all their lives, so there must have been some sort of equitable arrangement. Anyway, the presence of these neighbors encouraged the boatman to moderate his demands of the gullible foreigner.

With the prosperity of recent years, one of the first investments each family chooses to make is to fix up its housing. Everywhere you go in the countryside you see evidence of amateur construction. But now, with the rain and with the planting, many of these construction sites were temporarily idle, and I had a chance to poke around and have a closer look. In this particular area, where the basic houses were all made of brick, the most popular renovation was to add a second storey. People were knocking off the old tile roofs and using pre-cast concrete slabs to lay a second floor and then again to form a flat concrete roof. This presumably committed them to cooking thereafter with briquettes instead of firewood, because there were no chimneys. If they were to build a wood fire, there would no longer be any way for the smoke to escape. Previously it would just seep through the tiles.

In any developed country, concrete floor slabs would hardly be a topic of much interest, but in rural China they're high technology. In the traditional Chinese house the floor is of packed earth, stone or perhaps concrete. In the days of central planning, building materials were hard to get, and the housing stock became disastrously run down. Now that the peasants are starting to earn a little money again, the prevailing fashion is for two or even three-storey houses. Building with wood is out of the question in most areas, so how to add a second storey? They adopt the technology of China's urban six-storey buildings and floor the upper storey with pre-stressed concrete slabs.

The amateur builders cast these slabs themselves or buy them from a local expert. A strip of flat ground at least 3m wide is covered with paper or plastic sheeting. A number of rectangular slab moulds about 2m long, 45cm wide and 10cm deep are then laid out side by side. A metal frame runs down each side of this casting floor mounted on stout stakes driven deep into the ground. Turnbuckles are mounted every few centimetres along the frames, and wires are strung down the length of the moulds connecting turnbuckles at opposite ends. The turnbuckles are tightened, tensioning the wires, before the mould is filled with concrete. After the concrete has set, the moulds are removed and the wires are cut free from the frames. As the tension is released, the wires try to shorten and pull on the surrounding concrete, compressing it lengthwise toward the centre of the slab. This greatly increases the slab's strength. Which is just as well, as amateur slab works in the countryside often mix their cement using sand which is neither sharp-grained nor clean, and so tends to make weak concrete.

In truth, it certainly seemed to me that only a small proportion of the slabs I saw under construction were actually getting any pre-stressing. They all had wire in them, but in many cases the system for tightening it up before pouring wasn't very effective, if it was used at all. This could have been because the slabs were being made for sale. Stress in the wire isn't something the customer can easily check, and once the building is erected it's too late. On the other hand, it could have been one more legacy of the old commune system. You could imagine that making the slabs was once a well-organized craft on the commune, which followed properly designed methods passed down from the central planners. People who learned to do it properly continue to do it that way. Young guys just casting a few slabs to expand their house may simply be copying. They put wire in their slabs, but perhaps they don't understand the importance of tensioning it properly before pouring the concrete. It could be that they're copying the form and missing out the essence.

In addition to the stressing wire, each slab is cast around four lengths of pipe which leave hollow channels 7cm in diameter down the length of the slab. This greatly reduces cement usage and the weight of the finished product. It also makes the finished slab easier to carry, as a length of bamboo can be threaded down one of the channels and carried from each end.

Before communism, China's economic development was hampered for centuries by an unwillingness to invest in productive resources in the face of a vast surplus of labour. Now that the peasants have the opportunity, they're reverting to this ancient pattern and investing their first cash in raising their standard of housing. As a result, temporary amateur brick works and slab factories are springing up everywhere in the countryside.

A second result is that all the new homes are being built with 2m rooms. It must rather limit your options as a geomancer, always dealing with rooms of identical size and shape.

It was unusual to see these building sites temporarily idle during the planting season, but what was even more unusual was to hear babies crying. The Chinese traditionally practice some of the elements of Western hot-house child rearing, and in normal circumstances you don't often hear a baby crying. But at this time of year I was hearing them every day. I speculated that the person who's usually at home taking care of the baby is temporarily out in the fields, and for these few days someone else, an older sister perhaps, is taking over. She doesn't take care of the baby in quite the usual way, so the baby cries. It had to be something like that.

Then, one afternoon a couple of weeks after I'd left my friends the tinkers, I ran into a couple of itinerant musicians on the trail. They weren't from the local area and spoke clear Mandarin, so we stopped for a minute to chat. They told me that they wander around the country working primarily for room and board. "We play for weddings, funerals, all sorts of celebrations."

"Yes, weddings are the best because we can always enjoy the banquet."

"But surely there aren't enough weddings and funerals around here to keep you busy."

"Well, we can play for anyone. We know everyone, so we can usually get someone to give us a room for the night and some supper."

"Does anyone pay cash?"

"Sometimes, a little. But mostly at weddings."

I suggested that business must be pretty slow, but they explained that they manage to find an audience almost every night. It's an ancient craft, but in the past only the big landowners could afford to hire entertainers. These days the pool of potential clients is much larger and more democratic. Of course they face competition from television in the cities where there's reliable electricity, but out here in the country they're busier than ever, at least for a few more years.

There were only two of them, and each was carrying an *erhu* – a kind of miniature two-string cello. With just two strings they don't sound as rich as a cello, so a band of just two *erhus* would have a pretty whiny timbre. But I suppose they sing as they play, and maybe they had some percussion instrument in their baskets, which they play with their feet, or something. I would have liked to hear a bit of their repertoire, but we were going in opposite directions. I wished them well in the age of television.

9

In the Cradle of Chinese Communism

Westerners calling for democracy in China assume that the place will be pretty well hopeless until the Chinese have managed to turf out the Communist Party as the Russians did. Actually, it's a little-known fact that since the early '90s China has been developing elements of a pretty vigorous grass-roots democracy. The irony of this development is that it has taken hold most easily in the areas which were once most firmly under central control in the days of the communes. One such is southern Hunan Province, birthplace of the Great Helmsman, Mao Zedong.

With their native son in power, it's only natural that the Hunanese should have been vigorous in implementing his policies. Communism ruled through the communes, each running an area about the size of a county. Each commune was divided into production brigades (what an outsider would normally call a township) and each brigade was divided into production teams (the villages). Everyone's production quotas, rations and work points were controlled from the centre.

Since the collapse of the communes the links between these various levels seem to have weakened considerably. Each village is now supposed to be run by its elected governing committee implementing policies set at the township level (especially with regard to delivering grain for taxes, birth control, forest conservation and that sort of thing.) "Elected" in the Chinese context usually means that the township draws up a list of perhaps 11 candidates for 10 posts and submits it to the village for ratification. It's assumed that any Communist Party members in the village will be included in the governing committee, and that the committee will work closely with the township government to ensure that central government policies are implemented at the village level. Nevertheless, the formalism of an election does seem to be followed in many areas.

In some villages the system works more or less as designed. In particular, villages which operate a sawmill, a small mine or some other profitable venture need a formal structure to carry on the management, now that the commune framework has disappeared. The elected committee may also have its uses in villages where the families have more than one surname. The township authorities can select a slate that balances the interests of the different clans in village affairs.

But it's safe to guess that in most villages the new elected committee structure has probably been subverted by the ancient system where the family patriarch calls the shots, advised by the heads of the major branches of the clan. In these cases it's unlikely that the birth control regulations are too scrupulously observed, or that the taxes get paid in full and on time.

In some villages it was difficult to perceive that the communal structure had been dismantled at all. Of course, all the physical plant was still there. People still lived in barracks-like buildings and made use of a communal day care centre and dispensary. But out in the fields there were still loudspeakers, which still played martial music during the day and the national news from Beijing at 7 p.m. After lunch, even during the planting season, the fields would be empty while everyone enjoyed his constitutionally-mandated afternoon nap. Almost everyone could speak pretty good Mandarin, as well as the provincial Hunanese and the local dialect. It was clearly a region which had taken Maoism to heart, and many villagers had seen no compelling reason to change their ways.

Other developments had a more personal significance. After 10 straight days with rain, it finally cleared up. There were still areas of flooding, but I was gradually able to walk my shoes dry. The hills persisted, but became gentler, so that I was rarely climbing or descending steeply, rather winding back and forth from valley to valley over gentle passes. And I was leaving the deep countryside for a less remote, more sophisticated part of the country.

I even at one point compromised my principles by visiting the minor city of Shi Wan, shown on the map by something significantly larger than the smallest type of dot. I did so because I needed to reach a ferry to cross the Xiang river, one of the major tributaries of the Yangtze. I could ignore my principles with confidence, because Shi Wan is on the main trans-national rail line, and so is almost surely open to foreign visitors. I even fantasized about visiting a fancy hotel on my way through and having a Western-style meal.

That proved to be a pipedream. The town turned out to be a centre of chinaware manufacturing, and it was clear that the local factories had been as slow as some of the surrounding communes to adapt to the new economic climate. Every available space, even in vacant shops on the main street, was being used to store crates of unsold crockery packed in straw. The factories were apparently government work units, which still had output targets they were trying to meet regardless of whether or not anyone wanted to buy the product. It used to be that the planners just distributed the products around to various government shops and people who needed a teapot had no choice but to buy one. These days, the planners have lost control over the retail end of the chain, and any excess output just piles up. Shi Wan was bursting at the seams with unsold porcelain. It would make good ballast for road building, but it had been shown on the books of the factories as output, so probably if it were scrapped, the factories would be driven to bankruptcy. That is to say, formal bankruptcy. In fact they were bankrupt already, but the planners were twisting and turning trying to avoid acknowledging it. Meanwhile, Shi Wan was stuffed with crates.

The ferry crossing turned out to be a few kilometres northwest of Shi Wan at a place called San Zhang, and to get there I had to follow a dirt road. I didn't reach San Zhang until the next day, because on the way I had my first experience of what I later came to refer to as a parade. In this relatively sophisticated part of the country the kids had their own bikes to ride back and forth to school. Late in the afternoon, a gang of half a dozen of them decided that I was about the most interesting thing happening in Shi Wan, and they began following me. Along the graded road there was no way I could shake them off. It was like giving a rolling press conference where the newsmaker had no opportunity to say, "I'll take one last question." Worse, every time we came to a village one of the kids would race ahead and announce our arrival, so that by the time we got there the whole population would be lining the road to watch us pass. It was uncomfortable, but what could I do?

I was thinking of just striking off into the hills in hopes that the kids wouldn't want to leave their bicycles. Then we came upon an interesting sight. In front of a rural general store on the edge of a village, an old man was turning wooden handles for rubber stamps on a hand-cranked lathe. I immediately threw down my pack and asked the storekeeper for a beer to give me an excuse to sit and watch awhile.

The Chinese are very fond of rubber stamps to authenticate their signatures when signing documents. The handles are simple enough, but turning them on a hand-driven lathe appeared to be a pretty good trick. One hand pulls back and forth on a bow that turns the lathe, a bit like playing the cello or trying to light a fire without matches. The other hand holds the chisel and controls the shape of the handle. The old man told me he does 50 handles a day and gets half a yuan each for them, so each day he devotes to handle turning earns him 25 yuan. Not bad by Chinese standards. I don't suppose he has to pay for his wood. He might have to take a motor rickshaw to town to deliver the product, but he'd probably have to go there shopping anyway. It seemed a pretty good living.

While chatting with the carver I had an idea how to break up the parade. I finished up my beer, said my good-bys and started out back the way I'd come. It worked. The kids were on their way home from school and had to be home for dinner. They couldn't afford to follow me all the way back to Shi Wan no matter how interesting the spectacle. I put in a few hundred metres then, my enthusiasm for walking sapped by the beer, cut off into the bush and camped for the night.

After a spectacular star-studded night, my first in weeks, I rose early and finished up the road to the ferry crossing without incident. The town of San Zhang was a case study in urban morbidity. It was apparently subject to annual flooding, and so had been built within a system of massive dikes sealed by removable gates. The town had outgrown its enclosed area, but apparently hadn't mastered the construction of buildings more than three storeys tall. So the area within the dikes was a hothouse of packed buildings threaded by a warren of narrow alleys. Space-intensive amenities like the public market were set up outside the walls, but flooding was apparently frequent enough that there was no point in constructing any permanent facilities out there. All in all, it was a strange little place.

And it was in San Zhang that I met Mr. Xia, a strange little fellow. In retrospect, I think he may have had some sort of mental or personality disorder. He was a nice enough guy, but he had somehow convinced himself that I might be able to get him a job in the promised land of Guangdong province. He was quite insistent about befriending me and insisted that we exchange addresses. He spoke good Mandarin, but no Cantonese. I tried to explain that this would be quite an obstacle to finding any sort of responsible job in Guangdong, but he would have none of it. In the end, he gave me a brief tour of the town and put me on the ferry after I'd bought him a hot breakfast.

The tour of such an unusual place was, in fact, pretty interesting. The area within the dikes had originally been a little hill, and down by the water the town overlooked the river from the top of a steep bank. In an attempt to make more room, an extra street had been added in the form of a boardwalk hanging out over the water. It was along this boardwalk that we had our breakfast in a very grotty hotel. The ceiling was falling in; the walls were peeling. In the gloom, I tried not to think about the vermin that must have infested the floor mats. It wasn't a place that I would have chosen for breakfast, but the food was good, the proprietress was friendly, and after breakfast I was able to bid Mr. Xia good-by with a clear conscience. The owner was probably a Xia clansman.

The Xiang River, like the Bat Gong, was diked all along its length, and on the far shore I was immediately able to leave the road and strike out north along the levee. It was quiet, scenic walking, but unfortunately it lasted only an hour or so until the river launched itself into a sweeping bend to the east. At that point I again struck off to the northwest through some pine forest.

Having crossed the main rail line and the river, I had one more obstacle before me: the main north-south highway. I was asking directions to a town on the highway called Bai Shi Pu. On the basis of my rather inadequate map, I was guessing that at Bai Shi Pu I would be able to cross the highway and pick up some sort of trail across country to the town of Shi Tan Ba farther west. That would quickly get me away from the highway and all its development.

As my trail through the pine forest approached the highway, I could hear it from a long way off. Chinese drivers use their horns incessantly, even on the open road. Emerging from the woods, I asked the first person I saw and was dismayed to learn that Bai Shi Pu was five kilometres up the highway. From there I could indeed pick up a trail cross-country to Shi Tan Ba, but I'd have to do five kilometres in the traffic first to get there. The highway was wide, but the paving was in terrible shape. I was probably legal along such a major highway, but the traffic was going to be nerve-wracking and not a little dangerous. Five kilometres would take me about an hour. All I could do was push along as fast as possible and try to get through it safely.

Well, in the end there was no need to spend an hour in the maelstrom of the national artery. It was actually half an hour. The five kilometres quoted by the local resident was in fact two and a half kilometres. This is a very common confusion, even on a major highway with kilometre stones marking off the distance.

Just as most Chinese continue to use their local dialects rather than the national language, so they continue to prefer traditional Chinese measurements to the official metric system. In the case of weights and measures at the market, traditional Chinese units are sometimes used even in cosmopolitan Hong Kong. Buying vegetables by the catty and eating rice by the *leung* can safely be attributed to nothing more than inertia, but when it comes to road mileages the persistence of the traditional Chinese mile makes good sense.

A Chinese mile is defined so that an adult can walk ten miles in an hour. That makes it about 500 metres. Meet a Chinese on the trail and ask him the distance to the next village. Of course, he's never measured it, but he knows it takes him half an hour to walk there. So he'll tell you that it's five miles. In fact, you normally aren't really interested in how far away it is in miles. You too are mostly interested in how long it will take you to get there. When he says it's five miles, you immediately understand that he's describing it as a half hour walk, and you can then estimate how long the trip will take you at whatever pace you're going. This wouldn't be very convenient if you were driving a car, but ordinary Chinese don't use cars, and most of China's "roads" aren't motorable. For pedestrians and cyclists the flexible mile system works pretty well. If you look in an encyclopedia or a Chinese-

English dictionary, you can find the Chinese mile defined precisely in terms of metres and centimetres. This is baloney. Experience suggests that it takes half an hour to walk five Chinese miles whether the route is along a straight cement irrigation canal or over a mountain trail. The mile expands and contracts to suit the terrain. It's more useful that way.

My brief encounter with the national artery had the unexpected effect of pumping up my self-esteem. Even on that short rural stretch, it seemed as if every excuse for a shack had been converted to a restaurant. It has become conventional for such highway restaurants to employ one or two young female "greeters" to sit out by the roadside in their best clothes trying to lure in patrons from the traffic speeding by. Prostitution is under wraps in most of China because of the system of neighbourhood committees, which keep track of everyone's comings and goings. Reporting on your neighbour wasn't entirely a communist invention. In China it has always been encouraged by the authorities. But out here on the highway the motorists, mostly truck drivers, are far from home. It's their best chance to enjoy a little on the side. And traditionally, "enjoying the flowers" has a long and respected pedigree in Chinese culture, just as it does throughout Southeast Asia. Travelling at a fast walking pace rather than speeding by in a truck, I came in for more than my share of "greeting."

In any case, I survived with life, limb and virtue intact, and took the first opportunity to climb the steep ridge to the west, putting the noise and pollution behind me. In my eagerness, I in fact took the wrong trail, but the little-used ascent was garnished with some ripe raspberries. At the top of the steep climb I was able to find a ridge-top trail that brought me back to the right path.

Since the weather had cleared, I'd found afternoon temperatures climbing uncomfortably high. I had no means of getting a precise reading, but it seemed like 26-28 centigrade. I spent the rest of the afternoon walking in narrow valleys where I was glad of the shade. The narrow valleys took me through people's front yards, and I was interested to see that the laundry hanging out to dry included sweaters and long underwear. This overdressing must have a sound traditional basis, but I don't know what it could be.

Here, even more than before, decorative tile work had become a staple of house renovation. The modern flat roofs often were trimmed with an ornamental tile railing about a metre tall. They looked impressive, but what an enormous amount of hauling to bring in the heavy tile fittings on a shoulder pole. Many of these places were an hour's walk from any motorable track. The fashion was a pretty sure indication that those ornamental fittings are made not too far away, so that reject pieces are available on a cash and carry basis.

The fancy trim was also a good indication that the electric power in that area is probably none too reliable. Otherwise, people would be inclined to invest first in simple home appliances. China now produces a complete range of rice cookers, electric kettles and televisions. The quality isn't very good. In fact the Russians love them, while the Chinese themselves prefer Japanese products. But availability is usually the determining factor. In contrast with a few years ago, if you're willing to buy the local product you can find them for sale almost anywhere. The fact that these people were installing fancy ceramic balustrades and not television aerials says a lot about the work of the local power bureaucracy.

Although I was now within about 200km of Changsha, the capital of Hunan Province, I was surprised to find living conditions in some ways even more primitive than before. It was here, for example, that I used for the first time a motorless ferry poled by an old man. He charged 0.2 yuan a trip. At five or six trips an hour, he was taking in 15 to 20 yuan per day. A pretty good living by rural standards, but it would be an awfully strenuous lifestyle.

I was continuing to attract little parades. With the hot weather I was taking more time off in the heat of the day, so more of my walking was outside of school hours, and I would pick up bands of small children running to keep up with me and yelling "foreigner, foreigner" to bring all the locals out of their houses to see me pass. The sun was strong and, taking a cue from the farmers, I was wearing a hat through most of the day. Unfortunately, my hat was a blue and white baseball-style cap. These are very popular in Taiwan, but almost unknown on the mainland, where straw hats are about all that's available. The strange headgear made me even more conspicuous.

With my longer lunch hours I was really enjoying the local cuisine. In this region I was usually able to find a restaurant serving steamed meat dumplings and noodle soup. Back in Hong Kong I had always considered soup and dumplings to be Shanghai-style cuisine, but here it was clearly the local tradition. Better yet, close to the capital I was in a part of the province where the electric power was reliable enough to support an ice cream industry. Even small shops in the villages would sometimes have a tiny deep freeze in the front yard. Eating uncooked food is a pretty risky business, but the ice cream was often too tempting to resist.

Soda, too, was more generally available. It was the safest form of liquid, and I drank a lot of it. I was buying it in the big 1.5 litre bottles that most people buy only as gifts or for special occasions, but even so they weren't hard to find. On the other hand, sometimes these delicacies weren't all that they seemed. I was compelled to become an expert on counterfeits. The top-of-the-line soda in this part of the country was Pepsi, so that was the brand most often imitated. In some cases the sharks had faithfully copied the Pepsi label and cap, and it wasn't until the first mouthful when you were hit with the metallic taste of cheap artificial sweetener that you could tell you'd bought a knock-off. In other cases, they skirted the law by calling the stuff "Bepsi" with a label design that would seem like the real article to anyone unfamiliar with the English alphabet. Bepsi copied the Pepsi ingredient line right along with the rest of the label, though the sweeteners listed bore little relation to what was inside. I even bought bottles with a Pepsi label and a Bepsi cap. With China a big producer of sugar, it was surprising that the knock-offs would choose to use artificial sweetener. You'd imagine real sugar would be cheaper. It was probably a distribution problem. Sugar was probably traded through some sort of government marketing organization. The fly-by-night bottlers were probably private companies without the connections necessary to assure them of a steady supply. The artificial sweetener may be more expensive, but one drum goes a long way.

Paradoxically, closer to the capital I ran into many more people who spoke no Mandarin. I had expected educational standards to be higher there, but I later figured out that it was a mobility issue. Land nearer the capital and nearer the railroad was more valuable. For the first time, I saw shops that had been erected on bridge-like structures over the irrigation ditches so as not to take up agricultural land. With land and its products so valuable, there was little incentive for anyone to migrate elsewhere in search of work, and no industry to draw in outsiders. Whatever the standard of classroom instruction, people spent their whole lives among their clansmen and never had occasion to keep up their Mandarin. Back in the mining country many of the workers would have been imported from elsewhere, and that kept everyone speaking Mandarin as a lingua franca.

At the opposite extreme, it was here that I began for the first time to run into relatively fluent English speakers whom I could quiz about some of the things that were puzzling me. One Saturday afternoon, for example, I was following an irrigation ditch when a fellow came along in the opposite direction with a bedroll on the back of his bicycle. I nodded hello and thought no more of it until a few minutes later when I heard the clank of a bicycle chain coming up behind me, rattling over the rough track. I hugged the edge of the ditch to let it pass, but nothing came by. Finally, I turned my head and was surprised to recognize the same fellow who had passed going the other way a few minutes before. "Hello," he said in English. I replied in Mandarin, but he came right back with, "can I talk to you?" An English speaker, a nice surprise at the end of a long day. I hadn't met one in a week or more.

"Sure, do you want to speak English?"

"Yes, English." Then a long pause as he prepared the next question. For all the anticipation, it came straight from the catechism. "Where are you going?"

"Is this the way to Nan Zhu Shan?" I asked.

"My school is at Nan Zhu Shan."

"Oh, is that where you are going now?" No answer. "Are you going to Nan Zhu Shan?"

"I'm going home." A longish pause. "What is your name?"

And so it went on. I eventually established that he was a high school student returning home for the weekend after a week at school. This was his final year, and he was just preparing for his exams. The exams are the primary criterion for deciding whether he'll get into university and to which university he'll be assigned. He was hoping to become an English major, so when he unexpectedly ran into a native speaker, he realized it was worth turning his bike around in the hope of some practice. I later bought him some dinner, and we spent a couple hours practicing. Once he had warmed up and got a feel for my accent, we were able to converse reasonably well.

China has nine years of compulsory education, and my friend confirmed that after the 9th grade only a minority of students manages to hang on until the last year of high school. The only reason to do so would be a desire to attend college, and of those who sit the final exam only about half succeed. Success in this context means that they'll get into some university or other. The choice isn't primarily up to the student. He has expressed his interest in studying English or medicine or economics, and the authorities look at his results and decide which university would suit him best. A brilliant student might be assigned to one of the national universities in Beijing or Shanghai, but for most people the peak of ambition is a university in the provincial capital.

Financial considerations are not that important. During his high school years, my friend's parents had been paying 800 yuan a term to cover his school fees, including room and board during the week. That's a hefty sum, but it covers everything except books and incidentals. If he gets into university, he will, in effect, have been singled out as a national asset. He'll almost surely graduate, and on graduation he'll be assigned a state job as a worker. This is the classic route for someone born a peasant to earn a promotion into the worker class with all its state benefits. The benefits begin right away, as a college student draws a state salary, which covers most of his costs. His parents have to kick in only a little pocket money. It's not surprising that my friend was so anxious to try anything to prepare for his exam. And, in fact, his English wasn't bad. After so long in Mandarin, I found speaking with him a real treat.

Chinese universities are coeducational, and so is the army, the other main route from the peasant to the worker class. But China has a state-mandated target age for marriage, which varies from place to place but is always in the early 20s. University students and soldiers get no dispensations on the marriage policy, so they lead a pretty tame social life until after graduation. And by then, most Westerners would say, they've missed their chance. Mainland universities are not known for their social life.

With my friend ordering, I was able to have a proper restaurant meal, and with two of us conversing at the table, we weren't bothered by curious bystanders inviting themselves to sit down and ask questions. We had a couple of bottles of beer and a very convivial evening despite the difference in ages. We broke early to save my friend a long ride home in the dark and to give me a chance to get through town and find a campsite on a bluff overlooking the town and its river. The brief encounter with an English speaker had been like a vacation.

The next morning, I realized that the whole episode had worked out much better than I had realized. I rose early and ducked back into town for a hot breakfast before crossing the bridge and striking north along a minor road. I quickly realized that had I continued this way the previous evening I would have had a terrible time finding a place to camp. Yesterday's hills had disappeared at the river, and here the land was dead flat with every square metre devoted to rice paddies. I was only 100km or so due west of

Changsha, the provincial capital. Land around here was too valuable to be allowed to lie fallow.

There were other signs, too of city influences. The houses, my standard indicator of prosperity, here were all glazed, usually with one room screened as well. Many eaves sported gutters and downspouts. There was plenty of traffic on the road, even on a Sunday morning. And I saw people wearing sunglasses and shorts. Some of the bicycles were mountain bikes. That really was just conspicuous consumption. There was no need for gears in this flat country.

On that Sunday near the city I saw as well people indulging in recreation. That's something extremely rare in China. You can often see kids at school shooting baskets or kicking the soccer ball. Adults engage in group dance and Chinese exercise for reasons related to indigenous concepts of health maintenance. But true sports and recreations are not normally a part of Chinese life. That Sunday I saw a few people fishing with hooks and poles. It was the first time I'd seen it in China.

While angling is said to be one of the world's most popular recreations, the Chinese simply haven't enough leisure. Country people get very little meat in their diet, so given the chance they'll fish enthusiastically, but for food, not for sport. Most surface water has been channelled into irrigation canals, and the favoured technique is to build a rectangular bamboo frame as wide as the ditch and quite a bit deeper. One end of the frame is hung from tripods like a sort of trap door. A net is attached to the frame and the whole affair is lowered into the ditch so that the net screens the entire flow. Fish descending with the current accumulate on the upstream side of the net. The bottom edge of the frame is attached by a rope to a homemade winch based on a log with pegs driven into it for handles. After an appropriate interval, the winch is wound up to raise the net and check the catch. Any fish can be retrieved with a small net on a long handle.

Unfortunately, there are rarely any fish to retrieve larger than your thumb. The fishing rights seem to be allocated village by village. As in all hunting and fishing, there's no incentive for any village to conserve stocks, which might be taken by its neighbours. With nets at each village, the only fish surviving in the canals are those small enough to slip through the mesh.

By late morning I had learned why this part of the country seemed so citified. I wandered through the enormous Gong Nam Machinery Factory – another of those work units,which is really only a factory but seems to all outward appearances to be a small city not marked on the map. Gong Nam seemed to employ thousands. Many were apparently engineers, as I saw homemade solar water heaters on the roofs of some of the housing units. Just as I was leaving the place, I ran into my second English speaker in two days. She was the English teacher at the local secondary school. Apparently the factory offered particularly good schooling to lure trained workers from other parts of China to live so far from the city.

I wondered, of course, what Gong Nam might produce, hoping it wasn't some sort of secret munitions factory. The lady explained that they were pushing the envelope of Bepsi technology. They made the Nussan van – automobile knock-offs! And they seemed to be doing well with it.

"Are you going to walk all the way to Chairman Mao's museum?" The teacher assumed that I intended to visit Chairman Mao's hometown, not far away.

"Well, no I'm not really going that way."

"But you must visit the museum. Have you been there before?"

"I haven't, actually, but as you say, it's quite a walk." True to my principles, I resisted detouring to any sort of tourist attraction.

"Many people will be going there today. If you continue this way for about two kilometers, you will come to the highway where you can get a bus."

"In fact, I was planning to continue north across the highway toward Fa Ming Lau."

"Oh, Fa Ming Lau. Yes, that's good. It's very interesting . . ." and then she proceeded to give me some very useful directions in excellent English.

That got me thinking about the old Chairman and noticing yet another relic of his idiosyncratic rule. This area was swamped with small rural pharmacies. In the recent rage for setting up private shops, stalls selling soda, beer and cigarettes are the most popular. Haircut jockeys would be next. But around here pharmacies competed with both. Some stocked Western potions, some Chinese traditional herbs, many both at once.

These medicine shops are probably what happened to many of Mao's famous barefoot doctors. His idea was to bring universal health care to the countryside by training peasants in the rudiments of public health, prevention and diagnosis so that there would be basic care for the most common problems available in every commune. You could imagine that here, in Mao's homeland, the barefoot doctor system, like the communes themselves, must have been particularly thoroughly implemented. These days, people have to pay for their health care, so they're no longer willing to rely on a half-trained farmer in the next village. Some of the barefoot doctors have received further training and become a sort of second-class doctor, but many seem to have capitalized on their experience by going into the dispensary business. Most traditional medicines can be gathered on the hillsides if you know where to look, so the margins would be pretty good. But even so, in this region there were so many so-called pharmacists that it's hard to believe that they all could be making a living.

My own health was holding up pretty well. With a Spartan diet and plenty of exercise, my most serious complaint was sore feet. But I was now entering country where clean water was getting hard to find. I could usually count on the locals for a bottle of boiled water to drink, but I was now reduced to washing and shaving in the irrigation canals. They're pretty heavily contaminated with both animal and human waste, but in this flat land there was no alternative. There were no streams or ponds that hadn't already been through a series of paddies. Skin infections and worms are very prevalent among the peasants. Normally you'd hate to even wash clothes in the surface water. Shaving, it's best not to cut yourself.

Another holdover from more collectivist times is the tradition of wall posters. Before radio and TV, until the last few years in other words, painting slogans on walls and cliffs was a favorite government means of communicating with the citizens. Though less important, it's still used today. Back in the hillier country, the slogans had mostly been about the importance of keeping the kids in school. Here the favorite was about using electricity safely. I came to realize that this interest in safety was really code for, "Don't steal electricity."

Walking along the irrigation ditches, from time to time you'd come across a big pump perched on the edge of the ditch transferring water to an adjacent field. Some these pumps were driven by small diesel engines, but often the power came from a large electric motor. The whole setup had evidently been carried in on shoulder poles and positioned where overhead power lines crossed the ditch. Leads from the motor were stripped of insulation and bent into two little hooks, which were simply hooked over the power lines to tap off power directly through the insulation. There was no proper connection and, of course, no metering. The pump hookup was very temporary, but then I began looking more closely at some of the new houses and I realized that some of them were hooked up in the same informal way. Eventually, I also saw more explicit signs saying, "Electricity is a product. Pay for what you use."

Wider access to electricity has been one of the very first fruits of the recent liberalization of Chinese society. Previously, connection to the grid and the amount of power supplied were both subject to the whims of central planning. The planners, as you might expect, tended to give priority to government agencies, urban areas and major factories. Rural villages, even during the commune era, tended to be last in line. The relaxation of controls immediately led to a great deal of amateur craftsmanship in the electrical field. Villages had a well-developed system for mobilizing communal labour. They knew the route of the nearest pole line, and they quickly decided that the wire to reach it wasn't beyond their joint means. In a matter of months, thousands of villages were brought into the 20th century through private initiative.

Private initiative didn't, however, build any new generating capacity. Nor did it install any meters on the new connections it was rigging up. Power shortages, always troublesome, quickly became much worse. As in some other spheres, the dismantling of communism brought a reduction in privilege and a more egalitarian distribution of resources, but this amounted to more equitably spreading the shortages around.

By late afternoon I was approaching Fa Ming Lau. I stopped to ask the way and was surprised to receive directions, not to the town of Fa Ming Lau, but to the birthplace of Liu Shaoqi a few kilometres away. Suddenly, I realized why the mention of Fa Ming Lau had diverted my friend the English teacher from her mission to send me to Chairman Mao's birthplace. Liu was head of the Chinese government for much of the time that Mao headed the party. I had never realized that they came from villages within a few kilometres of one another. It was the old story of Chinese relationships. Mao's right hand man was a home boy from his old home town. How very interesting.

True to the lesson of the Fei Lai gorge, I had no intention of visiting Liu's birthplace, but when I got there a big thunderstorm broke and I ended up dashing up the entrance road to shelter in the door of the museum. It was obviously a pretty big tourist attraction and very busy on a Sunday. Chinese don't take vacations in the usual sense, but factory workers sometimes go on excursions organized by the factory and the union. Those organizations remain under firm party control, so it's clear that Liu's shrine would be a favorite destination for excursions of that kind. Thinking back, I realized that I'd been following roads, which, even though they weren't marked on the map, were maintained to an unusually high standard. The homestead too seemed very well maintained. I'll bet it didn't look like that when Liu was a boy.

I'd had a very interesting day, but all along I'd been worried about finding a place to camp in such flat, open country. Fortunately, early in the evening I came across a hill that had been given over to a tree plantation. I hadn't seen any in this area, but in fact they're very common all over China. Every tree is the same species, about 8m tall, 15cm thick at the base and spaced about 3m apart. It's hard to escape the conclusion that they all were planted about the same time in some sort of national reforestation campaign. Any time I could spot one about nightfall I could be pretty confident that if I could slip off the road without being noticed I could spend a peaceful night. Deep in one of these plantations there wasn't much danger that anyone would come along to pore over every item of my gear and put me through my catechism.

On this particular evening I was a bit early for camping. People might still be in the plantation working or walking through on their way home for supper, so I killed a half hour by heading back into town to pick up a couple of bottles of beer.

If you enjoy a cold beer after a long day walking in the hot sun, well, China is not the place for you. Of course, there's plenty of beer. It's one of the staples of the little private shops springing up in all Chinese villages. And the price is certainly right. A 750ml bottle normally costs about 2 yuan. If it were cold, it would be among China's greatest attractions. The difficulty is that it's invariably warm, often above body temperature.

It's not clear why there should be so many brands. Most economies find it efficient to produce their beer in a few giant breweries, but China seems to have a local brewery in just about every county seat. It may have to do with the poor transportation system. Almost all Chinese beer is sold in 750ml bottles, which are returned for refilling. The shipping cost is probably one of the major elements in the price.

In the present situation you might expect that there would be great potential for a beer formulated to be served warm. Not warm like the cellar of a British pub, but warm like a cabana in Miami Beach. This breakthrough hasn't yet materialized. Instead, the universal formulation is an ordinary lager with a low alcohol content. Many brands list alcohol content on their labels as low as

3.8 per cent. Most Chinese drink only rarely, so they find this enough to give them a buzz.

Pondering thus, I spent a peaceful evening among the pines. The next day the violent thunderstorms were back before noon, but I was gradually pulling away from the provincial capital and away from Mao's touristed heartland. Gradually, I got back off the gravel roads onto much more appealing walking tracks through the hills. By late morning I was even able to find a spring that seemed pure enough to risk brushing my teeth.

It was only a few minutes later, teeth immaculate, that I almost managed to step off a cliff in the midst of a wind and hail storm. The trail I was following looped around the head of a valley and disappeared over a spur. Suddenly, it veered off sharply at the brink of a cliff. When I'd recovered my composure and descended a few metres to where the wind wasn't quite so strong, I discovered why. My cliff was in fact the brink of a small open pit coal mine. The trail used to cross through what was now a vast pit and was only gradually being rerouted along the brink of the cliff as mining progressed. There was no-one working, but the place wasn't completely idle. Once I'd followed the trail down to the bottom, I came across a large area completely dry despite the rain. It was the roof of a large underground coking oven. I was able to inspect another one nearby, which was just a large underground igloo of firebrick. As far as I could tell, one first stuffs it full of full of fresh coal then ignites it with very limited draught. Some of the coal on the bottom is able to get enough air to burn, and the combustion products heat the rest of the pile and turn it to coke.

That, of course, was the end of my walking track. The trail out from the mine had been upgraded to a rough road for shipping the product. There was no traffic, though, and no one about in the fields. The peasants will work under the blazing sun, they'll work in the pouring rain, but the sound of thunder sends them for shelter. A human head is automatically the tallest point in a rice paddy.

The houses in this area were yet of another style. The first storey featured the traditional central door with windows on each side, but around here most dwellings had been upgraded with a second storey. The second storey design had apparently been copied from the better housing units of city factories. It had four separate rooms each accessed from a balcony running along the front. It's as if each householder were expanding his house into a motel. You could see how this would work well in a factory where each bedroom would be occupied by a separate family or a separate office. But in a one-family house it's a bit odd to have the rooms connected only via an external balcony. No wandering around naked in these households.

The explanation probably hinges on the idea that each district has only one construction team, and that team only knows how to build to a single design. There are no trained architects out in the countryside, and there are no written plans. If you want to extend your house, there's no choice but to accept the design that the construction team knows how to build. So your new house ends up identical to your neighbor's.

Indeed, most of the renovations were done at about the same time. In this district people had taken to inscribing the construction date on their new second storey. The ones in plain brick were all dated 1983 and 1984. Another lot decorated with tile facings were built ten years later. After two construction binges, there were very few unglazed windows left in these villages. And asbestos roofs, too, were pervasive. That was a pretty sure indication of an asbestos roofing factory somewhere in the vicinity. An asbestos roof would be a lot lighter and easier to install than tiles, but it then commits you to heating and cooking forever with coal or coal briquettes. Chimneys weren't part of the standard design, and with no chimney a wood fire would fill the house with smoke.

Late in the day I came across another sure sign that I hadn't yet escaped the influence of the provincial capital. It was raining lightly, and a lady passed me sheltering her head under a comic book. It had been a while since I'd seen any reading material apart from kids with their schoolbooks.

More worrying, there seemed to be a fashion for keeping pet dogs in this part of the country. Hills were becoming rare, and with them, woodlots. Much of the time the country was just flat paddy fields as far as the eye could see. There was hardly so much as a place to sit down, much less a secluded campsite. I was reduced to walking until it was quite dark before ducking into some tiny woodlot for the night. After dark I was normally quite safe from intrusion, because a local would be inclined to fear strangers and not approach me. With no private property, he wouldn't in any case have grounds for challenging a stranger about camping in a grove of trees. But a dog would have no such inhibitions. If a dog scented me and came over to investigate, the owner would be forced to come and retrieve him. Finding a foreigner, he'd of course be obliged to invite him to the village for the night, necessitating unaffordable hospitality for owner and endless repetition of the catechism for me.

10

Across the Yangtze

Northern Hunan province is dominated by the enormous Dong Ting Lakes. The Yangtze River rises in the Himalayas and flows East to the sea, dividing North from South China. The land along its lower reaches is one of the nation's primary grain producing areas. The river naturally tends to seasonal flooding, and indeed its lower reaches are diked continuously for thousands of kilometres. But the flooding of the Yangtze is mitigated considerably by a series of large lakes along its course. The Dong Ting Lakes are the first set, farthest upstream to the West.

At most times of the year the lakes are hardly lakes at all, but an interconnected network of lakes, swamps and channels over an area about 140km in diameter. At these times, the lakes are actually separated from the course of the Yangtze and drain into it via another large river, the Xiang, which you may remember our crossing at San Zhang with the help of Mr. Xia. But the land separating the lakes from the Yangtze is low and flat, and when the Yangtze floods, it quickly overflows this barrier and begins filling the lakes. The lakes' vast area can absorb an enormous amount of water in the course of rising a few metres, so they act as a huge emergency surge reservoir to moderate changes in the level of the Yangtze.

A bit like the Nile, this annual flooding makes the area very productive, and it has been the site of many of China's ancient civilizations. The Chinese are very keen on his sort of thing and speak highly of the Dong Ting Lakes as a cradle of world civilization. Be that as it may, these days the area doesn't offer much to attract the tourist.

For the walker, the approach to the lakes can only be described as flat and rather boring. Gradually, though, the drainage ditches became wider and the dikes became higher, to the point where I eventually found myself walking atop a giant levee following a watercourse that reminded me of nothing less than the ship canal at the mouth of the Rhine. Well, okay, there were no ships and no factories, but it was a big ditch.

It was up there, straining into the teeth of stiff breeze, that I was overtaken by Mr. Ngaan on his bicycle. During the entire 18 hours I spent with him, I could never make out much of what he was saying. His Mandarin seemed even worse than mine. In fact, I'm pretty sure that most of his words were actually borrowed from some local dialect and strung into pseudo-Mandarin sentences. But out there in the wind he eventually made it clear that he was inviting me to visit his home. Pretty well worn out by the incessant wind and the strain of trying to keep pace with a bicycle, I was glad to accept.

Mr. Ngaan lived in an entirely typical country house consisting of three rooms with an attached cooking shed (See photo number 19). The house proper has a central door leading into a main room, and from that main room doors lead off to the two rooms on either side. In this case the cooking shed, rather than being at the back or in some detached position, is in fact tacked on to one end of the house as if it were a fourth room. Mr. Ngaan, his wife and his son have the use of only the cooking shed and the one adjacent room. The other two rooms of the house proper are used by his older sister. Since the cooking shed has a door to the outside, Mr. Ngaan normally uses the door to the cooking shed as his front door, leaving the main central door to his sister.

The house is built of fired brick with a roof of asbestos sheeting. The floors are cement, but rather pitted and rough. The main room has a false ceiling of lathes and what appear to be flattened cardboard boxes. From this hangs a single fluorescent tube. The windows at the front and back of Mr. Ngaan's main room are both glazed and screened. In addition, they have wooden bars designed to repel intruders when the windows are left open in the summertime. The one window of the cooking shed has only the wooden bars.

The cooking room contains a mud stove with openings on top for two large woks and a smaller one for a pot or kettle. There are two holes in the roof to let out the smoke, but no flue. And smoke there is aplenty, as the main fuel is dried grass collected on the levee. A large and incendiary pile of it fills most of the room not occupied by the stove.

Mr. Ngaan's living room measures 5x10 metres. At one side is a new wooden sideboard where he keeps his dishes and leftover food behind screened doors. Other furniture consists of two chests of drawers, a dressing table, desk, a folding table for meals, several low chairs, and a bench-cum-sofa along the wall under the front window. Mr. Ngaan and his wife sleep in a four-poster bed in the centre of the room. This is arranged as a sort of partition so that their son's bed at the back is a bit isolated from the main living area. Both are hung with mosquito netting. A television set sits atop one chest of drawers, but the voltage is often too low to receive any programs. In addition, the Ngaans own a desk lamp, a fan and a treadle sewing machine.

Unusually, Mr. Ngaan has decorated his home with large colour pictures from various 1988 and 1989 calendars. 1989 may have been the year of his wedding, when he and his wife took over this portion of their extended family's stock of accommodation.

Around behind the house are a pigsty and a latrine. There's a pump outside the door of the cooking shed, but it doesn't work. Instead, Mrs. Ngaan must fetch her water from a pond across the road about 40 metres away. It's a pretty poor arrangement. The water is dirty, and after lengthy boiling they find that it still has a filthy taste. Mrs. Ngaan tries to improve the flavour by adding a heavy dose of salt to her tea, but a visitor might question whether this is much of an improvement.

When we arrived, Mrs. Ngaan wasn't at home. Mr. Ngaan sat me down with a bowl of salty tea and went to fetch her from the fields where she was helping the family with the planting. After 20 minutes or so he brought her back to face the prospect of unexpected company, accompanied by their son Wai See. As it happens, Wai See is also part of my Chinese name. I tried to explain this to the toddler, but of course he spoke no Mandarin at all, and I wasn't very successful.

I wasn't enjoying the tea in the least, but Mrs. Ngaan immediately lit the fire and brewed up some more. She went at it more ceremonially than her husband. It involved first crushing some rock salt in the bottom of each bowl. She then added one or two berries the size of grapes but with the texture of dates, and topped that with the tea leaves and boiling water. I suppose we all needed the salt after spending the day out in the wind, but over years of drinking salty tea perhaps they'd become insensitive to the flavour. Anyway, to my palate it tasted more like warm seawater than tea.

I was glad when, after a couple of bowls, we shifted to homemade liquor. It was homemade not in the sense that Mr. Ngaan distilled it himself, but rather that he had bought some commercial rice liquor and doctored it up with a selection of his favorite local herbs. This involved crushing up the herbs in a big glass jug, then filling it up with the raw liquor. The brew had apparently been infusing for several weeks by the time I got there. As his various relatives arrived to carry out their share of the interrogation over the course of the evening, all agreed it was a good brew. Among us, we finished off a giant jug of the stuff.

Mr. Ngaan was apparently the youngest of his clan. You could tell because, although everyone was gathered in his house and drinking his liquor, it was Mr. Ngaan who was passing out cigarettes. At one point we were up to eighteen in his tiny sitting room. Despite that, the catechism was less hectic than usual because there were only two or three high school girls among the crowd who could speak Mandarin fluently. Only they could converse with me reasonably smoothly, then they had to do all the translating. With the others it was mostly sign language. In sign language the most fluent was Wai See, who was intent on playing with my glasses. They were probably about the only pair he'd ever seen. Neither eye testing nor prescription lenses would be available to villagers. The nearsighted in rural China make do with squinting.

I was glad to be in a warm bed during the night. The strong winds apparently preceded some sort of front which brought a few hours of heavy rain. I heard it because I had to get up in the night and rummage in my pack for the remains of a bottle of Bepsi. After the salty tea and the liquor we'd dined on two kinds of pickled eggs, pickled bean curd, then spicy vegetables and more tea. It was like eating a pizza before bed. I was dying of thirst. When I set off in the morning, my first priority was to find a shop where I could buy more soda. As usual, with no refrigeration Mrs. Ngaan had no choice but to serve the remains of the salty dinner for breakfast.

During the course of the morning I came to realize that, although the giant ditch I was following reminded me of the mouth of the Rhine, in fact it wasn't very deep. Someone had bridged it with a trestle lashed together entirely from bamboo and wire. There must have been about 150 piers, presumably lashed up on shore then floated out one by one and driven into the bottom. The deck was about 70cm wide and made from split bamboo stood on edge and lashed into a flat bundle. You don't normally think of the privatization of public works in the Chinese context, but this creation was apparently the work of some of the nearby villages, and they were charging 0.2 yuan to cross it. I paid willingly to do my bit for capitalism, but also because I could see a shop on the far shore that probably offered the soda I was craving.

Because the shape of the Dong Ting Lakes changes so much with the seasons, it's hard to say when you've actually reached the lake shore. But in late morning I reached a town where Mr. Ngaan's relatives had suggested I could get a boat across. They were partly right. There was a dock, but there was no sign of a ticket office and no one around. I called in at a nearby barber shop and learned that at this time of year the boat came only once a day, and that from there it didn't cross the lake but went to the city of Xiang Yang about 40 miles up the shore. In Xiang Yang I could catch a boat for the crossing.

You'll recall that 40 miles in China means 4 hours walking. The boat to Xiang Yang wasn't coming until late that evening, which would dump me in the city after dark. I was better off walking. Chinese barbers always wash your hair, so I had a haircut, then set off again following the long, straight levees.

Along the way there was plenty of evidence of seasonal flooding, despite the enormous levees. For the first time I saw houses made of a sort of wattle and daub – reeds and sticks plastered with mud. Some had been whitewashed. With their thatched roofs it made them look English Tudor. But very, very poor. Hovels, really.

The system of interlaced water courses began to get pretty complicated for my rudimentary map, but after a couple of ferry crossings I at last reached Xiang Yang in late afternoon. In doing so I was, of course, violating central guiding principle number three about never visiting cities. Here, though, I was probably legal, as the main rail line and trans-national highway passed a few kilometres East of the city. Better, I wouldn't have to spend the night. A worker at the dock informed me that a boat would leave at midnight for Mau Tau Je on the north shore of the lake. It was like going on vacation. I had a couple of hours to wander around town and find a good meal. For weeks I'd been walking dawn to dusk. Here, for the first time, I had time on my hands, followed by a long boat ride.

I would have liked to celebrate my day off with a couple of bottles of beer, but it wouldn't have been a good idea. Recall that the second reason I was avoiding large towns is because that's where you find most of China's criminal elements. An overnight boat trip would be a likely haunt of pickpockets or worse. I might need all my wits about me. I decided to celebrate with a bottle of genuine Pepsi.

And, of course, I was taken. The label was a perfect copy of a Pepsi label, but I forgot to check the cap. Wanshi. Wanshi isn't, strictly speaking, a knock-off brand. Its label looks a lot like a Pepsi label, but the different brand is clearly marked. The name is a take-off on Pepsi's name in Chinese, but clearly different. The stuff I'd bought is apparently sold as a knock-off sometimes of Pepsi and sometimes of Wanshi. But not, presumably, both at once. On this bottle they'd either gotten confused, or run out of fake Pepsi caps and used a fake Wanshi cap instead. Either way, it wasn't much good.

My boat ride was a salutary lesson in why it's best to walk across China rather than taking public transportation. As midnight approached, the waiting room at the dock began filling up with my fellow passengers. About midnight, a horn was heard announcing that the boat was arriving at the dock. A couple of hundred people picked up their bags and bundles and jammed themselves against the iron grill sealing the dock entrance. Uncomfortable minutes passed. Through the grill we could see disembarking passengers leaving through another exit. Then, suddenly, the grill was opened and the whole crowd rushed as a body for the gangplank.

Yes, the gangplank. Up to this point it was exactly the system they use to control crowds in railway stations. But railway stations have several wide stairways leading to the platforms, and dozens of doors leading into the train. Here the whole throng had to squeeze across a gangplank over the swirling river. In the dark.

I was bigger. I was faster. I carried less luggage. But I was playing a contact sport where I didn't know the rules. Suffice it to say that I didn't get a seat. But it all worked out pretty well. Poking around in the dark, I found on deck a cargo of what seemed like sacks of melon seeds. They were mixed with other sacks that contained something soggy that seemed a bit like seaweed, but by rearranging things a bit I was able to make myself a dry and soft bed to catch a couple of hours sleep before the scrum at the next port.

Fortunately, the sacks weren't consigned to one of the ports where we stopped during the night. In fact, I slept intermittently through until morning. Then, at first light I had a chance to look around and discover what I'd gotten myself into. My first discovery was a set of crude and filthy washrooms featuring hot water. In short, a bonanza. Yesterday a haircut, today a hot water shave.

The Chinese have very little facial hair. Sitting in the park or riding on a train, you can often see Chinese men shaving with tweezers or a pair of nail cutters. Chinese haircuts don't include a shave, and that's why I was so glad to find a source of hot water the day after sitting for a haircut. For the visiting Western businessman, these Chinese shaving customs are often a source of frustration when he finds that his hotel has hot water only in the evenings. To keep up appearances, the Westerner finds himself learning to shave with boiled water from a vacuum flask.

On a walking tour this cuts the other way. Because they shave only once a week or less, Chinese men are always sporting a bit of stubble. Indeed, many rather value a bit of facial hair as a sign of maturity and masculinity. A Western visitor who can manage to shave two or three times a week will fit right in, especially in the countryside. He shouldn't, however, expect to rely on locally purchased blades and razors. He'd be better off with nail clippers. A woman walker, on the other hand, would probably find shaving even more of a problem than elsewhere. Chinese women have so little body hair that they don't shave their underarms and don't need to shave their legs. A Western visitor who tried to follow their example would attract a lot of attention and some very uncomplimentary comments when walking in shorts. A Western man who wears his shirt open will sometimes inspire local men to pull in wonder at the hairs on his chest. A Western woman who failed to shave her legs might well inspire similar curiosity. Whatever turns you on.

Better groomed than I'd been in weeks, I nibbled a few of my supplies and set out to tour the ship (See photo number 20). My second discovery was a set of cabins on the upper deck. In my haste to find a bit of unoccupied sleeping space, I'd missed them the night before. By morning's light they looked reasonably clean but unreasonably crowded. I decided I had been just as well served sleeping on deck. If nothing else, I'd deferred until morning my interrogation by fellow passengers.

I peered into the bridge. It was pretty basic. No radar. Nor radio. Not much of any navigation gear except the wheel, the engine controls, a spotlight and a picture of Mao. The captain was getting plenty of advice, though. All the locals seemed to prefer riding there.

I found the galley. They were serving breakfast, but I wasn't tempted. If they weren't using lake water for the cooking, they were almost surely using it for dish washing. Fortunately, by that time I'd met a fellow passenger who owned a restaurant in Mau Tau Je and had invited me around for lunch.

Winding through the complicated passages of the lake system gave plenty of opportunity for studying the countryside at leisure. Which was a nice change. I could again see evidence that this area had once been organized into communes. It was tempting to speculate that communes might have been established here specifically to reclaim swampy parts of the lakes country and to build flood control works. Each town had a water tower, normally seen only in cities and factories. The main product seemed to be reeds and swamp grass that had been cut and stacked along the waterways in huge structured piles resembling large buildings. A fellow passenger told me that the fibre was used to make a kind of paper. There was a plant at Mau Tau Je. That kind of large-scale harvesting probably indicated some remnants of the commune organization still operating. Each of the little villages seemed to be electrified, though there were no television antennas – a pretty sure sign that the power wasn't very reliable.

With maps so hard to get in China, acquaintances were always anxious to study my maps of their local area. Many people weren't too adept at map reading, but on the boat there was ample time for the maps to be passed around, and a few of the old soldiers were able to correct for me some of my map's many inaccuracies. The lakes area, with its swampy topography, was particularly poorly shown. Of particular interest to me, my informants claimed that the drainage canal I had intended to follow from Mau Tau Je to the Yangtze River was, in fact, not a canal at all but a dry ditch at any time outside the flood season. It had been constructed as an emergency drain to relieve pressure on the Yangtze levees when the water level reaches a certain height. Coming into port they pointed it out to me. It looked like just what I needed: a straight route north that hadn't been planted with crops, and so should provide plenty of camping spots along my journey.

The boat was late, and after a relaxed restaurant lunch I didn't get on the road again until 2p.m. It had been a pleasant break.

The first thing that struck me after leaving town and finding the flood drain was the prevalence of horses. Farther south I'd rarely seen them. You'd think that in most parts of China horses would be competitive with the little tractors used for farming. Perhaps farther south there was no place to graze them. Here the drain was a couple of hundred metres wide and supported goats as well as horses.

Outside the drain, the way was lined with brick and floor slab factories, and in the factories horses, actually ponies, seemed to be providing most of the motive power. They were hauling in clay from the pits and hauling away the finished product. Ponies were certainly preferable to little tractors from my point of view. Not only did ponies do less to tear up the track along the top of the levee, but they also made a lot less racket. As far as I could figure out, a new layer of clay must be deposited in the drain every time it floods. This boon then supports a dense ribbon of brick factories. Using the clay for bricks, in turn, was a kind of maintenance for the drain, keeping it clear with the bottom at the designed elevation. But who was buying all the bricks? There must have been an awful lot of building going on around there somewhere.

The top of the levee was straight and flat, and it had been marked off with kilometre stones. So I was able to measure my walking pace. I was doing about ten minutes and six seconds between stones, so about six kilometres an hour. Not bad. Measuring my pace that way ate up the afternoon, and that kind of pace ate up the map. I wasn't meeting anyone up on top of the levee, and I had no need to ask directions. The only thing that delayed me was the discovery of wild strawberries. They weren't very sweet, but I suppose if they had been more palatable they would have been picked clean long before I got there.

Along with the strawberries were plenty of wild flowers as well. Apart from the green fields and the blue of the sky, anything colourful is rare in the Chinese countryside, so the flowers, though tiny, really caught the eye. In areas with few cattle grazing, brilliant purple thistles predominated. They were a welcome touch until I started coming across bee hives. Whoever owned them seemed to have no hesitation about lining them up along the top of the levee to threaten passers by. I had no trouble with the bees, but I made a couple of detours down into the ditch.

As it turned out, I never did have to camp along the emergency drain. Late in the afternoon the levee passed near a town and I met another English student, this one rather unsuccessful. He'd graduated from high school the year before and gone south to take a job as a waiter in a fancy hotel. His English wasn't up to it, and now he was back home farming with his family. I had a cup of tea with his mother and father while he went and fetched his English teacher from the local high school.

The teacher, Mr. Chan, spoke very good English and insisted that I spend the night at his school and speak to a couple of the English classes the next morning. He put me up in the quarters of one of the teachers who was away on a course and whipped up a tasty meal with a bottle of beer in his own housing unit down the row. The teachers lived together in a row of barracks-like accommodation. Originally each family had been allocated a 5x5metre bare brick box. They had been expected to take their meals with the boarding students in the school cafeteria. Later it had become permissible to add a little shed on the front of each unit to serve as a kitchen, adding about 50 percent to the floor area. Mr. Chan lived there with his wife, also a teacher, and his young son.

While he was cooking dinner I had a chance for a sponge bath at the teachers' bathhouse. It was just a bare cement room with a drain hole in the floor draining into the adjacent ditch, but from somewhere Mr. Chan brought in a pail of hot and a pail of cold water, so I could have a good wash. Too bad about having to get back into filthy clothes after class the next morning.

In the end, I spoke to three different classes, telling them a bit about the school system in Hong Kong and answering questions. I enjoyed it. It was mid-morning before I got back to my six-minute kilometres.

During the evening I'd had the chance to ask Mr. Chan about the new crop that had taken over from rice north of the lakes. A trip to the dictionary revealed that it was rape. Rape is China's most popular vegetable, but around here it was allowed to grow far beyond the succulent stage and the seeds were being harvested for oil. It was everywhere.

The tall woody stems are harvested by hand with a sickle and stacked to dry in the sun for a few days. When the stalks have dried enough to be brittle, they're spread on hard flat ground and flailed with bamboo flails to break off the seedpods. The stalks are then bundled for forage and the dry pods are rolled with a stoneroller to break them up and release the tiny seeds. The roller is a tapered stone cylinder with a hole drilled down the middle. A wooden pole through the hole serves as an axle, so when pulled along by a water buffalo the taper automatically makes the roller turn in a circle. After rolling, the broken pods are separated from the seeds by winnowing in the wind. The mixture is tossed in large trays tightly woven from reeds until the wind has carried off all the pod fragments and left a pile of pure seeds in the tray. The seeds are then spread on sheets of plastic or canvas for further drying before they can be sold to a presser. The pods are burned and the ash spread on the fields. Flat level spaces are at a premium in China, where every square metre is under cultivation. During the oilseed season, harvesting activities block up the minor roads and even narrow the major highways as the peasants take over the verges. The crop's distinctive odour fills the air.

The levees offered wild fauna to divert me as well: tiny toads not larger than a small fingernail. You could visualize that all the larger species had been killed off for food. Perhaps these little guys survived only because they were too small to bother eating.

I came across a group of ladies spinning some sort of vegetable fibre into thread, and I realized that they may have been spinning flax. Their raw material was probably the same as the huge piles of reeds I'd seen from the boat that were grown for the paper mills. That had probably been a variety of flax as well. With the right equipment it would probably make a pretty good grade of paper, and it was certainly a lot more productive than growing trees.

A bit later I came across an old guy who had erected a shack, which he was using as an incense factory. It was a bit surprising, as I was under the impression that the main raw material for incense was the bark of a tree, a bit like cinnamon, that was ground up into a paste and formed into incense sticks. Out on the levee there wasn't a tree in sight.

It's said that just such a little factory is how Hong Kong got its name. Apparently there used to be an incense industry on Hong Kong island at a place that today is called Little Hong Kong in Cantonese. The incense was shipped out by boat, and the place became known as Incense Harbour, which is one translation for Hong Kong. The British came, corrupted the name and applied it to the entire island.

All together, it was a most unusual day for me. The emergency drain had been driven directly across the country, missing most of the traditional villages. I had no need to ask directions. So it was an entire day spent alone with my thoughts. I saw a few cowherds, but spent most of the day without speaking to anyone. It was a nice change, not having to recite my catechism, but it began to get on my nerves. I was glad, about lunchtime, to come to a junction with another giant drain served by a ferry in the form of a man rowing a flat-bottomed skiff.

The two big drains came together in a T intersection, so there were actually five different levees intersecting. The oarsman kept busy ferrying people back and forth in the various possible directions. The water was low and slack, so the trip was short and easy, but he told me he had no motor to use when the water was high. Those must be difficult days.

Chinese boatmen traditionally prefer to row standing up. Their small ferries are flat-bottomed skiffs which row easily (if not very straight) but are quite stable for carrying cows, goats and all sorts of barely imaginable farm gear. The boatman stands at the stern facing forward. Just ahead of him, a stick about 5cm thick and 20cm long stands up from each gunwale. Each stick has a gentle knee, so it stands up straight at first, but then the last 7 or 8cm bends gently toward the stern of the skiff. These are the rowlocks. A piece of rope is tied to each oar and formed into a loop, which passes over the rowlock. Each oar has a short cross handle at the top like a racing canoe paddle. The rower grasps the handles and pushes the oars forward ahead of him using the rowlocks as the fulcrums of the two levers. He may row cross-handed, especially in shallow water.

I lingered a few minutes enjoying a bit of human company with the ferryman. He wasn't busy during the siesta hour, though he had to keep an eye out for passengers appearing at the other landings across the two watercourses. Soon, though, I pushed on and at 2p.m. noted from the kilometre stones that I'd covered 43 kilometres in 24 hours. Not too bad considering I'd given some English classes in the morning before starting. It was almost surely a record, as my normal day was spent more in asking directions, then standing around answering questions, rather than walking.

I pondered my strange situation. As I walked along the levee, even far out in the countryside, there was almost always a house or two in sight somewhere. If I'd had any need – if I'd broken an ankle or needed clean water, or food, or a place to spend the night – those people would almost surely have helped me. They'd have been glad to. And I, at the same time, was interested in finding out more about how they lived. Yet still I was avoiding them.

One man I tried to chat with that afternoon was a cormorant fisherman. Unfortunately, we had very little Mandarin in common. The cormorant fishermen around the tourist Mecca of Guilin are quite famous, but I was surprised to see a fisherman returning home from a day on the almost-dry ditch. At Guilin they use proper boats, but this fellow was carrying on his back a tiny catamaran. It was about a metre and a half long, just big enough that he could stand with one foot in each pontoon and one cormorant perched on each of the bows. He apparently just poled himself around standing up, unable to change his stance for hours at a time. Worse, on that particular day he didn't seem to have caught anything.

I had been on the road only a few minutes the next morning when I came across one of the few villages that lay near the course of the drain. It was a lucky break, as I was able to find a dumpling seller for a delicious hot breakfast.

The town was unusual primarily because it had a church – the first I'd seen, and a sight that in general is very rare in China. It was a real European design with a steeple crowned by a cross, and tall windows with round tops. It looked as if it would hold a couple of hundred people. It would be quite surprising if it were able to draw such a large crowd from the environs of such a small village. I'd heard that Christianity was making a bit of a comeback, but this was the first evidence of it that I'd seen in many weeks on the road.

Apart from the church, this particular area looked notably impoverished. The town had cows and horses grazing in the main streets. The shops stocked almost nothing. The houses weren't falling down, but there wasn't much evidence of renovation work, and there was no evidence at all of the tile fronts and other decorative touches I'd seen earlier. Television antennas were few and far between, and there were no freezers at the shops, so no ice cream. Together, these hints were pretty conclusive evidence that although the area was wired for electricity, the supply was actually unreliable. Kids seemed to chew on sugar cane for a snack rather than store-bought candies. Adults bought glasses of cold tea and water chestnuts. But however poor they might be, the people were still smoking factory-rolled cigarettes. Perhaps the soil in the area wasn't suitable for growing tobacco.

Then I saw a little girl with a sack collecting cattle dung. It might have been for fertilizer, or it might have been for fuel. I didn't ask. But it's a recycling extreme that I hadn't seen before in China.

Later that morning I crossed the provincial boundary from Hunan into Hubei. I'd entered Hunan a month before in a sparsely populated mountain area. In that situation there had been no obvious, sudden change at the boundary. Here it was different. First, the boundary itself was marked on the levee with a boundary stone. Then the kilometre numbering system started over, marking now the distance to the Yangtze. And the dialect changed abruptly. I couldn't speak Hunanese or Hubeiese, but they were different enough that I noticed immediately.

For the first time, most of the houses had been built with a cast concrete sill up under the eaves. Formerly the rafters had always been nothing more than round poles set directly on the top of the brick walls. It wasn't a question of prosperity. None of the houses had any glass in the windows. It was just a different provincial style that had probably become established when the construction teams in the two provinces were under the control of different sets of central planners, and ordinary citizens weren't permitted to travel.

In some things central planning still rules, and I saw an example a few minutes later. A road crossed the drain at a ferry. In Hunan all the ferries had been little private operators with their rowboats, but here they were using a barge pushed by a substantial tugboat. No doubt, when the water was high all this was necessary, but there was very little water at this time of year. So little, in fact, that they'd had to excavate a bit of a lake in the bottom of the drain to float the tug. The whole crossing was only about three times the length of the barge. It would have been easier and far cheaper to rig up a cable and just pull the barge back and forth with a winch. Or even by hand, if necessary. The government just wasn't able to get to grips with details like that. And, unfortunately, that kind of transportation infrastructure is one aspect of the economy that the central planners are very reluctant to privatize.

The Yangtze is one of the world's major rivers, so I couldn't just cross it anywhere. I knew I was going to have to violate one of my principles by using the ferry marked on the map at the city of Shi Shou Shr. The best I could do was try to slip in on a country lane and skim right through without getting myself into any trouble.

I knew I was getting close when my country lane began to accommodate garbage trucks. Apparently the city had municipal garbage collection but no landfill. Their solution was simply to truck the rubbish to the outskirts of town and dump it by the roadside. Put that way it sounds a bit too high-handed even for the urban Chinese with their contempt for the peasants. Perhaps there was some concept of eventually widening the road based on the garbage fill. But such rationalizations didn't have much weight with the garbagemen who were actually doing the dumping. It was just rubbish by the roadside to them, and they dumped it as they pleased. To the passing stranger it appeared nothing more lofty than an unhealthy mess.

The land near the river was generally flat as a billiard table, but the city had been installed around a lone rocky crag standing a few hundred feet above the river. In ancient times it must have been a useful defensive position controlling traffic on the Yangtze. These days the crag seemed to be a sort of park with a pagoda on top. I didn't climb it, but approaching the city it was visible from a long way off. In the flat countryside, pedal rickshaws were popular. They seemed a practical way to haul the groceries home from market, though they must have given a pretty rough ride on the bad track I was following.

Apart from the big buildings, the rickshaws and the traffic, my brief brush with city life offered me a welcome treat. Out in the countryside I had sometimes come across shops with electric freezers selling ice cream. I could sometimes find restaurants with refrigerators. But the proprietors never saw fit to use their equipment to offer the patrons cold drinks. Regardless of the establishment's furnishings, the beer and soda was always kept on a shelf and served at room temperature – which was now getting to 30 degrees centigrade on most days. This seems to stem from the Chinese medical theories of yin and yang, the hot and cold essences of life. Many people seem to feel that cold drinks are bad for the health whatever the weather. In the city they'd conquered those inhibitions, and I took the opportunity to enjoy a cold bottle of soda in a roadside shop while surveying in safety the deadly traffic in the street outside.

I had guessed from the map that I would be using a major ferry crossing. I was surprised to find that I had to ask the way repeatedly before finding the dock at the end of a lane underneath the crag. It was obviously a government-run ferry, which is why it was shown on the map. But it took nothing larger than a bicycle. Of course, any ferry across a river the size of the Yangtze has to be considered a major business. The trip took about 20 minutes. The boat was just a metal pontoon with a small cabin for shelter and an inboard engine. The dock on the city side was nothing more than the last ferry that had expired making this run. It was now permanently moored to the shore, and the travellers sat about on deck waiting for their ship to come in. On the north shore there was no dock at all. The pontoon simply nosed up to the muddy bank and everyone jumped off. It would be a messy business in wet weather, as the chocolate current carries a heavy load of clay that's deposited in the annual floods to form the banks.

Stepping ashore after a half hour of intensive interrogation, I was at last in North China. The Yangtze is considered the dividing line. I'd been on the road a bit more than six weeks, and in absence of any real idea where my route would take me, I could consider this about half way on my trip. The Great Wall was by no means on the horizon, but now I could convince myself that I was going to make it.

The Yangtze levees were a cut above any I'd seen before, in China or elsewhere. They were massive. They were well maintained. They had a smooth trail along the top with houses about every hour occupied by flood watchers. I later learned that they lived free in these places in exchange for guarding the levee in times of high water and mobilizing repairs in case of trouble. Down below the levee on the riverside, the meadows had been planted with trees to break up the current when the meadows are flooded and lessen erosion of the base of the levee.

Walking on such giant levees had its drawbacks. For one, there was no shade. And the trail stretched straight and flat far into the distance. It was pretty boring. There was no water up there, and when the levee passed a village, it was usually a detour of a kilometre or so to climb down, buy a bottle of soda and climb back up.

On the other hand, the levee was about 20m above the river and the surrounding countryside. There was always an excellent view. The fields weren't spectacular, but the river and its traffic were interesting. The scenery changed only slowly, but it was memorable. And when it came time to camp for the night, the campsites were terrific. The river was so big that, as long as the campsite was screened from the top, there was no chance of anyone coming along down by the riverside. The sand bars made a luxurious cool, soft bed. Between the stars and the lights of the passing boats, you didn't want to go to sleep.

The levees were fast, easy walking, but on the whole the scale of the scenery was just too grand. I'd hit the river at a point where it was flowing south, but in general it flows east to the sea, and after a day or so its course swung away from my route. I also wanted to get off the levee before it reached the major city of Shashi, so I was glad enough to leave the river and strike off across the fields to the north.

That left me with the old problem of finding secluded campsites. In the flat land near the river, every square inch was cultivated. There were no rice paddies now. There was rape seed, there were soyabeans, plenty of wheat fields and a variety of other crops I couldn't identify. But woodlots were a thing of the past, and not a hill in sight. For a couple of days I was under pressure to find decent campsites.

Trudging the country roads, it was easy to notice things that were done differently here in Hubei province. The farm machinery industry was apparently still operating with the old socialist distribution system. Most farmers did all their work with the help of what in other countries would be described as garden tractors. In any particular area, all these tractors are identical. Back in Hunan they had all been made by a single factory in Hengyang, hundreds of kilometres to the south. Cross the border into Hubei and those tractors disappeared to be completely replaced by a slightly different design made in Wuhan, Hubei's provincial capital.

But many farmers didn't have tractors. Around here the two-wheeled horse or donkey cart was popular. These were simple things made of wood, though they had rubber tires. Every farmer had one, but not every farmer had a horse or a donkey. And so you could see farmers pulling these carts by hand along the country roads. Back in Guangdong I'd become accustomed to seeing the man of the family walking with a child while his wife came along behind carrying all their goods on a shoulder pole. Here the custom was a bit different. Apparently the sight of a wife straining in harness so her husband can ride is a bit too much for even the Chinese male sensibility. The husbands did the pulling while the wives rode.

The Hubei dialect was better entrenched than Hunanese had been. When asking directions in my lousy Mandarin, I'd developed the technique of beginning with, "Excuse me, I'm sorry to bother you. Could you tell me..." The stock greetings gave my victim a chance to figure out that I was trying to speak Mandarin and to get a feel for my foreign accent before I got to the meat of the question. Around here that was generally useless. My stock greeting again gave them time to figure out that I was using Mandarin, but most people didn't speak Mandarin, so they'd immediately break in with, "I don't understand." I eventually found that in Hubei I had much more success starting my question right off the bat with the name of the place I wanted to ask about. "Shi Shou Shr is which way" People expected me to be asking directions, so immediately hearing a place name they could recognize got me off on the right foot and less often summarily rejected.

From my point of view, the problem with that system was hearing the name of each place the first time and getting the Hubeiese pronunciation. China has one official language, several regional languages and hundreds or perhaps even thousands of local dialects. In the countryside it's the dialects that prevail, hence the need for flexibility in asking directions. Every Chinese village has a name. In most cases the name is thousands of years old, and it was given by the local people speaking a local dialect. These are oral dialects with no writing system. Centuries later, the central government tried to map the nation and sent out surveyors and cartographers to record these villages on their maps. In each case they tried to find standard Chinese characters to write on the maps which sounded a bit like the local name. Some of these efforts have been more successful than others.

You may have studied a lot of Chinese. You may be travelling with a Chinese friend. You may have a dictionary. Nevertheless, don't expect to be able to ask directions straight off a Chinese map. The best approach is to show the map to a local person and ask him the way. (Yes, him. You'll do better asking men, as illiteracy is much higher among women.) Listen carefully to his pronunciation of the names, and perhaps make some notes in some sort of English phonetic spelling. Just reading place names off the map using a dictionary is likely to generate some pretty puzzled looks, and even contradictory directions on occasion.

Hubei villagers were busy rebuilding their houses, just as in Guangdong and Hunan. But in Hubei the building frenzy extended from the villages into the towns as well. Almost every town had a long street of new shop front buildings either under construction, or newly finished and waiting for tenants. Most often the partly finished new buildings had been taken over by sharks who'd set up pool tables in them to earn a few yuan while awaiting permanent tenants. Each town had so many new shop buildings that you got the impression the sharks might be there a while.

One town had built an entire new quarter featuring what was apparently intended to be an industrial park. The vast park had at least two new factories nearly complete, but the new shops were mostly empty. There was a new bus station, not yet occupied, surrounded by new restaurants and tiny private hotels, for the most part not yet open. I spotted one that seemed to be in business but without patrons, and realized it would be a good opportunity for a hot meal in new facilities, still relatively clean. Over dinner the proprietor convinced me to have a look at his rooms on the upper floor. They were brand new, and he was asking only 20 yuan for the night. Thus did I enjoy one of my very few nights in a hotel bed. It was great.

A remarkable fact about the new hotel is that the proprietor never asked my name. China, of course, has long been a place where the traveller was obliged to register his every move with the local police. When you stayed in a hotel, they took your passport, and it was probably taken to the police station during the night for checking and recording. Even when staying with friends, there was a similar registration procedure. The town of my hotel break was probably closed to foreigners. Under the old system I would have been visited by the police during the evening, then shipped out to the nearest city by bus at my own expense. In fact, I simply paid my 20 yuan. There was no checking in, no checking out. If there were more hotels like that one, it would make China a much nicer place to visit. Anyway, for that one night it was a welcome change from camping.

1. Wet feet right off the bat.

2. Not wheelchair accessible.

3. Central Guiding Principle Number Two: Stay away
from tourist attractions.

4. Not the Golden Gate.

5. Well ahead of the Joneses.

6. Down on the commune.

7. The long road north.

8. Power to the people.

9.   In the karst belt.

10. A charcoal kiln.

11.   Mr. Yam's terraced house.

12.   This far from the road, even the pipes are made of wood.

13. If only the water were clean enough...

14. A hot meal in prospect.

15. In Hunan they know how to coddle the traveller.

16. Unloading sand at Mr. Lee's commune.

17. Amateur coal mining.

18. Bridge, deluxe model.

19. Mrs. Ngaan's cooking shed and its useless pump.

20. No radar, no radio.

21. Fish, perhaps, but leeches for sure.

22. Wall building gets out of hand.

23. 1.2 billion Chinese, but not right around here.

24. Passengers will please remove shoes before boarding.

25. Once a troglodyte, ever a troglodyte.

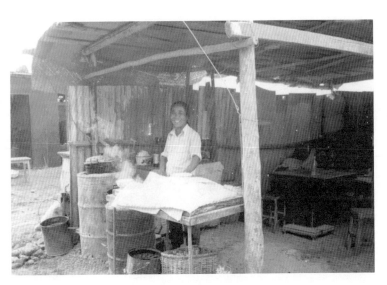

26. Private enterprise.

27. Tourist attraction. No tourists allowed.

28. Lunch with the Lis.

29. A rural highrise.

30. The Wus welcome a breakfast guest.

31. Winter's coming in Huang Tu Wan.

32. The Great Wall. Vandalized, but still Great.

33. And on your right, Inner Mongolia.

34. The Yellow River. Nice gorge, pity about the quicksand.

35. "You can't miss it."

36. A chance for a few minutes rest.

11

On the Han

Densely populated Hubei province is a difficult place for walking. The topography is flat, the roads were straight and sunny, and I was having some difficulty finding good camping places. My solution was to strike north from the Yangtze to the banks of the Han River, a major tributary that cuts through the middle of the province in a roughly north-south direction. I expected it to be heavily diked against flooding, so the levees would form a fast and uncomplicated route across the densely populated heart of the province.

And so it proved, but before I reached the Han I had another brush with urban life as I crossed one of the nation's main east-west axes: the highway from the provincial capital of Wuhan to the famous Yangtze gorges and the notorious Three Gorges Dam project. Unprepared by my map, I stumbled first across a new super-highway still under construction. The section I saw seemed to be awaiting the pavers, and when I reached it, there was no one around. I took a cool break in the deep shade of a new underpass. A few kilometres farther north I came to the old highway, lined with noodle shacks and retail businesses of every kind. It was teeming with heavy truck traffic. I crossed quickly and continued north on a tiny track through the fields.

It was there that I met Mr. Lee, another English speaker, my first for weeks. Some version of his story could be told by quite a few ambitious people in the countryside. He'd graduated from high school relatively adept in English, and had gone south to Guangdong province in hopes of finding hotel work. He'd been unsuccessful, not because his English wasn't good enough, but because he couldn't speak any Cantonese. Despite the influx of foreigners, local plutocrats and visitors from Hong Kong remain the life blood of the Guangdong hospitality industry, and such patrons aren't willing to speak Mandarin or English.

Discouraged, my English-speaking acquaintance returned as far as Wuhan, the capital of Hubei, where he tried to make money in the trendy new profession of selling insurance. That didn't work out either. He didn't try to explain why, but I'll bet it had something to do with his country accent when speaking Hubeiese.

So now he's back in rural Hou Kou, very dissatisfied after experiencing life in the big city and apparently unemployed, since he had time to pedal along with me for an hour or more and practice his English. I imagine that there must be many dissatisfied peasant graduates in rural China these days. In an important way they're probably the motor for the current phase of national development, relying so much, as it does, on the dynamism of the rural and township enterprises. Better than many peasants I met, Mr. Lee understood that I wasn't in a position to help him. I could only hope that he gets his life moving before becoming too discouraged.

He finally bid me good-by after guiding me to a ferry across a major irrigation canal. This particular canal was large enough to be one of very few marked on my map. The crossing was normally about 100m wide, though it was much less on the day I crossed, as the water level was low. The ferry was a cable job, with a ferryman who pulled the cable by hand. It was cheaper than buying fuel for a motor, and in principle it should have been easier than either poling or rowing, though in this case the skiff itself was terribly heavy. It was made of concrete. A well-made concrete vessel can be almost as light as a wooden vessel of the same size, but this one wasn't well made. Mighty durable, though.

From that ferry crossing north to the Han River, although my map was no more useful than usual, I found that I never needed my compass. All the fields, the roads, the ditches, were laid out in perfect north-south alignment. And for much of the way, the fields were enormous by Chinese standards. I saw some that were 100m wide and at least 800m long. They were certainly big enough to profit from modern tractors and farm machinery, though I didn't often see any. The long straight roads could get boring, but it was never any problem to shift over 100m to the next drainage ditch and find a smaller path along the bank. Even in flat, open country, following a tiny track where you'd have to watch where you were putting your feet made for an interesting walk.

There in the heart of Hubei province I unexpectedly came across an oil field. A small one, nothing fancy. Just a few pumps nodding in the fields. At first I thought they might be pumping brine. China has a few modest oil fields, but I had never heard of one in central Hubei. Later, though, I passed a couple of shipping terminals with their distinctive crude oil smell and a bit of oily spillage here and there.

On another occasion I was following a tiny trail along an irrigation ditch and came across a sizeable pile of what appeared to be large mussel shells. Another puzzle. I had always considered mussels a saltwater mollusk. The large, uniform shells suggested that someone had been farming them around here and, rather than shipping them out for sale, had chosen to eat at least part of the harvest. There was no sign of any installation for raising mussels in the ditch, so the whole thing remained a mystery. I intended to ask someone about it, but the word for mussel was neither in my vocabulary nor in my dictionary, and in the end I forgot to ask.

Despite the relatively large, open fields, the only time I saw large Western-style tractors at work was when I inadvertently visited another prison farm. The Chinese believe in the twin concepts they call "reform through labour" and "re-education through labour." The distinction between reform and re-education can be a bit obscure to Westerners (or at least to me), but the labour part is usually farm labour. I had a chance to view a bit of it in action. The prison farm was certainly an area closed to foreigners, but as usual the idea never occurred to anyone on the spot, and I was able to walk right through unhindered.

I first noticed something amiss as I was following a rather bushy and unkempt trail along a ditch and suddenly came across a field fenced in with a square mesh of razor wire. Chinese fields are never fenced. At most, thorn bushes might be planted to form a hedge. But razor wire? Perhaps the field contained some really valuable crop. Opium poppies under the control of some local bigshot? No, the crop didn't look different from any of the others around. Then I realized that there were two other things quite out of the ordinary. A few fields away a half dozen men were working with some very large and noisy piece of farm machinery. I couldn't tell what it was, but from the noise of the engine it was certainly many times the size of the conventional garden tractor. And apart from that group there wasn't a soul around. All the other fields were empty as far as the eye could see. That was really unusual, because it was nearing sunset, and the farmers always take advantage of the last cooler hours of the day to work in their fields right up until dusk. I was puzzled, but I had been looking for a campsite, and the empty landscape offered me my chance. I found a bushy, overgrown stretch of ditch and quietly made camp.

The next morning the mystery was solved. They lock up the prisoners early, but they rouse them out even earlier. By the time I hit the trail at 6:30, last night's empty fields were already well staffed. I knew they were prisoners right away, because they were all working in heavy dark blue jackets with a distinctive yellow stripe across the shoulders and down each sleeve. In that attire they must have suffered incredibly from the heat during the day. But each had a straw hat, a necessity in the hot sun with their distinctive super-short haircuts. It must have been a pretty low security institution, as the prisoners were working with sickles. The guards had simply marked the corners of the area where they were allowed to work and turned them to it. The dangerous types were presumably confined to the fields with the razor wire. I was walking with my sleeves rolled up, and seeing that I was wearing a watch one of the prisoners called out: "What time is it?" "Ten minutes to seven", I replied, and he gave me a wave. The guards didn't seem to mind, but I kept walking pretty briskly until I was well away from the scene of my crime.

As I progressed I realized that this was the first region I'd seen where there wasn't much house renovation going on. It could have been simple poverty; television aerials were few and far between.

But more likely the ownership rights still hadn't been adequately confirmed. In practice the communist state is far from monolithic, and central government policy can be implemented very unevenly in different counties and districts. The land around here was very productive, so perhaps the state hadn't yet given up as much control as elsewhere. Perhaps people weren't yet sure enough of their tenure to invest in home improvements.

The renovations that I did see were of a completely new type. Instead of adding rooms, or storeys, or tile decorations, people investing in their homes were walling them in by erecting a wall around the front yard to form a courtyard. Courtyard houses are traditional in northeast China. There, rooms are built around three sides of a central courtyard. The fourth side is closed by a wall with a fancy gate. The houses around here were originally built as three adjacent rooms all in a row, just like Mr. Ngaan's. A few occupants had gotten their hands on enough bricks to build three walls and a gate around the entire front yard. It would give a bit the feel of a traditional courtyard house once you're inside. If everyone did it, the street would look traditional from the outside too – each block would be just a blank wall on each side of the street punctuated by a few gates. In this region it hadn't yet reached that point.

"Property is theft!" Remember that one? You don't hear it much anymore, even in China, but you can still see its effects. Walls and fences remain a bit controversial. One factor that makes walking in China such a pleasure is that you need never worry about trespassing on private property. Not just the farmland, but even people's front yards are public property open to all, at least for innocent passage. For decades, fences were considered at the very least anti-social, often illegal. So even today fences are very few wherever you travel. In recent years people have begun to experiment a bit with planting thorny hedges around particularly valuable fields. Some thorn bushes will regenerate from cuttings, so if there were a return to the old morality the farmers could pretend that their hedges had grown up naturally and simply had never been cut back. For the most part, though, when people have a valuable crop like tomatoes or watermelons reaching ripeness they post a family member on 24-hour guard in the fields. Far better than fences, these bored sentries are happy to see a passing walker, and will probably invite him over for a chat and to sample the crop.

It was late one afternoon when I finally spotted in the distance the towering levees along the Han. And none too soon. I was getting tired of walking the long, straight ditches. Up on the levee I could again look down into the riverine villages and out over the passing boat traffic. I again had kilometre stones to mark my progress. I'd hit the river at kilometre 266, which suggested that the numbering system must start at Wuhan where the Han joins the Yangtze.

With so many irrigation canals running due north, I'd had little occasion to ask directions over the past few days. I now celebrated reaching the Han by stopping for a hot dinner at a small village restaurant, and I was amazed at the change in the people. Everyone was even more friendly than before and asked innumerable questions, but their standard of Mandarin was incredibly low. We were speaking mostly sign language. And for the first time in China the restaurant was serving potatoes. I'd seen them growing and in the markets, but these were the first I'd eaten since leaving Hong Kong.

Over a second bottle of warm beer, I lingered longer than I should have answering questions and ended up having to find a campsite in the dark. There were plenty of spots down by the river outside the levee, but cutting stakes with a Swiss army knife and rigging my fly in the dark was a complicated business. I was also surprised to find that I had to clear an area of stones to have a place to sleep. The soil in central China is mostly a fine silt, especially along the banks of a large river. I realized during the night how the stones had gotten there. The thunder that had impelled me to rig my fly turned out to be all-night blasting.

As I hit the trail in the morning, I saw a hill ahead upriver. It was the first I'd seen since the isolated crag at Shi Shao Shr along the Yangtze. The hill was clearly the scene of the blasting, and as I approached I saw as well how it had come to supply the stones along the shore. There wasn't much left of the hill, because quarrying had consumed most of it and would soon finish it off. The rock was blasted, crushed a bit and loaded into little two-wheeled wagons to be hauled to the levee by the ubiquitous garden tractors. There it was being loaded into barges by a simple expedient akin to walking the plank.

The quarrymen apparently worked in some sort of groups. It wasn't clear if they were separate families, or departments of a larger enterprise, or what, but each group had constructed its own loading dock. These consisted of board walkways cantilevered off the steep levee and hanging high over the water level. A barge could be moored underneath secured to the bank. Loading consisted of backing out onto the walkway and dumping the rock out of the cart down into the barge with a tremendous clatter. The morning I passed there were four barges loading and a few empty berths. The whole business was crude and dusty in the extreme, and a certain amount of the product ended up in the swirling current, but everyone seemed to be making money. They were too busy to stop and grill me.

Despite the giant levees, flooding seemed to be a way of life in this part of the country. Many of the houses were built on square

stone platforms about 3m above the general level of the
countryside. The faces of the base were armoured with large slabs of
cut stone to resist erosion. They looked a bit like the bottom layer
of a Mayan pyramid with a house installed on top. The outbuildings
that you would expect to be built of adobe, here were either built
from big blocks of stone set without mortar or from very flimsy
wattle and daub. It must flood every year.

Most of these platforms were built far back from the river – a
kilometre or more. This left the farmers with a long walk to and
from their fields. For the first time I saw parades of farmers traipsing
out for work in the morning riding on their water buffaloes.
Elsewhere I'd seen only little kids riding them.

Walking on the levee was a bit lonely. There was no need to
stop and ask directions every few minutes, and all the farmers were
working in fields far below. There were cowherds up there watching
their cows and sheep grazing on the banks, but they tend to be the
oldest, the youngest or in some way the most useless people in the
family, and little inclined to talk with a stranger. The old folks had
no glasses and probably couldn't see well enough to make out that I
was a foreigner. The young kids were too intimidated. The levee
was, though, used as a highway by a few people. Travelling peddlers,
for example.

I met a man hawking bean curd. Fresh bean curd is wet and
heavy to carry. He had a special system where his racks of curd were
suspended from the ends of his shoulder pole on braided cords. The
cords would stretch and take up some of the motion as he walked.
Otherwise, the bouncing would tend to squeeze out the water and
ruin the product.

The steamed bun man didn't have that problem. His wares
were much more voluminous, and he carried them on a bicycle in

two giant wicker baskets rigged as panniers. The baskets were lined with a bag, and the buns were wrapped in a cloth to keep out the dust. They were just what I needed. I could eat as I walked. Five for a yuan.

I met another pair of itinerant musicians. These two were blind, which meant I couldn't really stop and talk with them. My poor Mandarin wasn't much use in Hubei province, and to make myself understood with sighted people I had to rely on lots of ancillary sign language. With the blind I was helpless. They were walking close together carrying their instruments in their arms while one felt ahead with a white cane. Carrying their instruments that way presumably encouraged people to approach them and ask for a song. As they came to each village perhaps they'd set up and busk awhile. Even with a bit of vision they'd be hard put to seek out clients and solicit business. Still, they didn't seem to be starving or ragged. They were hanging on by roaming out in the countryside one step ahead of television.

One day I met a postman. It was a brief encounter, but it was nice to speak with someone whose Mandarin I could understand. He quickly pedaled on, but left me with a newspaper. It wasn't clear how he could divert to me someone's personal subscription addressed with his name on it. Maybe he knew the guy was away. I was starved for news and looked through it quickly, but my simplified characters aren't really good enough, and newspapers are one of the most difficult kinds of text to read in Chinese. They use all sorts of specialized constructions to expedite typesetting. Then, of course, there isn't much news in a Chinese newspaper. The whole content is a bit like the "At Court" column in a newspaper in Britain. They report the official appearances of the leaders and the official texts of their speeches, and that's about it.

I was better off studying the butterflies. For a few days they were everywhere. And everywhere there were kids with little nets running around trying to catch them. The colourful scene made a nice complement to the broad vistas over the rolling river and its traffic.

It was high summer now and the daytime temperatures were getting up into the 30s, about typical for central China. I was glad to be walking north with the sun at my back. The brim of my hat shut out the bright sky, but the clay of the path had dried to a light gray that hurt my eyes. I found myself squinting and getting headaches by the end of the day. I needed sun glasses, but there's nowhere to buy them out in the countryside. Fortunately, the farmers had the same problems, and were religious about taking a long siesta in the middle of the day. I too took to knocking off about 1 p.m. in the deepest shade I could find and not setting off again until 2:30. At that time of day I could sit out in plain sight confident that no one would come by to disturb my siesta. At 2:30 it was still hot, but only for a couple of hours before it started to cool off for the evening. My clothes, of course, were perpetually soaked in sweat and looked like rags most of the time.

With the long break at noon, the farmers were working right through dusk until it was too late to see properly. This meant the fields were very busy just at the hour when I was looking for a campsite, and every evening's hunt was a chore. Once it got dark there were always plenty of campsites down by the river, outside the levee, but after camping in the dark I'd have to move on again early in the morning, as the farmers were out at the crack of dawn while it was still cool enough to work comfortably.

I solved this problem one night by camping on the grounds of a police post. Around suppertime I came across what appeared to be a factory perched right on the levee overlooking the river. In China, any sort of compound surrounded by a high brick wall looks like a factory. The fields outside the wall were untilled. Exploring further, I saw that the compound had a substantial dock down by the river accommodating a police patrol boat. I found a quiet spot outside the walls and sat down for a bite to eat and to see what might happen. Over the course of an hour or so there was no sign of life, so I decided to treat myself to an early night and a quiet, scenic campsite with a nice view over the river traffic. It was a risky move because the area was almost surely closed to foreigners and there might well be someone at the police post who would be aware of the fact. In fact, no one came along and I had a restful night.

Perhaps because of the flooding there weren't many substantial towns along the Han, but eventually I came to a place marked on the map as Lin Kwong. I was another case of a major work unit housing thousands of people but treated by the mapmakers as just a village for political purposes. Kwong means mine, and Lin Kwong seemed to specialize in quarries and lime kilns. They were shipping out the lime by barge and importing sand. The quarries were a couple of kilometres back from the river, and they moved the product down to the docks with their own miniature railway. I neglected to measure the gauge, but I had a chance to watch a miniature steam engine about two metres tall pull a string of tiny hopper cars away from the dock and off up the track. The hopper cars were like mine cars, small enough to be pushed by hand, and the whole rest of the railway had been built to the same scale. The factory's living area was, in effect, the largest town I'd seen for a while, so I took the opportunity to stop for a hot meal. I was pleasantly surprised that, sitting in an open-fronted restaurant, I didn't draw a crowd. The other patrons were anxious to chat, but didn't insist on reading my map or pawing through my gear. It was a nice change.

Leaving town, I was glad I'd hit Lin Kwong on a Sunday. The road north of town was literally ankle deep in dust. The dust was fine and white like talcum powder, and at each step my feet would disappear, like walking in fresh snow. I had to follow the road only for a couple of hundred metres, and there was little traffic, but had the quarries been in operation the dust would have been horrendous. Of course, my feet and legs and everything else about me were pretty dusty long before I got to Lin Kwong. But many of my fellow pedestrians were out in their Sunday best – ladies in frilly dresses with pink plastic shoes. They were really struggling to keep clean, and not very successfully.

It was a bit sad to see the younger set around Lin Kwong wandering around with small transistor radios pressed to their ears. Every day I was meeting cowherds who sat on the levee all day long with absolutely nothing to do. They really needed radios like that but didn't use them. The reason, I suppose, is that they couldn't afford the batteries. As one evidence of their poverty, I was forever coming across broken tethers where a buffalo had been tethered to a stake to graze on the levee but had broken the tether and escaped. The tether was broken because it wasn't made from any kind of rope. It was rubber that had been cut in a spiral from an old tire. A cowherd who couldn't afford a proper tether wouldn't be spending his money on batteries and would in any case be too busy chasing his cows to listen to much radio.

That same afternoon I came across a more bucolic Sunday diversion. It centred on a construction project where they were building a new outlet weir for one of the streams flowing into the Han. As part of the construction, they had diverted a couple of streams into a temporary pond, and the people in the adjacent village had decided that this was their one opportunity to harvest all the fish that normally would flow past to other villages. Well, reasonable enough, except I doubt if there were actually any fish. It was really just another example of how so many Chinese are addicted to gambling. Nevertheless, 30 or 40 people, virtually the whole village, were immersed in a frantic fishing derby. At least it was an exciting way to pass a Sunday.

From my point of view it was interesting to note that as soon as the people had something else to do, they'd leave me alone. I'd noticed it before when following a road. Everyone would follow me and ask questions except people who were shooting pool or playing cards when I approached. They'd greet me and keep right on playing. Clearly my attraction wasn't good looks or scintillating conversation. It was primarily that many people spend all day with nothing much to do.

At one point the Han looped in a bit of an oxbow and I cut across country for a day or so. I passed through only one town, but this one was a real town, not a work unit like Lin Kwong. It was interesting to contrast them. Lin Kwong was too busy making money to worry about civic improvements. Here they had demolished a whole street of shops, widened the road to dimensions which seemed to rival those of the Champs Elysee and built at least 30 new shop-front buildings which still stood empty. At the central intersection they had installed a giant gilt statue in a traffic circle. It was like a special madness of mayors, this craze for redevelopment. Where did all the money come from? I never found an answer.

As I progressed farther north, more and more people were living in houses enclosed in walls to make a compound. One unfortunate result is that people were discouraged from setting up small shops outside their doors, because their houses didn't front directly on the street (See photo number 22). This made it harder for me to replenish my supplies, as shops I visited never had everything I needed. So I was looking forward to reaching the sizeable town of Yi Xiang where my map showed a bridge over the river. My plan was to avoid going into town, but I expected to see a long line of shacks on the approaches to the bridge serving the passing truckers. Unfortunately, I was disappointed. The long approach ramp was bare of commerce. The bridge itself was at least a kilometre long, so I felt I'd better buy some supplies before crossing. As a result, I embarked on what proved to be a long walk into town. In the end my search for supplies took me so far afield that I decided to continue on the west bank of the Han and never did cross the bridge. I did, though, enjoy in Yi Xiang one of my increasingly rare restaurant meals.

A Chinese peasant meal, be it breakfast, lunch or supper, is basically a large helping of a starchy staple garnished with some sort of tasty sauce. The staple varies from one part of the country to another, from rice to noodles to steamed buns to millet and even potatoes. The sauce varies from season to season depending on what's ripe in the garden, but it's always a stew of vegetables, sometimes supplemented with egg or bean curd. Even a foreigner usually finds this sauce delicious. It's seasoned with soya sauce, vinegar, onion and garlic, herbs grown and collected locally, and in many areas lashings of hot peppers. From a nutritional point of view, this diet is a bit like eating three meals a day of baked potatoes with various toppings. Even today, peasants rarely eat meat. But notice that the Chinese toppings contain negligible sugar, no dairy products and no fat other than a bit of cooking oil. The Chinese drink a lot of tea, but most have never tasted coffee. And they don't have much opportunity to snack between meals. It may not sound appealing, but foreigners living in China usually get to like it, if they can once get over their caffeine addiction.

After lunch, rather than walk all the way back to the bridge, I continued on the west bank. I paid for my laziness over the next couple of days as both hills and a highway began to encroach on the riverbank. The hills brought the end of the levee and the need to pick my way through riverside villages. The highway meant that there were few trails for inter-village travel. Everyone walked out to the highway and caught a minibus. I came to realize, however, that there was some sort of rule to the effect that farmers weren't allowed to cultivate right up to the top of the bank at the river's edge. Although they were cultivating every possible square metre – all sorts of ditches and slopes – there was always a narrow path left along the top of the riverbank. Anywhere else you might imagine that it was some sort of expression of riparian rights, but in China it's probably organized for the sake of flood surveillance and control. This uncultivated right-of-way wound and twisted, dipped and dodged as it threaded its way along the top of the tall clay bank, but in fact it was interesting and scenic walking once you got over the conviction that it was sure to peter out just around the next bend.

For some reason, despite the hills nearby just across the highway, the villages along the river were equipped with cement water towers. There may have been some hydrologic reason why this was necessary, but more likely it was another example of central planning at work. Water towers are a great convenience to most of the villages throughout central Hubei, so you could imagine provision being made and a campaign being organized to install water towers in all of them. Since these villages were under the same administrative authority, they too got their water towers even though a spring-fed system would have been more appropriate.

Although I was just a couple of hundred metres off a major highway, at night I had no difficulty finding spectacular campsites.

The eroding clay of the river bank had slumped away in landslides that had left an array of more or less level benches all down the face of the cliff. In wet weather it would have been muddy climbing down through the clay, but in fact the weather held dry. I surprised at least one farmer early in the morning as I was setting off. He had seen me passing late the previous evening and had wondered all night what I was doing and where I was going. When he went back to his fields the following morning he saw me again and this time stopped me for a chat. Of course, he couldn't believe that I'd spent the night camping on a little bench down over the edge of the bank. In fact, that particular night had been cold and windy, but it had been a spectacular campsite high above the river and its traffic.

As the river and highway converged, I began to run into factories, which barred my way by occupying all the land from the highway right down to the water's edge. In some cases it was necessary to cut out to the highway to get around. It was an interesting example of how privacy and property rights work in China. In theory, no one is supposed to own any property. Anyone can walk through the peasants' fields, through their villages, through their front yards. Along the Han the peasants were obliged to reserve a trail along the cliff tops uncultivated. But the factories, previously all owned by the state, are always very careful to erect high brick walls, usually topped with broken glass, around any property they've been allocated. Along the river that included running their walls right down to the water's edge and out into the river. The factory doesn't belong to anyone in particular. It belongs to the state. So it belongs to everyone and therefore (somehow) it's all right for the factory to wall off "its" property. It's a good example of the unequal treatment given the agricultural and industrial sectors.

My brief exposure to highway walking was risky and unpleasant, but I did see another side of society that I'd been missing out in the fields. There were plenty of long distance trucks passing, and the locals had set up stalls by the roadside to sell them local produce. The particular attraction in this area seemed to be some sort of special local tea and strings of garlic. Walking along the levee I could often smell the garlic on the breath of people passing, even very early in the morning, but I hadn't realized that they had been indulging in a local specialty. There were, of course, lots of restaurants along the highway, and I treated myself to a couple of hot meals, which certainly featured plenty of garlic.

The passing truckers were mostly from Sichuan Province and points west. You could tell from their licence plates, but also from the fact that most of the highway restaurants advertised Sichuan cuisine. Many had their signs written in Arabic characters as well. It put me off ordering a meal, because Sichuan cuisine is renowned as one of the spiciest in China. For some dishes they not only load up with hot pepper, but they then add another spice which numbs the tongue so that you can eat more and eat faster without the normal agony. Apparently hot spices are addictive. They stimulate the body to produce natural painkillers that are morphine analogs. The same phenomenon turns Westerners into compulsive runners and triathletes, but the Chinese find eating Sichuan cuisine much cheaper and easier.

At the outskirts of the city of Xiang Fan the authorities had erected a tollgate. It wasn't for any particular bridge or tunnel. The highway was less driveable after the toll than before. It was just a scheme for raising some money from the truckers to support the city budget. It's a common ploy in China. Pedestrians didn't pay, but I spent a few minutes there anyway, watching the fun.

The Chinese are intensely loyal to their family, their clan and to other groups to which they belong. But outside those groups they're lacking what Westerners would describe as public spirit. The tollbooths had several lanes open, and of course the truckers were jockeying back and forth trying to get into the shortest line. Not just the shortest line on their side of the road. Any lane in either direction with no-one waiting would do. So all the toll collectors all across the highway were being attacked by vehicles from both directions at once. Drivers were constantly diving for what looked like an open toll booth and then having to back up when someone beat them to it from the other side.

Why, you might wonder, do the toll collectors put up with it? If they refused to take money from the wrong direction they could stamp it out in no time. All I could imagine is that the violators are people who come through frequently and have gone to the trouble of developing a relationship with the toll collectors. Perhaps some extra cash changes hands, but more likely it's just cigarettes, some sort of Sichuan product, or a bottle of liquor from time to time. It doesn't take much.

You often see a related behavior at rail crossings. While the gates are down the waiting vehicles spread themselves over both lanes. Then when the train passes and the gate is raised, there are two solid walls of traffic facing each other across the tracks. They have to fight (sometimes literally fight) to filter through each other and clear the crossing before the next train comes. The lack of public spirit is certainly one of the least attractive features of Chinese life.

Having failed to cross the river in Yi Xiang, I was faced with having to make the crossing in Xiang Fan, a genuine city. This was a flagrant violation of the principles that had served me so well, but

I could excuse it on the grounds that it was time to renew my visa, which can't be done out in the countryside. Xiang Fan and its bridge were right on my route, and the city was a major rail junction and so surely open to foreigners. I'd still have to risk the city traffic and street crime, but it couldn't be helped.

Sure enough, while in Xiang Fan I had my pocket picked. The city proved to be a transit point for migrant labourers from the poorer provinces to the west, and the streets were crowded with young men on the make. Chinese cities are well equipped with public conveniences, but no toilet paper. Residents use newspapers, the lining from cigarette packets, whatever they can lay their hands on. I had splashed out on a small packet of tissues, which must have looked in my hip pocket a lot like a wallet. Every rich foreigner must carry a wallet full of cash, so some enterprising fellow stealthily slit my pocket and extracted his booty. He must have been heartily disappointed. Had he been caught stealing from a foreigner that way, he might conceivably have faced the death penalty.

Xiang Fan itself was just another Chinese city. Most of them look much the same. This one had the restored remains of a city wall, which, despite my rule about tourist attractions, was well worth a look. It also had a rather impressive new mosque. Elsewhere, a new mosque usually means Arabian oil money, but I doubt if that's true in central China. I poked into a few bookstores hoping to supplement my inadequate maps, but no luck. I got my visa extension and moved on.

12

Lost in the Wilds

I left the river at Xiang Fan. It bends sharply to the west; I struck out across the fields due north.

Right away I was experiencing something completely new. Here were gently rolling wheat fields reminiscent of central North America. The crop was just ripening – in every direction nothing but the classic amber waves of grain. But through it still ran the traditional rights-of-way: uncultivated grassy strips, some leading more or less north. It was great walking.

For most foreigners the thought of China automatically brings rice to mind. But many Chinese eat more wheat than rice in the form of noodles, dumplings, steamed buns and even types of pan-fried bread. Wheat grows without all the fancy irrigation needed for rice. It grows well through most of the north of the country. The fields are small and oddly shaped, so the work is done by hand. Even harvesting is still done with a sickle, a few stalks at a time. Some villages have begun to invest in powered threshing machines, but treadle threshers are still popular. You can see old women and children following the harvest through the fields scavenging up stray heads of wheat that have escaped baling. It shows the relative value of wheat and labour.

Unlike rice, wheat demands to be ground into flour for cooking. The villages have set up motorized mills to do this communally. The peasants store their wheat as grain to discourage infestation, then have it ground as required, one sack at a time. In areas where noodles are the staple, many housewives can pull their own noodles by hand, an impressive trick to the uninitiated. Even many men are able to make noodles chopped or shaved from a block of dough, and most can fry up a pan of bread if they have to.

But though the crop had changed, I was still in country under intensive cultivation, without woodlots or forested hillsides. Finding campsites was still a bit of a chore, although now, with wheat a less labour intensive crop, the villages were farther apart. My campsites were usually isolated patches of grazing land on a boundary between two villages far from the nearest house. Within the villages, wall building was running rampant. Wherever three or four adjacent houses were owned by the same family, they'd thrown up a wall around the entire cluster and divided the village into compounds. You could walk all the way through town, never meet a soul and pass completely unseen. The true courtyard houses that had been designed in that style from the beginning had no external windows at all. You could tell which houses had been retrofitted with walls, because they had windows at the back opening on the rest of the village. Some occupants had bricked these up once their wall was in place.

It was only a day or two after leaving the river that I crossed another provincial boundary, this time from Hubei into Henan. I couldn't detect any demarcation except the change in dialect. The borders seem to have been culturally delimited in the days of the warlords, where adjacent clans and their systems of fealty diverged along with their customs. There was no geographical break.

Whatever the cultural divergences, the economic trends spanned the border. New construction continued apace. At the turn of the 22nd century, people will still be able to look back and recall the 1990s building boom from the multitude of little boxes decorated with tile plaques over their doors. Sunsets, dragons, mottoes – all are very popular. Made from glazed tile, they'll last forever. The new houses, of course, were being used even before they were completed. But here again the towns were building rows of new shop buildings, which stood, at least temporarily, unoccupied. In one case, someone had decided to launch a new commercial strip from scratch at a country road junction. On the day I passed the shop units all stood empty, and there was no one in sight in any direction. It's hard to imagine what they were expecting when they decided to build the place.

I arrived in Yo Dien trailing the largest parade I'd attracted so far: 11 pedestrians plus six bicycles and a seventh who had ridden on ahead to recruit more. They had nothing to say, just hanging back a few steps and following me along to see where I might be going and why. When we reached the town I realized why so many were going there. There was some sort of ceremony in preparation. The only intersection had been draped with China's beloved red bunting, and there was a rostrum erected in the middle of the road. I couldn't read the posters and banners, but it was obviously some sort of civic occasion. I could sense that all I'd have to do would be pause for a moment to ask directions and, sweaty and dusty as I was, I'd be hauled up onto the rostrum and asked to make a speech. I was among thousands of bystanders lounging around with nothing to do before the start of festivities. A single pause and I'd be engulfed by the curious. I very calmly ducked under a low-hanging banner and kept walking. Heads turned, but no one made the first move. To everyone's amazement, I continued purposefully down the street and out of sight.

Just beyond the edge of town I had to wade a creek. To preserve my shoes I stopped, took them off and waded barefoot. You can do that sort of thing in the countryside pretty confident that your feet won't find any broken glass, or indeed rubbish of any kind. Everything is still too valuable. Of course, the water won't be clean. This particular stream seemed to carry a load of pulping liquor. I was hoping it would be good for athlete's foot. In any case, the festivities in town were so compelling that during the entire shoe changing and wading process I saw hardly a soul. The trail branched confusingly on the other bank, and I had to sit in the sun a few minutes drying my feet before someone came along who could tell me which branch to take.

Later that same morning I had another strange crowd control experience. I happened to pass a school just as the kids were coming out for recess. Of course, they came running over and walked along with me for a minute asking questions and making jokes to each other behind my back. Apparently, though, there was a strict limit on how far from the school they were allowed to stray during recess. As we reached the boundary, my parade dropped away. After another 150m I turned back to wave and saw the entire school, including the teachers, lined up along the invisible boundary watching me disappear over their special horizon.

Distribution of even the simplest products is hopelessly inefficient in China. Sometimes it's hard to predict where and when even necessities will be available. But I was now approaching a major highway crossing, and along the highway someone had arranged a system of ice cream distribution. Walking down narrow dirt tracks through the fields I kept encountering bicycle vendors with foam coolers full of ice cream bars for sale. What a joy it must be to knock off for a minute from work in the fields and sit down with your toddler to share an ice cream bar. Say what you will about freedom and democracy, it's surely this kind of innovation that has the peasants feeling prosperous, optimistic and patriotic about the changes in their country. I enjoyed a few myself.

The ice cream would be all the more welcome because this was one part of the country where many of the villages had never been wired up for electricity. It was by no means remote; a major highway and a rail line ran through the general vicinity. It seemed to be a case of simple poverty. I could judge pretty accurately from the sorts of things for sale in the little shops. No thought of Pepsi around here, or even Bepsi. The only beverages were beer and small bottles of a local brand of soda. (And a cheap and nasty brew it was.) The standard restaurant meal had deteriorated to consist of a deep fried dough stick eaten with a bowl of starchy water and a few scraps of fried cabbage. The ice cream vendors clearly were tilling virgin ground.

One noon hour I stopped to beg some clean water and was invited in for lunch. As it happens, I had just eaten one of the poorest restaurant meals I have ever found anywhere in China. It was largely my own fault. I asked the proprietor to hold the hot peppers, but that was about the only spice she had. Without the peppers, the noodles were so bland as to be pretty hard to eat – a bit like spaghetti boiled without salt and served without sauce with just a poached egg on top. Nevertheless, I'd eaten a big bowl of the stuff, so now I wasn't hungry. Nevertheless, I stepped in for a rest and a bowl of tea.

My hosts must have introduced themselves, but I never caught their names. They had been working since 4 a.m. taking advantage of the cool night air and the full moon to harvest their wheat. By noon they had already done a full day's work, but they were just in for lunch and a nap. At 2:30 they'd head back out again and work until late in the evening.

When I saw their luncheon arrangements I was glad I'd already declined to join them. After eight hours of hard work, their lunch consisted of a bowl of noodles with some fried cabbage and a hard boiled egg. One of the brothers made himself a second helping by breaking up a piece of steamed bread left over from breakfast into a bowl of the noodle water. There was just about enough food, but they needed all of it. I limited myself to a couple of bowls of tea as we chatted.

The family consisted of two brothers with their wives and children and their elderly father. The father and one brother served as doctors for the area. It sounded as if the father might have been trained as one of the famous barefoot doctors of 30 years before. These days they no longer worked from a communal dispensary, but kept a stock of both Chinese and Western medicines at their house.

The original house had been built in 1980 when the elder brother married. At first it was just the standard three adjacent rooms, but since then they'd built a second similar house at right angles to the first and then walled in the front yard to form a courtyard. This allowed them to build a separate cookhouse in the far corner where the wives worked together to prepare the meals on a common stove. They all ate together, in good weather, out of doors.

This was a village without electricity. They lived a very hard life, cut off in large part from the modern world. But they had a family solidarity that even a casual visitor could appreciate. I finished my tea and left them to their nap. A very pleasant interlude.

Wandering these wheat lands I was reminded of the Wizard of Oz. Like Dorothy, I knew I wasn't in Kansas, but in the hot afternoon air I began seeing dust devils sweeping across the fields lifting funnels of chaff into the air. Some were strong enough to pick up sheaves of wheat stalks standing in the fields. In the background, a steam engine passed on the rail line puffing coal smoke and pulling a line of empty boxcars. It could have been the 1930s in America.

The goats, though, didn't fit the Kansan stereotype. I'd been seeing more and more of them. I'd been assuming people raised them for their wool, but then I began seeing ewes with udder bags. Were the Chinese drinking the milk? Most Chinese are lactose intolerant. Doesn't goat milk contain lactose? I never found out the answers to my questions. I intended to ask, but it was difficult to find someone who spoke enough Mandarin.

I had other questions to trouble me. First and foremost, could all the growth and material progress be sustained? The farmers I met were expressing excitement and optimism, but what about the food supply? Despite a very successful birth control program, surely the population is going to double before it stabilizes. If all those people are going to live better, where's it all going to come from? Improving productivity isn't likely to make much of a contribution; surely the land can't be farmed much more intensively than it is today. I hadn't seen any vacant land waiting to be brought under cultivation. There are no new sources of water waiting to be exploited. Even today's farmers are eating hardly any meat or fruit, using almost no paper or metal and burning hardly any electricity. It's hard to see them maintaining even present standards as population doubles. Where's it all going to come from? Still, you feel as if you're going out on a limb making dire predictions. Malthus was wrong; the Club of Rome was wrong. Maybe there are still more green miracles coming. But walking around in the countryside it's pretty hard to believe it.

As I wandered farther north the towns seemed to have implemented a crackdown on taking over farmland to build new shop buildings. Where before you'd enter town past a long row of brand new but empty shop buildings stretching out into the countryside, here they were going to the trouble of demolishing and rebuilding streets of buildings within the existing town boundaries. That had the additional advantage of allowing them to widen the streets while they were at it. Though I must say that with the amount of traffic those towns get, widening the streets seemed like sheer bravado. The change was general enough that you had to suspect that someone at the county level had issued an edict to the mayors about chewing up good farmland in the interests of urban renewal.

The mid-summer harvest was in full swing, and again a few days later I was invited to dine, this time by a family of three breaking for breakfast in the shade of a tree by the road. It was again fortunate that I'd already eaten, as they of course hadn't brought enough of a picnic to accommodate an unexpected guest. They said they had started at 4 a.m. to take advantage of the bright moonlight. It was 8:30, and this was their breakfast. They'd knock off again about 12:30 for a long break through the hottest part of the day. For breakfast each was drinking a lukewarm bowl of starchy gruel (they'd brought it out in a vacuum flask) and a giant hardboiled egg, probably a duck egg. They had another flask of tea, and I joined them for a couple of cups and a welcome break. There was no traffic, but I'd gotten stuck on a long, straight gravel road that wasn't much fun for walking.

By late morning, though, I was starting to see a range of hills up ahead in the distance. I wandered just at lunch time into a little town which I could tell marked the end of the long straight roads I'd been following for the past few days. The town was on a minor east-west highway, and beyond it the map showed a different pattern of roads and rivers. Villages suddenly became sparse. I could now see why. I was at the foot of a range of substantial hills stretching right across my path.

There was a graveyard at the edge of town with some unfamiliar characteristics. In Hong Kong and in most of the parts of China I'd visited so far, a grave is a round mound of earth surrounded by a sort of berm and usually dug into a hollow in a hillside. Here, the mounds were either peaked like little miniature cathedrals or capped with a stone cap on the top of the mound. When I first saw the stone caps, I guessed they must be to prevent erosion of the mounds in the rain, but that made no sense in light of the cathedral shapes which had no caps and would be much more susceptible to erosion. It wasn't the kind of thing I could ask about with my, and their, limited Mandarin. I tentatively had to accept that the stone caps might be just a decorative feature.

The little town again featured a mosque. That no doubt had something to do with the fashion in graves. It was also one of the towns where they were practicing demolition and renewal in preference to ribbon-like expansion. The highway was already very wide, and now they had widened the town's only cross street to the point where you could U-turn a tractor trailer rig. I was tempted to pace off the width, but I had already attracted a big enough crowd. I guessed it might be 60m.

I stopped to buy some soda from a woman who obviously wasn't wearing a bra under her shirt. I had been surprised to find that the bra-less look isn't that uncommon out in the countryside. I decided that it's a bit like the old virginity charade in the West. Before the pill, well-bred girls were supposed to feign disinterest in sex, "saving it for their wedding night." But if they were widowed or divorced they were no longer expected to keep up the charade and could be as pragmatic about their needs as everyone else. China has free contraception, but the virginity charade is alive and well. Bras are a good example. Virgins are usually so flat-chested that they don't need bras, but they're the ones who always wear them. Mothers are the ones who need them, but they're the ones who sometimes don't bother. A few years ago there was a fashion for padded bras among city women, especially the young and unmarried. Poor quality padded bras on their basically very slim figures led to some truly bizarre sights.

I was looking forward to getting back into hill country, but I realized that I'd be well advised to have a substantial hot lunch in preparation. It might be my last for a while. There were plenty of joints near the highway junction, so I picked one and pulled up a chair.

As in many an open-air restaurant, the chairs in this one were homemade of split bamboo. The seat is about 30cm square and only a few centimetres off the ground. Sitting on one of these contrivances and you're just far enough off the ground to enable you to cross your legs Buddha-fashion without too much discomfort. In fact, with a little practice you can sit that way for as much as an hour and still get up again relatively smoothly. Which is just as well, as the table too is very low, much too low to put your legs, or even your feet, underneath while you eat.

The restaurant served noodles with some sort of spicy meat which seemed to be a home-made specialty. It was quite delicious if you could overlook the ambiance. The passing trucks were noisy, but not that frequent. The dust blowing in from the road was dry and probably pretty harmless. The cook came out and dumped a load of ashes from his stove along the roadside, but that was certainly sterile. The problem lay more under our feet. The eating area was on slabs of cement, which covered the open drain – the sewer serving all the premises up and down the highway. You couldn't actually smell it, but I wasn't reassured. I'll bet on a rainy day it would be pretty ripe.

I shared my table with six other travellers, mostly cyclists from neighboring towns. They took turns asking the questions, so they got a chance to eat while listening to the answers. I had trouble finding time for each mouthful. While juggling questions and chopsticks, I was at the same time trying to keep one eye on my watch so I could time their spitting. It was remarkably uniform. Each of my tablemates was either spitting or blowing his nose on the ground once every two minutes, on average. I don't think it was from any organic necessity. They were just cueing off each other. But the result was that someone was either hawking or blowing every 20 seconds with surprising regularity.

Meanwhile, the employees cooking and washing dishes were also handling the money. It's all you can expect from a small, family-run setup, but it certainly makes you think about hepatitis. The Chinese aren't bothered much by AIDS or diabetes, but they sure worry about hepatitis. About one person in three is a carrier.

Hepatitis comes in several forms. The most common are Hepatitis A and B. Hepatitis A is the endemic form that the carriers have. It weakens your liver and makes you susceptible to various liver problems, but it's not very contagious. Hepatitis B is the acute sickness that travellers get – the one that gives you jaundice and sends you to bed for six months with no alcohol. This one's very contagious and usually comes from food that's been contaminated with sewage and then poorly cooked. With China's unclean water, fish is the prime culprit. But you don't get much fish to eat while walking out in the countryside.

In a restaurant in China you'll often see the patrons rewashing their place settings in hot tea before the food is served. Hong Kong people visiting the mainland often carry their own chopsticks around with them. The reason is hepatitis B.

After more-or-less enjoying my delicious lunch, I set off into the hills. They were neither steep nor very high at first, and there was even a scattering of unmapped villages. Around here the houses had obviously all been built as courtyard houses from the beginning. They had no windows or other openings except the front gate. Well, with one exception. In some cases the latrine had been built into the outside wall so that the pit can be emptied from the street without carrying the muck through the courtyard. You could visualize how this architecture had evolved in the days of banditry. You could really lock up the house at night and no one had any excuse to open the gate until morning. Surely, it's not necessary these days. In most respects you'd be better off with a detached outhouse. But apparently it has become the traditional design.

I spent the afternoon climbing, and as I reached higher elevations the wells began to get deeper. For the first time in China I began to see wells with the classic winch and crank, the kind that's presented as the stereotype of a well in children's books.

Chinese water comes in three varieties: surface water from lakes, streams and irrigation canals that comes in handy for laundry and bathing; water from taps and wells for washing food and cooking; and boiled water from vacuum flasks, the only kind you can drink. It tastes better with a few tea leaves in it. Walking in the countryside you can, it's true, occasionally come across springs which appear to come directly from a deep aquifer and seem to be safe for drinking. Probably. But it's a bit like crossing roads against the lights. With care you can get away with it for a long while, but eventually...

By late afternoon the dusty roads were far behind. I was wandering through the wheat fields on little access trails left unplanted. There was a lot to see, with families in every field harvesting their wheat. From the tops of the ridges I could see a couple of kilometres in every direction, and over that area I could see 250 to 300 people harvesting. All that work, all those carts full of wheat heading back to the villages, and in all of it not a motor to be heard. And after sunset, no lights either. They have metal sickles. They have the wheel. But the overall picture was of an awful lot of people working by hand. I pondered it as I watched a golden sunset with a rampart of mountains in the background.

As usual, the only problem was where to find a campsite amidst all the agricultural activity. As I was looking, I came across a field of opium poppies. Well, of course, I'm not absolutely sure that they were being cultivated for opium. But they were the first field of any sort of flowers that I'd seen cultivated. And I recalled that I'd lately seen at least half a dozen different men smoking long wooden pipes with a small brass bowl and brass mouthpiece. Most people were still smoking factory-rolled cigarettes, but I'd seen more pipes that day than I could remember seeing in a long while. It was only a small field, but it was planted in an inaccessible position right on top of a hill. What else could it be for? I decided I'd better look a bit further for a campsite.

I spent the next morning floundering around looking for a route into the town of Chi Li Peng (Seven Mile Plain). The rights-of-way through the fields climbed the tops of the ridges, while the villages were in the bottoms of the intervening valleys to keep their wells to a manageable depth. I had no way to replenish my water, and as the sun mounted in the sky, it was beating right on the face of the escarpment before me. Those I met assured me I was on the trail to Chi Li Peng, but they said it in a way that let me know I always had a lot more tough climbing in front of me. "Just keep climbing," was typical. The trail deteriorated to a goat track, and then there before me was a long, long flight of marble stairs straight up the face of the escarpment. I should have counted them, but of course I only thought of that after I was part way up and I wasn't prepared to return and start over in the blazing sun. Three hundred metres of steady climb with three steps to the metre would come to almost 1000 blocks of beautiful marble quarried at the top, carried down on shoulder poles and carefully set in place. It was impressive. And so was the view whenever I paused for breath and looked back behind me to the south.

At the top, I was immediately struck by a drop in living standards. Suddenly, all the buildings were back to mud brick. The land was rough and rocky. Fields were small and few. Pretty much every flat space had been constructed by erecting a stone retaining wall and filling in behind it. Goat raising seemed to have replaced agriculture (which reminded me that I still hadn't figured out how they make any money from their goats). The streams ran milk white or inky black with rock dust from marble polishing, but the people didn't use stone in constructing their homes. The main road into Chi Li Peng forded streams. None of the stone was being wasted on bridges. Poor country indeed.

My difficulties speaking with the local people were getting even worse. I began to suspect that they might be some sort of minority group. The older ladies were often wearing traditional-style tunics buttoning up the side to a high collar. But the food seemed much the same: a bowl of gruel and some fried or pickled cabbage seemed to be the standard fare. For more energy, this was supplemented with a steamed bun.

Beyond Chi Li Peng the traditional trail had been upgraded to a rather rough road winding up into the mountains. There was very little shown on my map in this area, and when I came to one of the few towns that was marked, it proved to consist of just two buildings. One was a primary school; the other was almost deserted. It had apparently once been a store, but now housed only a small office for a guy who distributed electricity. By hand.

If that sounds rather a good trick, here's how it works. The supply to these remote areas is rather feeble and unsteady. On the other hand, there are only a few local buildings connected to the grid. Rather than brown all of them out when the voltage is low, the distributor has some priority rules for allocating the available supply at different times of day. When juice is short, he cuts off some of the lines. In this case, the distributor himself was an old codger who had probably been one of the leaders during commune times. These days, a post like his can be a pretty lucrative sinecure, as people are prepared to supplement his salary with under-the-table payments to get priority.

The two-building town reminded me of Britain where a town shown on the map sometimes turns out to consist of just one pub. At the same time, the whole area brought memories of Australia. The fords started it, but even more reminiscent were the flies. For the first time in China I was besieged by little flies which didn't bite but insisted on buzzing around and around in front of your face. It was possible, but not easy to swat them. Just easy enough to tempt you to keep trying. Walking with them was intensely frustrating. If I'd had a hat with a brim I'd have been tempted to try rigging up the famous Australian ring of bobbing corks around my head.

I spent about a day climbing the road from Chi Li Peng into the mountains. It was pleasant enough, as the road wound back and forth amidst interesting scenery. Whenever the road embarked on a series of switchbacks, the original trail would come back to life and pedestrians could cut straight up the traditional climb and avoid a lot of winding back and forth.

At one of these shortcuts a little stream crossed the road, and on the bank a lady had set up a stall to sell cakes of sticky rice wrapped in banana leaves. It was a dish I hadn't seen since Guangdong, where they're usually made with a bite of chicken in the middle. These cakes were sweetened slightly and contained a bit of sweet potato. I wondered where she got banana leaves. She was operating far north of banana country. I wasn't able to ask her properly, but as I finished each cake I noticed that she took the leaf and washed it for re-use.

At the top of that same shortcut I came across another cultural relic that I hadn't seen in a while: a roadside shrine. It may have been significant that this one wasn't actually by the roadside, but in its ancient location a bit down the traditional trail from the edge of the modern road. In that spot it was out of sight to anyone passing in a vehicle. Only the locals would know it was there. It appeared to have been fixed up and extended recently, and there were fresh cigarettes on the altar. It seems the people were still under some pressure not to indulge too openly in superstitious religious practices.

But the pressure doesn't manage to keep it completely under cover. Later that morning, back on the road again, I found the rock faces at some of the sharper curves pasted with paper amulets against traffic accidents. That's a custom I'd seen before only in Taiwan. The papers pasted on the rock face looked a bit unsightly, but in Taiwan they throw dozens of the papers from their cars on dangerous curves, and that looks much worse. What impelled this religious activism is this particular district? I was inclined to guess it was the steep brooding crags overhanging the valleys. The terrain was starting to get truly rugged.

Over the past couple of days, a dozen people had assured me that there was a trail over the steep ridges to the north. After almost a day on the road I'd reached the point where I was going to have to find it. I eventually found the turnoff by asking every passer-by (there weren't many) until I finally ran into one who told me that I'd already missed it. As I doubled back, I encountered a man who'd seen me pass earlier and had now come down to the road to meet me. The weather was hot, my shirt was half unbuttoned, and he was fascinated by the hair on my chest. He kept pulling at it as we talked. He eventually directed me up a dry streambed where, if you half closed your eyes, you could perhaps imagine that there was some sort of smoothed track through the cobbles. I was skeptical until, at the first fork, I found a red blaze painted on a rock by the shore. It led me to the west, which more or less corresponded with the sign language directions I'd received from the hair fetishist. After that I was sucked in.

I found another blaze or two, but most of the forks were sheer guesswork. There was no physical trail evident over the smooth cobbles of the streambed. Then I came to an isolated shack in the woods. Could it be that this was where the blazes were leading? There was no one around to ask, so I kept climbing.

By the time I'd accepted that I'd lost the trail, I'd climbed too long to turn back. The ridge was extremely steep, but by that time the summit wasn't too far above me. I explored several tributaries looking for an easy way up, and on each of them found one or two ruined houses. It looked as if this area had been depopulated by the communization movements 35 or 40 years before. There had probably been a woods industry up here, but then all the people were resettled into communes down in the valley, and the forest was allowed to go to seed. There was certainly no harvesting going on any more, but plenty of rotting deadfalls.

I eventually followed one of the tributaries as high as I could and then struck out bushwhacking for the ridgeline. I was climbing a rock fall, so there was a definite danger of falling or breaking an ankle. Either would be pretty serious so far from anything. I made it up in about three quarters of an hour, but it was a tough and tangled climb.

To my dismay, I then found that there was no sign of a trail along the razor-sharp ridge line. I struggled along through the underbrush for a couple of hundred metres in each direction and found nothing better than a rabbit run. That was a sure sign that the woods industry in this area was defunct. I was faced with bushwhacking again down the other side. Worse yet, across the valley to the North was another ridge that was just as steep and a lot higher than this one. I resolved not to lose the trail next time, and cast around for a place to descend.

I picked what appeared from above to be a smooth steep valley with no sudden cliffs part way down. In fact the smooth surface proved to be a deep bed of leaves and debris, which had collected in a chute, which had once been used for skidding logs. The ground beneath the leaves was steep and slick, and I did quite a bit of dangerous, uncontrolled skidding myself. Later, the valley degenerated into a rock fall, which had previously been bridged by wooden walkways, now almost completely rotted away. Climbing over the unstable rocks and through the tangled deadfalls was a difficult business, even going down hill, but the struggle only lasted a half hour or so before I came to a hint of a trail. That quickly brought me out to a larger trail where I eventually saw a red slash much like those I'd seen on the other side. So there had been a trail as advertised. I'd simply missed it.

I was completely filthy. I had bark and leaf dust in my hair, in my socks, under my clothes and all over my gear. Thankful to be down safely, I stopped by a stream before reaching civilization and treated myself to a cold bath.

I met a housewife almost as soon as I struck the winding dirt road in the valley bottom. She wasn't too surprised to see me, as by that time I was emerging from the marked trail. As before, she assured me that there was a trail over the next ridge. But, also as before, she warned me that it was difficult and dangerous. According to her, I should follow the road down to the highway and take the bus. Once I'd weaned her off that idea, she informed me that a little hamlet I could see down the valley was the only settlement for miles around. If I was intent on suffering, I could pick up the trail behind the store.

I was glad to hear there was a store and set off to see what I could buy to celebrate my escape from my own stupidity. There wasn't much, but they had the usual weak beer and some vacuum packed jars of peanuts. Good enough for me.

As I sat snacking, of course just about everyone in the valley came over to see what was going on. While they all agreed with my friend the housewife about taking the bus, a couple of the men had walked both the trail I had just failed to follow and the one I was now looking for, and they agreed that if I had gotten this far I would probably make it. Through this elaborate discussion I assembled a pretty comprehensive set of directions.

I tried to replenish my supplies, but about all I could find to buy was more peanuts and beer. I was packing them away when one of my informants who lived nearby invited me in for a hot bowl of noodles to prepare me for the climb. I tucked in eagerly until I realized that he was sharing his own rations, not an extra portion cooked up for me. It was too late to back out, so I offered him a package of my instant noodles in compensation. His entire supper consisted of a bowl of noodles (two bowls until I came along) topped with a bit of fried tofu and fried cabbage. I dashed back to the store and bought a jar of pears, which we split for dessert.

I was glad of the hospitality, but by the time I left it was too late to get over the ridge before dark. I climbed for a few minutes, then ducked off the track and camped for the night.

The lower part of the trail was actually a narrow dirt road, and as I was climbing it early the next morning a dump truck full of workers passed me. I was surprised, but glad to know that there would be someone up ahead to give directions. I kept my eyes open for side trails, but found nothing to tempt me astray. In this valley, in contrast with the last, the workers were cleaning out all the old slash and deadfalls from the long-dead logging operations. Most of the logs piled by the track looked pretty rotten, but they were apparently hauling them out and selling them for some use or other.

It was this effort which had led them to reopen the track up the bottom of the valley.

I'd been walking for an hour or so through beautiful wild country when I came across two men cooking breakfast over a campfire. They were in the process of setting up a mini-sawmill; actually relocating it from somewhere else. They had a pretty comfortable camp with a spectacular view, but they were plagued by the little flies. They had mosquito nets in their lean-to, but they must have found it a very long day trying to work with the flies buzzing around. They spoke good Mandarin and invited me to stop for a bite.

Need I say it? Breakfast was a bowl of starchy gruel, a bit like the water left over when you've boiled a pot of rice, supplemented with a bit of fried cabbage and some bread. But instead of steamed buns these guys were frying a kind of thin bread that reminded me of a French crêpe. Unlike my friend of the night before, these guys had plenty of supplies and we ate our fill. I was coming to enjoy fried cabbage. The only problem was picking the fried flies out of the pancakes. Once cooked in, they were tricky to find.

By the time I caught up with the truck full of workers, I'd already climbed up pretty close to the ridgeline. A couple of them were people I'd spoken with the night before, and they had complete directions ready for the rest of the climb. It wasn't far, but the trail was hard to find because they had spent the previous winter cleaning out all the old logging debris from the upper valleys. There were clear, well-worn trails everywhere, and only one of them led over the ridgeline. As I got to the top, I had to dump my pack and begin searching all the little draws one by one looking for the one which held the trail going through. It was a long process. When I found it, though, there was no doubt. It wasn't big or well used, but it was clearly a traditional trail. There was a little notch cut through the very summit of the ridge, and someone had mounted a log as a seat for taking a break and surveying the valley below.

Surveying to the north revealed yet more crags, seemingly steeper and certainly higher than anything I'd yet climbed. If I didn't get lost on the way down, I'd be in for another tough climb that same afternoon. I didn't have much leisure for surveying, however, as the ridgeline was the domain of a very possessive owl. As I sat there, he swooped at me repeatedly, calling and showing his talons. I concluded he didn't get many visitors.

The trail down again was by no means heavily used, but it was well graded and without too many tricky junctions. To my surprise, I again reached the bottom relatively quickly with far less descending than I'd anticipated. I was getting the distinct impression that each of these ridges could better be described as an escarpment rather than a ridge separating two deep valleys. In crossing them I was gaining altitude at each transition. Of course, my impression may have been distorted by anxiety. Perhaps the descents seemed shorter because I could simply keep walking with no decisions to make. On the way up it was essential to keep a careful eye out for the one correct trail at each branching. The others led to dead ends. Coming down, every trail leads to the bottom sooner or later. But the wheat crop in this new valley again seemed to be behind the crops I'd seen yesterday. On balance I had to conclude that I was gaining altitude.

When I hit the valley bottom, the first person I met on the road was a mute. I was surprised, because one of the men at the store the previous afternoon had also been mute. Could it be that there was some sort of genetic problem around here? Not likely, I decided. Although there weren't many kilometres between them, these valleys probably held two pretty independent populations.

More likely they were both deaf. Many children in China are deafened by overdoses of antibiotics, though these guys both looked a bit too old for that problem. When they were kids China didn't have antibiotics.

Just a few minutes later I came to a shop. There wasn't much for sale, but I bought a big bottle of soda and sat down to finish it off. It was the worst I'd tasted yet.

The shop owner and a couple of his customers seemed genuinely impressed that I'd crossed from Xiao Tang He in two days. None of them had ever done it, but they'd heard it involved a couple of tough climbs. They disabused me of my illusion that I'd crossed from the Han watershed to the drainage of the Yellow River. The little brook in their valley curved back to the south and eventually reached the Han near Xiang Fan. As usual, they suggested I follow it as far as the highway where I could catch a bus north.

In the course of these discussions a young boy came in and left again. Then, suddenly, the shop was full of kids. I hadn't realized it, but there was a primary school almost next door. A teacher appeared, and to my great surprise he spoke a bit of English. I offered him one of my biscuits and we sat back for a chat, which must have really impressed the shop full of kids and parents. He told me that he wasn't from around here. In fact, he wasn't from this province, but he had been assigned here after teachers college. He'd later managed to recruit a wife from his hometown, and the two of them had been trying to learn Henanese and to get used to the isolated life in this secluded valley.

As we were chatting, one of the students burst in with a bowl of gruel and a steamed bun for me from the school canteen. I suppose they'd already shared out all the cabbage. It was a nice gesture and I ate it with pleasure, but it was my third meal in a row sponged off these impoverished people. I did feel a bit guilty.

I bid good-by after lunch, armed with a fresh set of directions for the new ridge in my future. None of them had climbed this one either, but all assured me that it was an absolute killer. Weighed against the other directions I'd received over the past few days, it sounded to me as if I should be able to make it over before dark. To be on the safe side, I decided to pass up any noontime siesta. The crucial first junction wasn't far from the shop, and the teacher sent a boy with me to make sure I got started on the right trail.

In fact, this climb turned out to be my last for a while, and the easiest of the series that had begun with the marble stairs leading to Chi Li Peng. The trail had been widened for logging trucks, though quite a few years before. It wasn't easy to lose. It was obvious that few came this way, because when the track began switching back to climb the steeper sections, there were no shortcut trails cutting off the switchbacks. Without logging, no one had any reason to make the climb except perhaps for a bit of hunting. For me it was just a beautiful, decision-free walk. The cliffs overhead were spectacular.

The old logging road petered out near the top, but the route from there on up was pretty obvious, and in two hours I was at the ridgeline. Another 45 minutes and the trail on the other side brought me out on a beautifully maintained gravel road with hardly any loss of elevation. My theory about gaining altitude with each ridge seemed confirmed.

My new surroundings presented a bit of a mystery. Not the least of it was which way to turn. The road wound back and forth in the bottom of a narrow valley under spectacular pinnacles and sheer rocky cliffs. The forest was quiet and beautiful, and the stream in the valley bottom was a clear deep blue, a real rarity in China. I felt as if I were in a park in the Canadian Rockies.

After walking for the better part of an hour among the squirrels, I finally came across a fellow human being. He was grading the road. In fact, he was attempting to grade the road by hand with a scraper on a long handle like a push broom. It seemed an endless task, but he assured me that the road got very little traffic. Which seemed reasonable, as his hand work seemed sufficient to keep it impeccably manicured. He couldn't read the map, and neither of us spoke enough Mandarin for me to extract any useful directions, but he waved me on in the direction I was going with some sort of assurance that I'd get directions farther down the valley.

13

Nabbed

It took me a while to realize it, but I was violating one of my basic principles. Certainly the beautifully manicured road I was following wasn't shown on my map, but after wandering along admiring the scenery for a while I came to a boulder in the stream marked with a carefully painted sign. That seemed odd. Surely no one around here needed a sign on their boulders, and in any case very few could read it. What was going on? I spent a few minutes trying to decipher the characters and realized that I had wandered into a tourist attraction. It made sense – the beautiful scenery, the clean water, the careful road maintenance. There was nothing shown on my map, but in fact it seemed a site well worth a visit.

Which isn't to say that it was getting any traffic. I walked for an hour or so and saw not another soul until I came to what was apparently the park headquarters. There was a whole complex of buildings including dormitories for the workers, garages, offices and a big hotel. None of it was new, but everything was decked out in banners and bunting for some sort of grand opening ceremony. I realized that here was an old commune, which had decided to try and make some money by converting itself into a park to exploit the beautiful scenery. A pretty innovative idea in the context of China.

I yearned to sit down in the hotel dining room and order a proper meal, but I was filthy and sweaty. I took a photo and reluctantly passed it by. I made it as far as the main gate. I had just stopped to ask directions of the ticket seller when a man ran up behind me calling: "Wait! Wait! Come back!"

"Oh, I'm just passing through," I said. "It's a lovely park, though. I really enjoyed the scenery. And so clean."

"Please stay for dinner. The manager invites you for dinner."

"Well, that's very nice, but I'm not really dressed for it. I've been walking all day, and I'm pretty scruffy. I need a shave."

But he wasn't taking no for an answer. "Don't worry, we have lots of rooms. You can have a bath."

What could I say? Back we went.

It turned out that the park had just opened. They were having their grand opening festivities, and tonight's program featured filming by a television crew from a small city not too far away. Hearing of my passing, the manager realized at once that he had an invaluable prop for his television feature. What better way to attract visitors than to show that foreigners were flocking in and loving it. I was taped enjoying a sumptuous dinner with the manager, commenting warmly on the scenery and facilities, and dancing (amid a crowd of employees in their best attire) in the hotel discotheque. In fact, there was no shortage of country girls dying to dance with a foreigner. It wasn't Hollywood, but for one evening I was a star. Better yet, I spent a night in the hotel between clean sheets. I had to pay for that, but at 20 yuan I'm not complaining. In the morning, the television crew set off to film the crags and one of the assistant managers bought me breakfast. All in all, it was a very pleasant interlude.

As I hit the road after breakfast I had to admit that the park had a lot of potential. Of course, a typical foreign tourist might object to the toilet facilities. After drinking beer all evening I'd found that the hotel toilets consisted of an eight-holer across the road, with no partitions between the holes. But most Chinese tourists wouldn't find that so remarkable. The manager's real problem is that I'd seen the place at its absolute peak. Everything was spic and span; everyone was in his uniform. But they have very few opportunities to do any marketing and build up their reputation. Inevitably, business will be slow at first. Employees will start to say, "Ah, no need to wear this dumb uniform. I'm going to take off these shoes." By the time a few people do start to trickle in, a lot of the initial enthusiasm will have worn off. The bunting will be a bit tattered and dirty; the uniforms won't be as they were designed. If that happens, it will be all down hill.

The television workers travelled around the region quite a bit, and for once I was able to get some informed advice about my route for several days ahead. On the other hand, they travelled everywhere by van, and part of their suggested route involved following a major road clearly marked on my map. I set out from the park by the only possible route, and resolved to play the rest by ear.

As soon as I got out into farmland, the flies that had been pestering me for days disappeared. I realized that either they were woodland creatures or, more likely, insecticide on the cultivated fields kept them in check.

The wheat in this district was nowhere near ready for harvesting, but the farmers were out in force anyway. They were planting corn between the unripe rows. This was a tricky business, but they did it with the aid of a pair of giant bamboo tweezers about 3m long. They'd stick the apex of the contraption into an old shoe and slide the shoe up the channel between two rows of the crop, a bit like pushing a wheelbarrow. The two arms of the tweezers gently push the rows apart so that it was easy to reach in and weed, or to plant another crop. Very crafty. The planting was apparently timed so that when they came through to harvest the wheat, the corn would already be well started. It's not something you could do in mechanized agriculture, but if you're harvesting with a sickle, might as well make the most of it.

The fields had been divided up among the families in accord with the new agricultural policies. No fences, though. Instead, every few metres along the little paths through the crops, you'd come to a stone about 10 or 15cm in diameter that had been carefully placed, painted white and lettered with the names of the families allocated the strip of land on either side.

I spent the first part of the morning descending from the hills into a broad river valley. The last part of the descent was on a paved road, and it was distinctly dangerous. The truck drivers heading down had the habit of shutting off their engines and coasting to save fuel. Because traffic was very light you didn't expect them, and had a tendency to wander out into the road as it twisted back and forth. They were on top of you before you heard the tire noise. I avoided the city of Miau Tze by cutting through the fields, but following the directions of the television crew then involved me in a couple of hours along a major highway just the other side of town. This featured much more traffic, but at least you could hear them coming.

This highway was shown on the map. It was only a short stretch, but I paid the price for ignoring my own rules. A jeep suddenly pulled up and out jumped a couple of fellows in uniform. The leader called out in English "Stop!" in a tone that brooked no argument. "Passport, please," said he, brandishing a police ID card. One side had his picture and so on, but, worse yet, on the other side was printed in English "Police Foreign Affairs Division." They all spoke good Mandarin and made it clear that they'd like me to accompany them down to the station. I'd been nabbed.

I sat at the station and had a couple of cups of tea while they passed my passport around various senior officers. Eventually someone came back to explain politely that foreigners aren't allowed to visit that part of the country. I feigned surprise and asked them how far the closed area extended, but they claimed, honestly as it turned out, not to know. After an hour or so it was decided that they would escort me to permitted territory, and four of us piled into a comfortable new Volkswagen sedan for a trip to the county seat.

Our destination turned out to be the major city of Luoyang. It was about two hours' drive. Luoyang was the capital of the Chinese empire in ancient times, and remains today a major tourist destination, even though it's no longer an important centre in modern China. The two-hour drive was basically to the east, so it knocked me off my original course, but at least it didn't set me back significantly on my way to Mongolia. At the end of it, we called in at the county headquarters of the Foreign Affairs Police.

The county office had a couple of pretty competent English speakers and quite a few others who were trying to learn, so I settled in for a long session of catechism. The questions were the same ones I'd been answering hourly for months, only this time I couldn't excuse myself when I got tired of it. Their first interest was to check the validity of my visa, but once that was established it was just a question of how long it would take before everyone was tired of practicing his English. My story was a simple one, and I stuck to it religiously: "I had no idea that China still had whole counties closed to foreigners. Why hadn't anyone told me? Just the previous evening I'd dined with a senior local cadre at the new park and a crew from a local television station. It was they who had combined to suggest the very route which had turned out to be illegal. If the police watched TV over the next few days they'd soon see my face advertising a new resort, which, as it turns out, I wasn't allowed to visit. I was very sorry for straying into a closed area, but how was I to know?" I'd long planned this line of defense for use in this situation, and it seemed to be pretty effective.

In fact, it's a distortion to speak of closed areas in China. It would be more correct to speak of open areas. Because on a straight hectare calculation most of China is still closed. A few years ago everyone, even a Chinese citizen, needed a pass to travel anywhere away from his home village. These restrictions have now been eliminated for Chinese citizens, and for foreigners too the open areas have been greatly expanded. A tourist on a package tour to see the famous sights need never realize that most of the country is off limits. But anyone setting out to walk through the countryside is sure to spend a great deal of his time in areas he's not legally supposed to see.

As I've explained, it's nothing to worry about. Like many systems in China, this one works rather badly. Not only are those areas secret, the fact that they're secret is secret. The ordinary people (and even most senior cadres) don't realize that China still has areas where foreigners aren't allowed, much less that they might be living in one. So in practice foreigners can walk through the countryside crossing in and out of restricted areas without ever realizing it. They'll only be made aware of their transgressions if they should happen to meet members of the special section of the police trained to deal with foreigners. These are the only people aware of the existence of the closed areas and more or less familiar with the boundaries in their local bailiwick.

Naturally, in this situation the penalties for infringing the law can't be very severe. China is a police state, but even the Chinese police realize that they can't expect tourists to know about the closed areas through mental telepathy. Of course, they have a free hand to throw the book at you if they wish, but normally about all they'll do is inform the transgressor that he's in a forbidden zone and assist him in getting away. At one time, this consisted of escorting him to the bus station and helping him to by a ticket out at his own expense. These days the police have more vehicles at their disposal and will often provide the transportation themselves, as they did for me.

Since there's no way the visitor can find out where the closed areas begin and end, the best approach is simply to ignore them. Go where you please and let the police worry about it. This might lead to encounters like the one I've described, but in my experience the Chinese police have always been very courteous and helpful. Though I should say that you'll never find a Chinese citizen who'd endorse my opinion. The Chinese themselves will go to great lengths to avoid any contact with the police.

Of course, I didn't tell the police that I was headed for Inner Mongolia. Back in Xiang Fan, when I left the Han River and set off into the hills, I'd mailed home all my earlier maps and diaries. So I told the police that I'd started in Xiang Fan and my intention was to walk from the Han to the Yellow River. The Yellow River flows just North of Luoyang, so according to that tale my trip was almost over. Before leaving the county headquarters I asked the experts which route I would be permitted to follow, and they all assured me that as long as I stayed down in the river valley out of the highlands I'd be okay. At that I floated the idea of following the Yellow River upstream for a few weeks. Right away they couldn't help me. Their knowledge of the open and closed areas ended at their own county line. The only officially approved system for walking up the river would be to take a train to the next county seat, visit the police and verify which townships in that county were open, then take the train back here to start walking. They said it with a straight face, but I'm sure they didn't really expect me to follow their advice.

My actual plans were rather different. The Yellow River was a few hours walk north of town, and a few hours north of that lies the boundary of Shanxi province. In Shanxi I had a clean record. I'd just have to be more careful in the future. No roads shown on the map. No towns larger than the smallest dot. I'd learned my lesson.

The walk out of town was all on the roads, so it was noisy and dangerous. Once I'd passed the airport the traffic tapered off, but it began to sprinkle, and that made it even worse. Many Chinese trucks have bald tires and dodgy alignment. Driving in the rain you see frequent and spectacular wrecks.

The Yellow River valley produces a lot of pears, apples and plums. They were piled high in the roadside stalls. Unfortunately, those are difficult fruits to eat in China. Apart from the insecticide residues, they may have been irrigated with sprinklers. The combination of chemicals and surface water would leave the skins thoroughly contaminated. The Chinese always peel them first, even in Hong Kong where they've been imported from New

Zealand or the U.S. I would have enjoyed a couple of juicy pears, but it was tough to peel them while walking. There were grapes for sale as well, but of course they were even worse. They looked nice, though. I wonder why from such beautiful grapes the Chinese manage to make such terrible wine?

After struggling with the traffic for a couple of hours, I managed to get off on a new road that was under construction and not yet open to regular traffic. That was a bit muddier, but much nicer and safer walking. It had been driven past some established villages, and it was in these villages that I came across the first of the cave houses popular in North China. They weren't natural caves, but had been excavated out of sheer banks of clay. The clay seemed to support itself without internal columns. Only the doorframe and window openings were reinforced with a row of bricks.

Here again, as I'd seen back in Guangdong, the new road cutting had exposed coal seams, and the locals were taking advantage. I passed deep crevices where the farmers had tunnelled their way into the banks extracting the coal. Their children were sorting the different sized chunks into piles along the roadside where it could be sold to a passing buyer.

Toward evening the new road suddenly plunged over an impressive escarpment, which, I supposed, signalled that I'd soon reach the river. I probably had time to get across before dark, but the escarpment itself was majestic and deserted, and I decided to quit a bit early and get my shelter up before dark. I picked a place with a great view, though the weather was so murky that all I could see was a cave village far below me.

It was a real contrast to villages in the south, where typically the whole village huddles together under a few trees. Here the caves were strung out on terraces cut into the sides of an eroded clay ravine. It was an efficient use of the otherwise useless gullies, turning them into vertical settlements without consuming any farmland. At the same time, the villagers must have been completely satisfied with the cave style of architecture, because off to one side, where the trail from the original village led up to the route of the new road, someone was building a couple of new houses out in the fields. Those houses were actually freestanding, but he was building them as though they were caves. He had used bricks to make three deep arches out in the field, like the arches of a bridge (See photo number 25). The three tunnels underneath were to be the rooms of the new house. He then presumably intended to bury the whole structure in dirt for insulation and to plant the roof with grass to hold the dirt in place.

The next morning, I had been on the road only a few minutes when I caught sight of the river in its gorge far below me. The road continued down through a series of construction sites where they were still completing various cuttings and short tunnels, until eventually it swung around a promontory to reveal a new bridge proudly spanning the flow. That was a relief, as I had expected to spend the morning walking the riverbank looking for a ferry. Instead I could clearly see the new road allowance descending smoothly to the brand new bridge, crossing the river and angling up the wall of the gorge on the other side to disappear over the rim.

Though the bridge itself was new, this was probably a traditional crossing place. A deserted World War II blockhouse stood on a knob surveying the scene. Some family of ferrymen had made its living here for centuries and was now out of business, but the new bridge had no toll plaza. In modern China that's probably a sign that it was built with foreign aid. Another tipoff was the statue on a marble-clad pedestal decorating one end. Once the road has been paved, the foreign donors will come for a grand opening ceremony and pictures in front of the statue. After that will come the tolls.

The Yellow River is one of the world's great watercourses. It's central to China's history, and still today absolutely vital to its agriculture. I had heard so much about it that I was surprised to find that it was only 250m wide. But it certainly carried quite a current, and the river was like chocolate milk, just as I had always been told.

The north face of the gorge was less steep. The construction camps were mostly spread out there, and at the northern end of the bridge a shanty town had sprung up to serve the workers. There were vegetable stalls and small shops selling beer and cigarettes. I picked a noodle stall and ducked in for a late breakfast. There were no other patrons, so I had a chance to chat at length with the owners.

Mr. Chan and his wife were, in fact, workers. The term "worker" means something special in China. It means the Chans are among the favoured 15 percent of the population that has been assigned to work in a state work unit. The work unit is then supposed to care for them from cradle to grave with a job, a place to live, food, health care, pension, all the benefits of socialism. Above all they have status. They're not peasants. The peasants are the other 85 percent who do the agricultural work that feeds the nation.

The Chans' work unit is in Taiyuan, the capital of Shanxi Province, a city about 350km north of the new bridge. So why, you may ask, are they camped in a shack in a muddy construction site instead of relaxing in the city enjoying their iron rice bowl? The reason goes to the heart of socialism as it has come to be practiced in the real world.

As in all the communist economies, most "workers" in China rarely do any work. Not because they don't want to. The Chans, after all, are out here cooking noodles in the mud of their own volition. Back home they have no work because the central planning system can't cope with running an economy from the centre. Work units are always short of one input while oversupplied with others. Work is always held up by bureaucratic interference. The workers (and there's never a shortage of workers) can't be productive in the context of a state work unit, and as a result they can't earn much money. They have plenty of security and (rather shoddy) fringe benefits, but no cash.

Like many others, the Chans have decided to take advantage of the new market economy to do some real work for a change. They've decided to set up a restaurant at the site of the new bridge.

The establishment in question (shown with its proud owner in photo number 26) is their own creation from the ground up. Their shack has about 2.5m frontage, and is 5m deep and 2.5m high. To construct it, Mr. Chan first begged some poles about 10cm in diameter from the construction crews. He dug six postholes 2.5m apart and erected his posts, then connected them with stringers around the top lashed up with wire. Anywhere else, the lashing would be some sort of vine or plastic twine, but here the wire could presumably be diverted from the construction site by the concrete workers. For stability, a second row of horizontal stringers runs around half way up the walls, except across the front and the front panel of one side wall which serves as the door. Some lathes of sawmill waste are laid across the top as rafters. Straw mats and collapsed cardboard boxes are then laid over this to form the roof, covered by plastic sheeting. More wire holds the whole roof together. The walls are sheets of corrugated asbestos roofing. Each sheet is 2m tall by 1m wide, and these are simply stood on end around two and a half sides of the structure and lashed to the posts and stringers with wire. That leaves a 50cm gap between the roof and the top of the walls for ventilation.

The furniture is as Spartan as the structure itself. The short front wall facing the road is blocked off by a table and two stoves. The frame of the table has been welded up from reinforcing rod from the construction site. The two stoves have been cut from oil drums. They burn coal dust briquettes. This is where Mrs. Chan spends her days, standing behind the oil drums and table selling steamed buns to the passers-by. Beside her, along the left hand wall as seen from the road, is a cupboard holding her various cooking supplies and utensils. Behind her, right in the middle of the enclosure, is a square hardwood table with four wooden stools perched unsteadily on the rough dirt floor. Across the back wall is a 1.5x2m wooden platform which serves as a bed. The rest of their possessions are stored under the bed in cardboard boxes. The only other furnishings are two wooden cases of beer and a wicker basket of empty bottles.

The Chans' main business is in steamed buns, which sell for 40 fen each. These have no filling. They're just large bread rolls about 10cm in diameter, which are steamed rather than baked. Mrs. Chan makes three or four batches through the day and tries to sell them hot. If someone sits down for a meal, her menu is limited to noodles in soup topped with fried vegetables and hot peppers. She stocks no meat, but her top-of-the-line bowl of noodles can include an egg stir fried with the vegetables.

The worst feature of this setup is that the Chans can never both leave home at once. With no walls, it's impossible to close the place up. Someone must always be at home to keep an eye on it. Not that there's anywhere to go. The Chans haven't so much as a bicycle in their current, perhaps temporary, home.

Nevertheless, they're not dissatisfied. The chance to leave their work unit in the capital and set up in this scenic location is in itself a great adventure. It's only in recent years that Chinese citizens were permitted to travel at all, even in their local area. And for all the hardships, they are succeeding in earning a little cash. For a year or two at least, the Chans are satisfied to be doing something useful for a change and to be getting paid for it.

The new highway climbed out of the gorge on a broad bench that was being cut into the cliffs. I opted for the old traditional trail, which took another route up one of the tributary valleys. At first this involved following the riverbank upstream to the west for a couple of kilometres. It was a scenic walk alone with just the roar of the current. Then the trail struck north away from the river toward the town of Da Yu. The people of Da Yu must have opened up their own access direct to the new highway, because the old track was in terrible condition. I had to take off my boots and wade the streams.

When I finally reached the town, it wasn't much better. There were a couple of shops, but in the beverage line they sold only beer. No soda of any kind. Eventually one of the shop owners invited me in for a bowl of noodles. I wasn't very hungry after my breakfast with the Chans, but I took the opportunity to avail myself of his latrine. This proved to harbour a resident snake. Not a very big one – about 15 or 20cm long and as big around as your finger – but bright yellow. I had a vague notion that it's the brightly coloured ones that often are the most poisonous.

The lack of bottled soda was my personal indicator of a very poor district, but in fact to see the poverty you needed to look no further than the quality of the soil. All afternoon climbing out of the valley the soil was sandy and stony. Cultivation was limited to tiny corn fields levelled out of the sides of the hills. The population was sparse enough that there were areas were the brush hadn't been cleared for firewood. At one point, I even saw children playing naked, though it may be going a bit far to attribute that to poverty. The children were striking because farther south I had often seen little boys swimming naked in the irrigation canals, but the little girls were always fully clothed even when swimming. Here both boys and girls were naked. It was tempting to ascribe it to extreme poverty, but it was probably no more than an example of the different customs in distant parts of such a large country.

One nice amenity they did have in this part of the country was a bird with a beautiful call exactly like the sound of a little silver bell ringing three times. I never saw one, and I never remembered to ask anyone about them, but I heard them frequently over the next few days.

That night, only my second on the road after my encounter with the police, I was discovered in my campsite by a passing farmer. He was surprised to see me, of course, and wanted to hear my entire performance with all the grace notes and cadenzas, but basically he seemed quite a nice guy. By the time we'd been through the whole story backwards and forwards, it was quite dark, and he insisted I come to his village for the night. I resisted tenaciously, and he eventually bid be good night, but I suspected my respite was destined to be highly temporary. I figured I had about 15 minutes before he got back to the village and began telling everyone in sight about his amazing encounter. Then I'd have another 10 minutes before the entire village turned up to marvel and to interrogate me far into the night. The moon was full. I was up and packing in a flash. Checking around as best I could by moonlight for forgotten gear, I grabbed my pack and made a run for it. The trail was black as pitch under the trees, but I put in a kilometre or so before concluding that they'd never find me without tracker dogs. I felt my way a few metres off the trail and flopped down for the night in the first somewhat level spot I could find. In the morning I was up and on my way at the crack of dawn.

This headlong flight might strike you as anti-social, and I admit that it was. I concede that sitting around answering questions is by no means such a hardship. But I reasoned that after the questioning was finally done and everyone had gone home, I'd then have to move camp anyway. Because by then dozens of people would know my whereabouts, and just one or two of them might reason (correctly) that I would be worth robbing. That, indeed, I was a gift from heaven to anyone in a robbing frame of mind. If I wasn't prepared to sleep in the village, secrecy was my only defence against those larcenous few. So I'd have to move anyway. Might as well do it right away and get some extra sleep for my trouble.

It was still early the next morning when the trail dumped me on a paved highway outside the gates of a school. It was 6:20 a.m. on a Saturday morning in mid-August, but I could hear the kids inside reciting their lessons in unison. Perhaps the school ran two shifts. School on Saturday is standard in China. But why was it in session during the hottest weather and during the harvest season? There was a woman by the roadside, probably waiting for a bus, but she didn't understand my questions.

I was able to learn, however, that my best route to the north and over the border into Shanxi province required me to cut east 4km on the highway to pick up a trail. It was mountainous country, and the woman seemed quite certain that she was revealing to me the only possible route across the provincial boundary, so I was back on a mapped highway again despite my pious resolutions. A stroke of bad luck might soon find me again in the familiar offices of the police in Luoyang.

I hurried through the 4km at a half trot. Fortunately, it was all downhill, and it was early enough that few vehicles had yet reached this stretch of road from their starting points in nearby cities. I made it down the hill undetected, though once again I had to keep an eye open for trucks coasting down with their engines off. Like me, they could hear any climbing vehicle a long way off, so, like me, they didn't feel compelled to stay on their own side of the road, and they cut across the insides of the sweeping switchbacks.

Silent careening coal trucks were exciting, but at the bottom, just as I found my turnoff, an even more perilous vehicle passed me. A yellow van decorated with posters cruised past at moderate speed and disappeared around a bend. A yellow vehicle is immediately startling in China. The posters made it more so in a land without bumper stickers. But the occupants of this van were shooting fireworks out the windows. Once I noticed them passing I didn't have time to decipher the posters before they disappeared. In Taiwan you'd assume they were electioneering, but of course that couldn't be the case on the mainland. Perhaps they were advertising something. Whatever their intent, I hope none of the rockets misfired. I'd sure hate to be trapped in a van with a whole carton of exploding fireworks.

The track north from the highway climbed beside a fairly clean rushing stream. The road itself was wide enough for a truck, but I saw no more vehicles the entire day. There were a few very small villages, but there was very little decent soil, and the valley quickly narrowed into a gorge, leaving little space for growing crops. There were some scrawny forests on the slopes that were apparently regenerating after having been cut over in the past, but everything was still too small to allow harvesting any useful timber. It was dirt poor country.

Poor or not, I met a couple of fellows who gave me a present. It was a moon cake: a special pastry filled with peanuts, candied fruit and sugar crystals that's eaten at one of China's major festivals at the fall equinox. We were still a month from the festival, but these guys had apparently just been given some moon cakes, and were passing one on to me. In fact, most people find moon cakes too rich to eat. They buy and exchange them as presents without actually eating more than the odd sliver. But walking all day burns a lot of calories. I brewed up some tea and had my entire moon cake for lunch.

I met one other group of locals during the day, and one of them wasn't so friendly. I found them sitting in the shade by the roadside, and gave them a greeting as I passed but didn't stop to chat. A few minutes later I heard a call from behind and turned to find the whole group of six or eight running after me. I leaned against a rock and waited for them to catch up, but when they'd caught their breath one old guy began a line of clearly hostile questioning. Questions being my specialty, I immediately feigned a complete ignorance of any known language and responded to everything with a quizzical look. Taking the offensive, I began repeating "Shanxi" in a questioning tone and pointing up the trail. They wanted to look in my knapsack, so I pulled out some of my meager apparel for their inspection. I feigned incomprehension of all their requests to see my passport. They didn't know the English word and had no equivalent ID to show me as an example, so I was able to get away with it. The old man appeared to be the instigator. He kept repeating "You can't go on. It's not for foreigners. It's not okay." But he couldn't say it in English, and I pretended not to notice him amid the babble. I just kept smiling and asking the way to Shanxi, and after everyone had satisfied himself that my knapsack held nothing more subversive than clothes, I eventually found a moment to abruptly bid them good-by and walk away. The old man protested, but his companions had already had their fill of uphill running, and I disappeared with a last friendly wave.

The old guy's attitude was typical of a certain strain of old-line party cadre. He was probably some sort of local party official who still gets to approve almost everything that goes on in that depopulated valley. Anyone applying for a marriage licence probably needs the old man's signature on the application. His real problem with me was just a general objection to anyone doing anything new without his approval. If no foreigner had walked up this gorge before, then in his eyes it's forbidden. There's even a chance that he might actually have been aware of the closed area policy from some long-past training course. But I doubt it. He was just being conservative in the most ironbound sense of the term. It's old cadres like him who don't want to give up the reins that are holding the country back. But in this case, by accident, he was right.

At the time it gave me quite a turn. Perhaps there was some secret military base farther up the valley. But wait a minute. Did they travel in and out by helicopter? They certainly didn't use this dirt track. What if he called the police to intercept me? One look around assured me that the valley wasn't even wired for electricity, much less telephone. The track was climbing steeply enough that they couldn't even chase me on a bicycle. It took me about 10 minutes to convince myself that I had nothing to fear.

14

Into Shanxi

As usual, I found little evidence of the provincial border between Henan and Shanxi. Over the next few days I spoke with few enough people that I couldn't even detect it in the local dialect. The track simply continued up the gorge and then eventually left the streambed and began a series of killing switchbacks aiming for the rim high above. The scenery was spectacular. A thick layer of sandstone over the mudstone in the bottom of the gorge allowed for spectacular overhanging cliffs eroded with caves. The track had no confusing junctions. There was only one route. Everything else was cliffs.

Finally, in late afternoon, when I had resigned myself to another hour of steady climbing, the track suddenly rounded a sheer buttress and disappeared into a tunnel. It wasn't a big tunnel. Just large enough to accommodate a truck. But it was long. I could tell from the long spill of tailings below the entrance, and when I looked in there was no point of light at the other end. Now what? I had no flashlight.

I wandered slowly in as far as the light from the south portal would take me, hoping against hope for a vehicle to come along and give me hint where I was going. Fat chance. I'd been on this route all day and seen nothing. But the light from the portal was enough to show me that if a vehicle had come along, I could have followed it all the way through without having to hurry much. The floor of the tunnel was a patchwork of extensive puddles. I could hear a lot of dripping in the dark.

I hemmed and hawed for a while, but with no place to sit down on the muddy floor I eventually decided to push on blindly. Blind was certainly the correct term. After a few minutes I could see nothing at all. The floor was badly potholed, and some of the puddles were well up over my ankles. I shuffled forward one unsteady step at a time trying to keep my balance in the pitch black. The water was icy cold.

How long did it take? I really don't know. It seemed to last a lifetime. Even after I could see the north portal gleaming in the distance it seemed to take forever before it gave any appreciable light to my path. I never fell down completely, but I emerged with both arms muddy to the biceps. My watch was still running, but perhaps the mud had protected it from the water. My clothes were soaked from being rained on. And I was chilled to the bone. What a business. I quickly dived off the trail and found a campsite for a bit of cleaning and reorganization. Only one or two trucks passed during the night.

After a whole day's climbing, I expected a long drop the following morning, but again I was surprised. As back in Henan, I wasn't crossing an ordinary mountain range; I was climbing onto the highlands that make up the northern tier of the country. My route the next morning descended for just a half hour or so before reaching the first village and its farmland. There had been no passing weather system, but the air seemed a lot less humid. I had gained a lot of altitude.

I reached the school in San Lin just as the students were going in to class. Amazed as always to see me, they thought they'd try out their English. They realized "Good morning teacher" wasn't appropriate, so they tried the only other phrase they knew: "Good morning class."

The scenery was by no means as spectacular as the day before. No cliffs, no pastures, no forests, just bare ridges with a few bean fields and some millet. It reminded me a bit of Northern Italy, but awfully poor.

There was even a castle on one of the ridge tops. I suppose it was a Buddhist or Taoist monastery. I wondered how they got their water way up there.

I tried to speak with a few people on the road, but their dialect was really impenetrable – nothing like any kind of Chinese that I know. I eventually came to understand that I was looking for a factory where I would branch off on another route heading northwest. Sure enough, I came after a couple of hours to a small factory hidden behind a high wall with a locked gate and no sign. There was a smell of sulfur in the air, so it could have been a small foundry or a fertilizer works, but whatever the product it wasn't producing any on that morning. There was no sign of a turnoff, so I continued on until I encountered a group of men chatting by the roadside. After the usual routine, they sent me back to the factory to turn on a tiny bicycle track running under the factory wall.

The track quickly matured into a typical rural trail, and indeed I found it much better walking than the road I'd been following since the tunnel. It crossed a couple of streams on stepping stones before

I came to one crossing where a work gang was out in force rebuilding the ford. In essence they were paving the river bottom with large stones to smooth the crossing for tractors and bicycles, and installing a new set of stepping stones for pedestrians. It was heavy but simple work, and most of the crew consisted of what appeared to be housewives. It was apparently a village work party organized under the traditional *corvée* system. Each family seems to have sent its least productive members for this sort of work, as among the lot of them they couldn't put forward anyone who could ask me questions in Mandarin. *Corvée* work looked rather like fun, actually. Like an old-fashioned pioneer house raising. And the part of the work that had been completed looked pretty well done.

As always, the idea of walking in a district where the main artery is completely devoid of motor vehicles had a certain primal appeal. It was a bit dry and stony, but a nice walk.

I realized that in the stony terrain I was no longer seeing any cave houses. I had understood them to be typical of Shanxi province, but I'd seen hardly any since leaving the Yellow River. The preferred setup around here was a two-storey stone or concrete structure with a balcony across the front and an external stairway. Two rooms on each floor, but no internal doors connecting them. Often the homeowners had added a single storey outbuilding at right angles to the original structure so that they could use the roof of the outbuilding as an extension of the balcony for drying grain and for storage. The architecture had changed with the provincial boundary, but also with the geology and the dialect. A puzzle for an anthropologist.

That evening I had dinner with another English speaker. He was a high school student, and his English was pretty weak, but I was happy to give him a chance to practice. I met him on the trail and he took me to his home. His parents weren't home when we arrived, and when his mother came in from the fields she took a dim view of his initiative. He had invited me to spend the night, but his mother pointed out that they had neither suitable food nor enough space to entertain strangers. In the end, she served us whatever leftovers she could rustle up from lunch: some millet gruel with peanuts in it, a sourdough steamed bun and several cups of tea. The student claimed they grew all the ingredients themselves. He excluded the soy sauce, and I suppose he was forgetting about the tea leaves. Surely they also raise vegetables, but presumably those had been finished off at lunchtime. You don't often think of sourdough bread in the context of Chinese cuisine, but I had been served it once before, and it certainly made sense that they would keep their starters that way.

I completely sympathized with the mother's discomfiture and hastened to excuse myself after dinner, but it left me in a difficult position. It was now pitch dark, and I had to stumble out of the village and find a campsite. Luckily the trail quickly broke out onto a treeless ridge top where I could see a bit by starlight. I cleared away the rocks from a small patch a few metres off the trail and flopped down without further ceremony. In fact, it worked out fine, though camping so close to the trail I had to get going again at first light.

The country became drier and stonier. There were no more grain fields and certainly no fruit trees. The fields were mostly of beans with sunflowers on the even drier ridge tops. My route was taking me northwest along almost-dry river valleys. The valleys were dotted with villages at regular intervals, but in each case the track bypassed the village proper and cut through the dry riverbed alongside. After seeing hardly a soul all morning, I began to reflect on this and realized that the track was bypassing the villages because it had originally been built for packhorses and human porters. The village houses were all of stone and the streets were very narrow. When garden tractors began taking over the transportation system the streets couldn't accommodate them. Widening the streets would have involved demolishing the adjacent houses stone by stone. So traffic began bypassing the villages, and that had now become the main route. It was faster for me, with fewer questions to answer and less scope for getting lost, but I felt a bit lonely walking all morning without my usual quota of interrogators. Seen from the trail, each village was nothing but a collection of blank stone walls.

In fact, one of the few people I did encounter was a beekeeper. He had set out a dozen hives in a grove of trees along the trail and was living there temporarily in a tent. I would have enjoyed finding out a bit about his profession, but when I passed he had a couple of the hives open and was hard at work in his headnet. I gave it a miss.

The beekeeper had picked that grove because it was one of the few still left in the district. In general, shade was hard to find. I was feeling the sun, and my lips were cracking from sunburn and the dry air. At lunchtime I was lucky to find a small overhanging cliff on the south side of the valley that gave a little shade. There wasn't much else.

It wasn't until late afternoon that I finally came to some semblance of industrialization in the form of a rural smelter. It wasn't in operation, but slag and cinder piles all across the riverbed gave evidence that it had been producing something fairly recently. They apparently depended on occasional flooding to dispose of their wastes. The place was clearly a government work unit, because one of the housing units sported a giant satellite dish on the roof. Only government units are supposed to have them.

After a whole day in the stony river valley, I eventually turned north up a narrow ravine which had eroded down to a smooth stone slab underfoot, but had walls all of clay. Part way up the ravine a family had set up a tiny factory quarrying the clay and manufacturing ceramic pipe and flue sections. This was no government work unit, but, in contrast with the smelter I'd seen earlier, here was an enterprise that was working full bore. It struck me as a promising venture. The quality of their fired work was a lot better than most of the bricks I'd seen in that part of the country. We chatted briefly. They gave me some directions and I wished them good luck.

The ravine brought me after a few kilometres to a proper gravel road, which led another kilometre or so down into another river valley and the substantial town of Tou Wu. I say the town was substantial, but in fact I saw only its most substantial feature: a large smelter and foundry. This one not only was in production, it was building rows of new housing for its workers. In one of the factory buildings fronting on the road was a restaurant open to the public. The proprietor spoke Mandarin and it was just about supper time. I needed no urging. Having seen hardly anyone all day, the evening catechism didn't bother me as much as usual. I had a litre and a half of beer and a hearty meal and left in a cheerful mood. The bill was 18 yuan for the lot.

My route branched off from the road just behind the factory without entering the town at all. It immediately scaled a steep and barren ridge, not easy on a full stomach and a couple of beers. I took the first opportunity to dive off the track and make camp under the stars with the fires of the blast furnaces glowing below.

The next morning, soon after setting out, I came across a man carrying what appeared to be a flintlock rifle with a barrel about a metre and a half long. He'd never be able to track a moving target with such an unwieldy weapon, so he couldn't be flushing quail. I had to assume he was after rabbits. I'd been seeing quite a few. The people I'd encountered over the past few days had immediately approached me to start a conversation, but this fellow wouldn't even return my wave. I supposed it was because he was stalking something, but as the day wore on I met quite a few people just as reticent. In this part of the country they were simply a lot less outgoing than the people I'd met farther south. Surely they couldn't speak any less Mandarin, but perhaps they were more aware of this limitation. Their behavior highlighted the fact that in the space of 50km the geography, economy and culture had changed dramatically.

As soon as I crested the first ridge of the morning, there were many more trees in evidence. That had to be the result of better forestry policies, so it was a pretty sure sign that I'd crossed into a new county. Occasional shade certainly made the walking more pleasant.

I came across a man ploughing a field with a wooden plough. Only the tip was iron. He had probably bought the tip at the store and made the rest himself. He was ploughing with two buffalo. It was hard to imagine why a man owning two buffalo would be using a wooden plough, but perhaps the buffalo were borrowed.

I'd been hearing blasting more or less every waking hour since reaching the Yellow River. This morning was no different, so as I walked along I thought nothing of it. I was therefore surprised to come across a new railway line under construction. There was no mention of it on my map. I followed the line of the construction most of the morning, and the blasting was almost continuous. It was only just before lunch that I escaped the noise and the dust, as the new line swung West and my route branched off up a steep hill to the North. At the top of the hill I took an early lunch, as the ridge top had been replanted as a pine plantation. I hadn't seen one of these shady plantations in weeks and I wasted no time before diving in among the pine needles for an extended lunch break in the deep shade. It was just as well that I did, because it was an isolated example. It was weeks again before I saw another.

The culture, the economy, the flora were changing, but as I progressed toward my goal, the geography was changing most of all. I was slowly climbing onto the top of a vast layer of fine, dusty soil that covers Northwest China. The rocky terrain near the Yellow River crossing was being buried in a thick layer of loess said to have been deposited by dust storms off the Gobi desert to the west. Up on top, all was bare and windswept. The top of the dust layer extended at a more or less uniform elevation to a very distant horizon in all directions. But this soft dust was then eroded into deep gullies by every tiny, intermittent watercourse. Each had eroded down through the dust to the layer of shale underneath. The depth of the ravines depended only on the elevation of the local bedrock. In most places even the narrowest ravines were 100-150 metres deep with absolutely vertical or even overhanging walls. Only the gully bottoms harboured a few trees that had escaped the stove. For the most part, the vast panorama was all thorny scrub and not much shade. My trails were taking a lot of time to wander back and forth avoiding these sheer ravines.

With the eroded soil, of course, it was back to cave housing for the inhabitants. Everyone lived in the ravine bottoms for protection from the wind and access to water, so several times a day I had no alternative to climbing all the way down a ravine and out again. It was always a long haul over switchbacks and crude stairs cut in the clay.

I visited late one afternoon with a man I met on the trail, who offered to fill my water bottles. In contrast with most of the people I'd met, he had an enormous house. From the outside nothing was visible but a blank adobe wall with the cliff towering overhead, but inside the gate lay an expansive courtyard flanked on two sides by cave rooms. The courtyard was set in a sort of corner cut out of the cliff, so the two sets of caves amounted to six rooms in total. I visited only one, perhaps the largest. It must have been about 10x6m with a brick floor and tiled roof. The walls were decorated with pictures from an old calendar advertising motorcycles. He must have had some city friend in the business. I estimated they had an extended family of about 10 living in the six rooms, but of course my call attracted a lot of visitors, so it was hard to tell.

The dry climate, the eroded canyons, the thorny scrub combined to remind me of the old cowboy movies of my youth. I even saw the odd tumbleweed. Camping was no longer a problem. The population was sparse, and most of the land was unsuitable for cultivation. When the weather was good, the walking was fine, though mostly it was too hot and sunny. There was only one morning when it rained, and even then not very determinedly.

It was a day or so later as I was climbing over a barren ridge far from the nearest village that I came to the abandoned temple shown in photo number 27. I hadn't seen many temples of any kind, and this one had been pretty elaborate – more a temple complex than a temple. There were two main temples facing each other across a courtyard, the whole complex surrounded by a wall. There were some other smaller outbuildings in the compound behind the main temple, and all around the inside of the wall were cells that looked now a bit like deserted garages. They could, of course, have been stables, but I guessed they were probably cells housing monks. The facades of the two temples had once been ornate, but now the whole place was in utter disrepair. The courtyard was full of roof tiles, and the whole compound was so choked with thorns and thistles that I didn't even venture to explore the outbuildings at the back.

In Penang, Malaysia a similar structure is one of the main tourist attractions. That one is a shrine to the ancestors of a single family. If this one had similar origins, I must have been looking at one of the vestiges of China's latest warlord era in the early 20th century, when major landowning families ruled their local fiefs like feudal lords. On the other hand, it might have been the monastery of a religious order. Either way, it hadn't fared too well under communism. There was enough of it left that it could be restored as a pretty interesting tourist attraction, but of course this wasn't downtown Penang. It would be little visited in rural Shanxi, even if foreigners were allowed.

In several of the larger villages I came across the modern communist version of these old temples. Standing alone, usually at the edge of the village, would be a big cement stage. Rather as if there had once been a giant movie house which had been destroyed leaving only the stage with its proscenium arch. The Communists destroyed most of the temples and ancestral halls in the villages on ideological grounds, but those buildings were also the only large halls for holding weddings and public meetings. So, at least in Shanxi, a stage was sometimes erected to fill the role. They must have come in very handy during the cultural revolution. These days the ones I saw looked disused and were invariably in poor repair. Perhaps the faded old Maoist slogans still discernible on the facade lessened their attraction as a romantic wedding venue.

I stopped for a cup of tea with a gang of clansmen operating a mini-brickworks. No state work unit this one. There was no wall around it, because there weren't even any permanent buildings. They had simply located a seam of suitable clay in one of the banks, channelled in some water from a nearby stream and buried their brick-extruding machine in the bank. I couldn't see the actual machine, but it must have been some sort of mixing gadget like a cement mixer. They would push soil into the hopper opening on top and add water through a hose from a holding tank, adjusting the flow by trial and error. As long as the clay came from the same vein they didn't seem to have to adjust the flow of water very often, but they couldn't shut it down. All during my visit a skeleton crew had to keep the machine running extruding bricks to keep the proportions in balance. The mixer extruded a rectangular sausage of clay onto a wet plate. The sausage was sliced into bricks by hand with a wire, like cutting cheese, and these were hauled away on boards to dry a bit, and then to be stacked in the kiln. It took a lot of labour, but it certainly seemed that they would turn out quite a few bricks in a day.

Some of their bricks were black. I couldn't thoroughly understand their explanation, but I got the general idea that they mixed coal dust in with the clay. This would vapourize in the kiln leaving a lighter finished product, though presumably not so strong. I hadn't seen much black brick in use, so I couldn't really figure out in what applications it was preferred.

I didn't tarry long with the brick crew, but as I walked away my attention was drawn to the fading rumble of the diesel driving their mixer. I realized it was the only motor I'd heard all day. Apart from that one engine, a man riding a bullock cart was the height of mechanization.

I was still seeing beans in the fields, but the main crops were now corn in the valley bottoms where there was a little water, and sunflowers on the dry tops. The combination was a happy hunting ground for chipmunks, and I was seeing them everywhere. I hadn't realized that China had chipmunks, but around here they were certainly doing well.

All in all, I was spending a lot less time answering questions. I was encountering fewer people on the road, and those I did encounter didn't seem so inquisitive. They'd ask a few basic questions, we'd chat a minute about geography, and they'd let me go with wishes for a safe journey. Though as I was walking away I could sometimes hear them asking each other, "Who was that man, anyway?"

Several people, however, wanted to buy my shoes. There must have been some sort of current supply problem in that part of the country. It happens in China. The shoes they were wearing were no different from the normal peasant garb anywhere I'd been: cheap gym shoes or plastic sandals. They didn't look very comfortable, but I suppose once you were used to them it would be difficult to change to wearing socks. My own Adidas trainers wouldn't have suited them at all. Without socks, they'd pick up little pebbles which would tear your feet to ribbons. Quite apart from the fact that one pair would cost a Chinese peasant a couple of years' earnings. People often asked me how much they cost, but they found the truth so incredible that I took to lying about it.

Apart from a shortage of cash, people in the countryside don't have access to a selection of shops, so they all tend to dress much the same. Plastic sandals, for example. At any given time there will be different models and colours available in different parts of the country, but within a county or district everyone's sandals will be very similar. Men who do heavy work sometimes prefer light canvas shoes with rubber soles, or heavier khaki sneakers modelled on army boots. These are pretty uniform all over the country. Socks are uncommon anywhere. Both men and women wear heavy drill trousers with a zippered fly and a light leather belt. In summer these will be rolled half way up the calf to save wear on the cuffs. Similarly, both men and women wear a long sleeved white shirt over a cotton singlet. Unmarried women will always wear a bra, but out in the countryside wives often don't bother. In summer, the men will roll up their sleeves. Everyone wears a wide-brimmed straw hat to work in the sun. In winter everyone piles on two to our more layers of long underwear and wool sweaters. They top it all with a heavy cotton drill jacket or, in the north, a calf length padded greatcoat with an ample collar. Home-knitted sweaters and scarves are popular. The women knit themselves colourful woolen hats, while the men wear store-bought padded caps, often with ear flaps.

Travelling through the countryside, the uniformity of dress is striking. Not only the styles, the colours too are highly standardized – a straw hat, white shirt, dark blue or khaki trousers. Apparel in a Chinese rice paddy is even more uniform than in an American high school.

In that context the people found me pretty shocking. My clothing, of course, stood out in colour and design. On close inspection, the quality was also quite a bit better. I was usually sporting at least a five o'clock shadow, but this never bothered them. The Chinese don't have much facial hair, so many men seem to pride themselves on a bit of designer stubble. The shocking bit was the condition of my clothes. A peasant's clothes might be ragged, but they'd be ragged from repeated washing. They pretty generally bathe every day and wear clean clothes. Compared with them, I was filthy.

After my encounter with the brick-makers, I was more aware of the lack of motor vehicles. I began estimating the interval between them along my way. I was following tracks wide enough for a garden tractor, but one day I went seven hours without hearing an engine. And when I met one it turned out to be the mailman. He would be one of the few people in the district with a cash income, and he had apparently invested some of it in a motorcycle instead of the bicycle that most Chinese postmen use. Chinese bicycles have no gears, so the motorcycle would have saved him a lot of pushing climbing out of the ravines. It's easy to imagine that the time he saves would be enough to enable him to take a second job and pay for the cycle.

Many of my trails, however, were too steep and narrow even for a motorcycle. I was switching back on one of these, descending a ravine late one afternoon, when I heard someone calling out behind me. I had passed a couple of young men in uniform a few minutes earlier, so I was immediately on my guard and pretended not to hear the cries. The hailing continued. I took a peek out of the corner of my eye and, sure enough, there were three guys in uniform scrambling down after me. It was all so reminiscent of my climb out of the Yellow River gorge and the old man and his cronies who had given me such a hard time. There was no way I could outrun them. All I could do was keep descending steadily and try to think of an approach to deal with them when they caught up. I feared the worst.

When they were too close to ignore any longer, I turned in surprise, gave them a hearty greeting and immediately proceeded to ask directions. To my relief, they greeted me warmly and suggested cheerfully that I follow them as far as the village at the bottom of the gulch where they'd put me on the correct trail to climb the other side. On the way down it was the usual interrogation, but they clearly had no ill intent, and I was answering questions much less frequently these days, so in fact I was glad enough of the company. It turned out that they were security guards at a small coal mine, which we soon reached at the bottom. They invited me in to spend the night, but I was still nervous from my previous reaction to being chased by men in uniform. I declined and accepted instead their directions to the best trail up to the north rim.

As Hong Kong has been discovering to its distress, many areas of life in China operate under the rule of men rather than the rule of law. An hour in Chinese city traffic is enough to introduce you to soldiers and policemen who feel entitled to disregard the traffic regulations. Unofficial privileges of this kind make impersonating a soldier or policeman a particularly valuable trick in China, and it's very often and very openly done. Surprisingly, the authorities don't seem impelled to impose much control.

China does, indeed, keep a large number of men and women under arms. Like many other nations, China operates a hierarchy of active and reserve military and para-military forces. The number of main force troops has been cut back significantly in recent years, but the main force soldiers are not in any case the soldiers most often seen on the streets. Real soldiers spend their time under military discipline in PLA camps, often in remote or border regions. The people one sees in uniform are reserves, the police and a hybrid outfit known as the People's Armed Police. They outnumber the active soldiers eight or ten to one. Though the reserves may undergo only a few weeks' training each year, they all have basic military uniforms, and until recent years these uniforms often doubled as their best dress suit. Military garb is so acceptable that people often buy miniature uniforms for their children. This is far more common in China than in other countries.

The real confusion comes with the police forces. China has a whole family of various police forces charged with different tasks, and these forces all wear very similar uniforms and insignia. Even factory security guards, like my friends who gave me such a fright, wear a tan police-style shirt with a shoulder patch very similar to that of any other police force. Any such uniform commands a certain wary deference in China, and the owners don't hesitate to wear them when off duty.

Police automobile insignia are even more useful. Genuine police vehicles have special licence plates, and these have come to be their only somewhat-reliable identification. All the other door and radiator badges, as well as the flashing roof lights, can be purchased in shops specializing in police insignia. The licence plates too can be forged, but this seems to be largely the province of smuggling gangs. The various forces are reluctant to challenge each others' vehicles at roadblocks.

It's not clear why the authorities tolerate this abuse of their own authority. Presumably, bullies who flout the law in this way have in place all the relationships necessary to protect them if anyone objects. It's the rule of men turned back against the rulers.

Down in the ravines, at places like the coal mine, I was always able to beg a bit of clean water to top up my bottles. But up on top of the dust layer the treeless wastes were hot, windy and dusty, and I went through my water supplies pretty quickly. I was eventually reduced to keeping one water bottle for water from dubious sources. This bottle always had a layer of mud in the bottom, and I kept it heavily dosed with water purification tablets. The other bottle I kept for tastier water from sources that I felt were more likely to be clean. Nevertheless, I found myself wrestling with occasional bouts of diarrhea.

In my search for water I had to follow up every lead. Once I saw a lady carrying two laden buckets on the ends of a shoulder pole. By the time I reached the spot where I had seen her, she had disappeared, but there were splashes in the dust, and I proceeded to track them back to her water source. They led me to a hole in the ground covered by a board lid and with a length of nice new rope coiled alongside. There was no one around, but I tied one of my bottles to the rope, lowered it into the well and, after a certain amount of experimentation, got it to sink and fill up. As I was re-coiling the rope and preparing to leave, I was fortunate that the lady returned and was able to convey to me that the water was undrinkable. What appeared to be a well was in fact a cistern for storing agricultural water, probably contaminated with all sorts of human and animal wastes.

She must have had a vegetable garden somewhere. It was getting rather late in the season to be planting. There were still a few fields of beans growing here and there. No corn, probably because it takes too much water. All the farm work was being done with donkey carts. The cave houses all seemed to have electricity, but no one had screening and quite a few windows were glazed with paper. I suppose it was too dry for mosquitoes, but life must be chilly there in winter.

On that occasion the lady solved my water problem by directing me to an isolated shop hidden in a little declivity in the vast, open spaces. I bought several bottles of carbonated soda made at the regional brewery, drank one and poured the rest into my water bottles. I bought out all the bottles on the very limited shelf space, so while I was drinking the lady tending the store went out back and brought in more. I was interested to observe that before she put them on the shelves she had to stick labels on them. They were shipped from the brewery in wooden cases, but apparently the ride is so rough that if they labelled them at the factory, the labels would be scuffed into illegibility by the time they got out to the villages. So the breweries deliver each crate of bottles with a separate stack of labels, and the shopkeepers stick the labels on themselves when stocking the shelves. That certainly must facilitate counterfeiting.

Erosion of the ravines really seemed unstoppable. The trails from village to village wound back and forth trying to stay on top of the dust layer to avoid the steep climbs down into the deep gullies and back out again. In many places the route seemed only one rainstorm from disaster. It would go far out of its way to cross a narrow isthmus where the heads of two ravines almost meet. At the narrowest point there would be just a metre or so of level ground left, just enough for the trail. You felt that surely after the next rain the heads of the two ravines would join and the trail would be cut. Anyone trying to rebuild the road had only dust to work with. It wasn't clear what could be done. The situation was redeemed only by the fact that this was clearly an area where it didn't rain very often.

Even in the villages, it was unusual to run into anyone out and about. When I passed through, the villagers were usually either working in their fields up and down the ravine, behind the walls of their courtyards or in homes cut from the ravine walls along terraces far above my head. Bei Han, though, was an exception. I happened to arrive on market day and the joint was jumping. The streets were packed with vendors and their customers. So crowded, in fact, that many people hardly noticed my passing. It was only when I stopped to buy some eggs to boil up with my instant noodles that I was mobbed by a crowd of the curious. Fortunately, in the bedlam there was no way for the crowd as a whole to launch a proper, lengthy interrogation.

The most interesting feature of my visit to Bei Han was the part of the market where several ladies were dealing in scorpions. I assumed at the time that they were selling them and I couldn't imagine why. I'd eaten them at fancy Chinese banquets in city restaurants, but I couldn't imagine the country people taking the trouble to prepare such a useless delicacy. Certainly not if they had to buy the ingredients. I later realized that the ladies in the market were buying, not selling. In any case, the sight of all those scorpions certainly gave me pause to think twice before putting on my shoes the next few mornings.

A few days later I visited the larger town of Gu Luo. There was nothing of interest in Gu Luo. It was larger only because it was on a paved highway. I got a bit of a break from the dust, as I hit the highway a couple of kilometres east of town, and the trail I wanted left the highway three or four kilometres west of the centre. It was late on a Saturday afternoon, so I expected plenty of bus traffic, as the kids would be coming home from their week at school. I hustled along trying to get off the highway as quickly as possible, but I needn't have bothered. Gu Luo was another town that had caught the redevelopment bug, and the highway was a construction site. The trucks and buses were crawling through the confusion raising billows of dust. In fact, I was getting through faster than they were, because they were held up by a truck which had strayed too far onto the shoulder and gotten stuck almost blocking the way. What a mess.

Even so, by the time I found my turnoff it was getting dark. Far from the deserted wastes I had been traversing for the past several days, I found that the area north of the highway had been planted with cotton, the first I'd seen. Worse, the cotton was ripe and, worse yet, the harvesters intended to take advantage of the moonlight to harvest well into the evening. Even after dark I was never out of sight of dozens of cotton pickers, so no place to camp. It wasn't until the moon finally set that I was able to get off my feet and wolf down some cookies and soda before bed. At least I didn't have to leave too early in the morning. It was a clear cold night with a brilliant star show. Dew had formed on the cotton by morning, and the pickers couldn't work until it had dried, so I had a bit more time to brew up some instant noodles for breakfast. It was just as well that I was able to sleep in. Coming from urban Hong Kong, I wasn't used to seeing the stars, and I'd been up half the night enjoying them.

I made a practice of burying my paper and bottle caps, but the bottles themselves I left by the roadside. I was pretty sure they'd be gone within a couple of hours. That's one thing about the countryside – there's no waste. Any sort of paper or rubbish lying in the road is a sure sign that you're within 50 metres of a shop. Trash is so rare that a scrap of paper on the ground just leaps to your eye. Country people would buy a bottle of beer only for some sort of special occasion, and they're always happy to have an extra beer bottle around for buying cooking oil, kerosene or soya sauce. Such commodities are still stocked in bulk in country stores, and it's much cheaper to buy them that way than pre-packaged.

The cotton fields must have profited from some sort of local irrigation system, because it took me only a couple of hours to walk out of them, and then I was back to the badlands of the wild west – goats, sheep and tumbleweeds. The land was so dry that the track had been eroded into a deep ribbon of dust like yellow talcum powder. In the middle of the road, if I placed my feet carefully, they'd disappear completely down into the dust layer. I could stand up to my ankles in fine powder, my feet completely buried. You'd need a respirator to drive any sort of motor vehicle over those tracks, but fortunately all the work was done with donkey carts. And for some reason those were all painted bright yellow. It was a striking touch in a land otherwise devoid of human decoration.

With all habitation hidden in the ravines, the view from the trail was a vast and desolate panorama. From any one vantage point the trail always appeared to wind on to the horizon without encountering any greater obstacle than the stiff breeze. But in fact the trail wasn't able to wind around the heads of all the ravines. Every couple of hours would bring a steep scramble down into a hidden gully, and then an exhausting haul back up the other side. These descents were hard work, but they provided my only opportunity to replenish my water and ask directions. The trail up on top was almost deserted.

It was in one of these narrow gorges that I met Mr. Li. The gorge seemed deserted when I first reached the bottom, but it sheltered a little brook, and by searching upstream I was able to locate one of the little springs that fed it. In that deserted spot it was a fine opportunity for a wash and brush up. Refreshed, I was just getting back into harness when I heard someone shouting. I went to investigate and found Mr. Li chasing a donkey colt, which had broken its tether. He was having a hard time of it until the colt suddenly saw me in my strange gear and halted dead in its tracks.

Mr. Li had finished his morning's work in his garden and was now heading home with a drum of water on his donkey cart pulled by the colt's mother. He invited me home for lunch. His village was on a bench part way up the north wall, and it was quite a climb for the donkey cart. The route cut across several terraces where the donkey would break into a run before scrambling up the next steep slope. I had no trouble on the slopes, but running across the terraces with a knapsack, I was hard put to keep up. I reached the village with my tongue hanging about to my knees.

Mr. Li, his wife and daughter live in a set of three caves excavated into the clay of the hillside. Each cave is about 6.5m wide and 16m deep, and the arched ceiling is about 4m high down the centre. The three caves are side-by-side. Such parallel cave houses often have internal doors between the chambers, but not this one. The Li family is obliged to go outdoors to pass from one room to the next. The three rooms all open into a courtyard surrounded by a mud brick wall 2m high. There's a stable in the courtyard and a latrine, but no well. Mr. Li and his donkey haul all his water, either from the spring, if he happens to be down there, or from a communal well elsewhere in the village. It serves about 200 people living in about 50 or 60 sets of caves.

On top of the cut bank about 3m above the Li family compound is one of the public areas of the village that's used, in season, as a threshing floor. The Lis' three chimneys protruding from the ground are the only indication that someone is living 3m below.

Each of the Li family's three chambers has a door to the outside, a main window next to the door and a smaller transom window higher up near the top of the arch. The Lis use the middle cave as a kitchen, a second as a storeroom and the third as a combination bedroom and sitting room.

This third chamber serves double duty because it contains the kang – a bed in the form of a brick platform with a firebox underneath. The door into this room is in the left hand corner of the end wall. As you enter the doorway, straight ahead down the left hand wall are two armchairs and a wardrobe. Across the back wall are a couple of old-style steamer trunks protecting most of the family's clothing and valuables. At the far end of the right hand wall is a conventional double bed, which their daughter uses during the summer. Just to the right of the front door, underneath the window, is the *kang*.

The Lis' *kang* is a 2x3m brick platform 1.2m high, with a wooden rim around the outside edges. At the far end of the platform away from the window is a small coal burning stove, also made of brick. The flue leads across under the surface of the *kang* before funneling into a chimney and up through the roof to the public square above. Deep underground, the caves stay cool in summer and are warm in winter, but during the winter months the *kang* is the most comfortable place in the house and the centre of all activity.

The walls of Mr. Li's caves are plastered and whitewashed, but also papered with old newspapers and pictures from calendars. If not papered, the clay has a tendency to crumble and gradually flake off. The windows in the end wall face southeast, so the interior is pretty dark most of the day. This is relieved by a single naked light bulb hanging from a cord over the *kang*. It's bright enough for knitting, but the Lis don't in any case have access to much in the way of reading material. They do, though, have a television set, which sits on the sill of the main window at the end of the *kang*.

On a hot summer's day, I found it a lovely cool, dark place to sit for a while out of the sun. We were into our second cup of tea when I suddenly found out about those scorpions in the marketplace back in Bei Han. I wasn't bitten, but Mr. Li spotted one on the back of my chair and suddenly jumped up in great agitation, spilling his tea. He quickly pulled me aside, and he seemed so agitated that I at first thought he must have seen a snake. But no, his agitation was not so much for my safety as that the scorpion shouldn't make good his escape. He grabbed a handy matchbox, opened it and slapped it over the tiny critter. He then carefully slipped on the lid and used the box to transfer his quarry to a bottle in which he was already holding two others. Mr. Li explained that they were worth 2 mau each (a mau is worth about one cent). No one around here would bother trying to eat them, but people in the cities apparently consider them a delicacy, so the locals collect them to sell to the ladies who buy them up on market days. According to Mr. Li they have a painful sting, and clearly there are plenty of them to be found in these cave houses. I was hesitant to sit back down.

I felt a bit better when Mrs. Li returned from her morning's work in the fields and we all moved outside for lunch *al fresco* in the shade of the arch at the courtyard gateway (See photo number 28). Their daughter had been preparing it while Mr. Li was on scorpion safari. On a formal occasion the Lis would serve meat, but this meal was strictly potluck and typical of what a family would eat on a normal workday. (In fact it was Sunday, but Sunday is a normal work day in the Chinese countryside.) The menu was based on steamed buns about 10cm in diameter called *mantou*. Each diner is expected to eat two or three. These were supplemented with boiled sweet potatoes, steamed squash and a radish-and-tomato relish. Anyone still hungry is expected to fill up with a bowl or two of millet porridge at the end of the meal. All of this, including the wheat for the buns, came from the Lis' own fields.

After lunch I quickly excused myself and let the family get down to its siesta. Mr. Li had given me thorough directions for the next phase of my journey, including an introduction to a navigational aid, which I hadn't appreciated. He pointed out that villages like his own often left one large tree standing on the rim of the ravine just above the village as a sort of guide post. The practice may also have some animist basis, but I now realized that whenever I saw a large isolated tree on the horizon, I could expect to find the lip of a ravine below it and, down in the ravine, a village.

We had heard shooting all during lunch, and as I hit the trail I came across the source. I wouldn't know a grouse from a quail from a partridge, but up on top some men were hunting some sort of ground dwelling bird (Well, where else would they dwell in these treeless wastes?) with long, single shot rifles. Despite all the shooting, they didn't seem to have bagged any when I saw them. It couldn't have been easy trying to bring down game birds without a shotgun.

As Mr. Li had predicted, I could soon see in the distance a tall pagoda on a mountainside. The mountains were the southern end of the Tai Yue range, a rugged and uninhabited chain that runs up through the centre of Shanxi province. The pagoda was a local tourist attraction. Visiting it would violate one of the guiding principles that had served me so well, but in this case I had little choice. As you would expect, such a prominent landmark in this featureless country formed the linchpin of Mr. Li's directions.

When I first sighted it, the distance to the pagoda looked like a half hour's stroll but, as usual, there were a series of three or four hidden ravines in between, each involving a rugged descent and climb. The last one, in fact, was right at the foot of the mountains and was given over to an active quarry and gravel pit. There was no fencing, but the trail suddenly disappeared over the face of a new quarry. Getting down involved a tricky detour down some very steep and loose slopes. It was a long way down. Though you'd probably survive the fall, I couldn't imagine that a stay in a country hospital would be at all pleasant, or even good for your health. I took it very carefully. Fortunately, they weren't blasting.

The track up the other side was less dangerous, but it led directly to the pagoda. It was about 20m below that I hit the first rubbish. The place had clearly been fixed up and was attracting local tourists. I was pleased to discover, however, that by climbing in this back way I'd avoided the admission charge. However little the charge, it didn't promise to be worth it. I avoided the pagoda proper and retreated to an outlying gazebo where a professional photographer was posing visitors. The gazebo had a welcome cool breeze and a great view out over the country to the west, but that's not the backdrop the photographer was using for his snaps. He'd brought his patrons out there because he had set up a platform where, if his subject stood on the platform and held his hand a certain way, it would appear in the photo as if he were dangling the entire pagoda from his hand like a Chinese paper lantern. Pretty kitschy by my reckoning, but it was pulling them in.

I didn't visit the pagoda. It had 15 storeys, and for one yuan you could climb the internal staircase. I had already done my climbing for the day. They had done a nice job of painting up the outside and hanging little bells from the pointed eaves at each layer. They tinkled in the breeze. But I suspected that the inside was likely to be simply a dirty old wooden staircase and a crowd of people anxious to put me through my paces. Outside the door was another fellow selling the opportunity to have your picture taken sitting on a camel. I sat in the snack shack instead and drank a couple of bowls of cold tea.

People had described the mountains to me as wild and uninhabited, but I found it hard to believe that they wouldn't be laced with trails nonetheless. I struck off from the pagoda hoping to pick one up, but to no avail. I discovered instead that, far from being wild and uninhabited, this part of the mountainside served as the local lovers' lane. As we've seen, the Chinese live in very close quarters at home, so necking *al fresco* is an important social phenomenon. I gave up my search for a trail and retreated quietly.

Not wanting to retrace my steps, I set off down a small, precipitous trail toward a dirt road I could see running north along the foot of the range. It proved a poor choice, and I had a tough time getting down, but it brought me out at a brand new brick temple that had apparently just been constructed at the foot of the mountain. There was no one around, and it looked a bit as if it were so new that perhaps it hadn't yet been consecrated. I'd previously seen various temples that had been newly restored, but this was the first new temple that I'd seen built from scratch on a virgin site. I later found out that it had been built to replace an older one, which had been incorporated into the tourist site.

15

Badlands

It started at the quarry below the pagoda. I spent a couple of days following dirt lanes north along the foot of the Tai Yue mountains, and the economy of the entire district seemed to be devoted to quarrying and cement making. Each family owned a little tractor and a great big cart, and earned all its money hauling rock from quarries at the foot of the mountains down to cement plants in the valley. Suddenly, there seemed to be no farming anywhere. In fact, the carts were of a special design. They were oversized carts useful for nothing but hauling rock down a gentle, steady slope. The carts themselves were heavy enough that, empty, the little tractors could just barely haul them back up the hill. Neither tractors nor carts were licensed. They travelled only up and down their one road to and from the cement plant. As you can imagine, walking with them was less than charming. Noisy, dusty, but most of all dangerous. On the way down they weren't under their drivers' complete control.

Fortunately, my way was along the hillside rather than up or down. I had a beautiful view of the clouds forming around the peaks to my right and of the broad valley stretching away to the west on my left. A few of the carts I saw were hauling water rather than rock. At several points villages had gotten together to pipe water down from springs in the mountains. They had constructed loading points where a cart could back in under a spigot to fill by gravity. These were standard donkey carts with 55 gallon drums permanently mounted on the back. A drum that size could supply about 6 gallons of water to each of eight or 10 families, so the supply system was probably organized by several villages working together, then each village ran its own cart. I confirmed this by asking one of the drivers how much he charged for his water and, sure enough, he told me he doesn't get paid. It's a clan duty. The system certainly solved my water problems for a couple of days. I had all the water I needed, and good quality to boot.

Camping wasn't much of a problem either. There were plenty of dry streambeds running down from the mountains. Of course, camping in a dry streambed, you're always worrying about the weather at higher elevations. But in that region even the fields were available for camping. Since they weren't cultivated, they remained littered with boulders. Just 100m off the track you could sit down anywhere and immediately be screened from view.

Very early one morning, I stopped to chat with a fellow who was holding the fort at a very rudimentary amateur brickworks. He was the only one around, because their brick-making process was simple in the extreme. As far as I could understand him, they simply packed the raw bricks into a pit with a lot of coal dust, then set the coal dust on fire. The pit had been cut into the bank of one of the dry streambeds, so there were vents around the bottom of the pile. Nevertheless, it was hard to believe that this kind of oven ever gets very hot. You can usually spot a brickworks a long way off by its tall stack. This oven had no stack at all. I could only suppose that maybe the local clay didn't require a very high temperature to make good brick. I came by in mid-firing, so I never saw any of the product.

Over a couple of days I got heartily sick of the dust and noise of the rock wagons. I was in a hurry to get away from the cement factories into a more peaceful district, but in my haste I took a wrong turn. I found myself in a narrow valley with cliffs 100m or taller on either hand and the cliff faces swarming with workers quarrying stone. It was a spectacular sight, in a horrible sort of way.

Standing warily in the track I could see perhaps 200m up and down the valley. In that short stretch I was watching at least 100 men attack the cliff face on one side and a similar number across the valley. They seemed to be working in independent groups and relying on independent tractor owners to haul out their production. The men up on the rock faces levered out huge boulders with iron bars and sent them rolling down to the bottom where they were broken up with sledges and chisels. No one was wearing helmets. There were no gloves or safety shoes. Each group would blast whenever they were ready. Surely some of the giant boulders must occasionally roll down onto the carts passing below.

You can read some quite horrendous statistics on industrial safety in China. But don't bother. Horrendous as they may seem, like all Chinese statistics, they've been concocted to meet a target or earn a bonus. The true situation is far, far worse.

When industrial enterprises were state-run, each would normally have a safety officer whose bonus depended on compliance with safety rules. The statistics would still be doctored, but at least there was an on-going effort to compel workers to wear their shoes and gloves. The new private enterprises are less well organized, and the safety effort is often strictly voluntary. Private enterprises out in the countryside tend to specialize in construction and mining, two of the most dangerous sectors in any economy.

Much of this risk to life and limb remains out of sight, but if you're interested in observing the life of the average worker, it's not difficult to watch quarrying in progress. Hang around and strike up a conversation. You'll quickly attract a crowd of workers. Check how many are wearing rubber sandals. Anyone have a pair of safety gloves? Has anyone ever so much as seen a pair of safety gloves? Watch the workers clambering around the rock faces levering out blocks of stone with crowbars and crying "look out below!" Anyone up there wearing a safety harness? And your conversation may well be interrupted from time to time by shouts of "Blasting! Blasting!" Each crew lets rip whenever it's ready. If it's all so dangerous, where then are the cripples and amputees? Yes, indeed. Well you may ask. Basically, they don't survive.

I knew I'd taken a wrong turn, but it was all so fascinating that I couldn't bring myself to retreat. It was the real modern China now that private enterprise has taken over. I was debating whether to keep walking and perhaps descend another circle into hell, when all of a sudden a well-dressed fellow drove up in a dump truck and invited me for lunch.

Mr. Leung was a most interesting host. He didn't actually live in the district. These days he was a cadre in the city. But he came from a nearby town and was home for a visit. He had intended to leave that morning until he'd heard from one of the rock wagon drivers that I was coming up the valley. He'd put off his departure and arranged the lunch specifically to meet me.

As soon as we met I felt there was something unusual about the guy, and when he revealed he was visiting from the city I realized what it was. Apart from being relatively well dressed, he was wearing glasses. He was the first person I'd seen in weeks wearing them. The Chinese have no better eyesight than anyone else, but most of their problems go uncorrected. Only city dwellers can get to a place with eyeglasses for sale. Not prescription eyeglasses, of course, but if they're simply nearsighted, city dwellers can often find a pair at their local department store ground to some sort of generic prescription that's close enough to let them read the paper. Country folk do without.

We stopped briefly at the Leung family home, but then continued on to the home of the head of the village. The leader was out, but his wife made us comfortable in his sitting room. The home was a cave not much different in layout from Mr. Li's humble place where I'd lunched a few days before, but the leader's walls were lined with brick, and in the corner was a radiator. Hot water heating in winter? It would be a real luxury if it worked. And, of course, the leader had much nicer furniture than Mr. Li.

Wood is scarce in China, and the Chinese don't waste much of it on furniture. City homes are too small to hold much; country homes are too poor. Chinese architecture doesn't run to closets, so the item of furniture found in almost every home is the sideboard or chest of drawers where the family stores its clothing. Almost every family is forced to supplement this limited drawer space with cardboard boxes, but these are subject to infestation. The Chinese use beds, but these are not as universal as the sideboards, because in much of the country the people sleep on a *kang*, which is more a feature of the building than an item of furniture. Another essential is, of course, a table. A Chinese meal features individual bowls of rice or noodles, supplemented with a few dishes of vegetables in the centre of the table, accessible to all. No individual trays in front of the television. But here again many families simply spread a tablecloth on the *kang*. Most families try to own at least one armchair. If there's room they'll have a sofa as well. Wooden designs with simple thin cushions are easier to keep clean and dry. Every family also owns a few low stools, about 30cm off the ground. In the south these are often very cleverly made of bamboo fastened with wooden pegs. Every family aspires to add a television to its suite, but many haven't yet achieved it.

I suppose it's one of the burdens of being the village head – coming home for lunch and finding a dusty foreigner in your parlour. I must say his wife behaved brilliantly. We had pears, walnuts, sunflower seeds, all from the local gardens. I'd visited at just the right time of year. Perhaps the harvest is what had drawn Mr. Leung home for a visit. All the various dishes served for lunch were prepared from wild plants the village head had gathered in the mountains. It was a nice change from cookies and soda.

We all went for a walk before lunch. I thought we were just passing time, but it turned out that the village had a certain historical significance. They took me first to see a stele erected in the 3rd year of the reign of the Ming Chuan emperor, which they calculated to be about 1370 by the Western calendar. It had been erected then to commemorate a much earlier emperor of the Tang dynasty who came from this village. His reign was back about 700 AD. They showed me a fancy evergreen, reputed to have been planted by the future emperor when he was a kid. It didn't look 1,300 years old to me, but I'm no tree expert. For many years this village was known as Sing Tang Si in honour of its famous son. It had many impressive temples and a big monastery. But all that tradition made it a prime target during the cultural revolution, and in 1972 the whole place was destroyed and the people were moved away. Only the stele and the tree survived. People have now moved back into some of the old buildings, and Mr. Leung was leading some sort of movement to restore the place as a historical monument. Though I don't suppose many tourists would find entering through a couple of kilometres of stone quarry as fascinating as I had. Indeed, over lunch someone recalled that they'd had only one other Western visitor in living memory, and he was a missionary before World War II. He's remembered as having red hair.

In fact, it was a great lunch. A delicious introduction to the local products, particularly walnuts, pears and jujubes. The conversation was on a considerably higher plane than I was used to, and in Mandarin that I could more or less follow. I enjoyed myself thoroughly, though I drank enough rice liquor to put paid to much further progress during the afternoon. It was all I could do to get through the quarries safely and find a quiet spot to camp. Even these cultured folk, however, seemed to really appreciate my offer to take some photos that I could develop and send back to them from Hong Kong. The village head had posters of Mao, Zhou Enlai and even Stalin decorating his walls, but no photos of his family.

I fell asleep early that evening, but was awakened later by fireworks and a loudspeaker broadcasting speeches and music. The next morning the source of the racket proved to be a funeral. In the first village I came to, everyone was wearing white and setting up giant steamers and a massive noodle press. Fancy funerals are an important element of Confucian respect for your ancestors. In this case they'd hired a funeral director who'd brought in a tent, an opera troupe and all the banquet-sized kitchen equipment. The bereaved had only to supply the food, the mourners and perhaps the wreaths. I would have liked to take a picture, but I couldn't predict their response, so I thought the better of it and just kept on walking. If it had been a wedding they might well have invited me in.

A couple of days later I had an opportunity to do some entertaining of my own. While there wasn't much farming in this area, every day I said hello to quite a few goatherds. I'd never had occasion to chat with any of them at length, probably because herding tends to get assigned to the least productive and able members of the family and, alone all day with the animals, they quickly lose their language skills. But one lunchtime I was boiling up some noodles in the lee of a bank, when suddenly a herd of goats began pouring over the top and swarming past me. What a mess! I grabbed my stove and tried to defend my patch, but to little avail until the goatherds showed up to help. Once their charges were under control, they of course launched directly into the standard interrogation, so I relit the stove and invited them for a bowl of instant noodles. As usual, communication was very uncertain, but I found out that they were cousins, both in their 20s, and neither had been educated past about the 4th grade. They did other work besides herding, but I never understood what it involved. At this time of year they left home every day at dawn and drove their flock around the district all day, returning home at dusk. Not much of a life, but at least they had each other for company. Most herders that I'd seen worked alone.

As I headed north, the basic geology – a thick layer of eroded dust over bedrock – was still the same, but the dust layer had gotten much thicker and perhaps a lot older and more stable as well. Where before I'd been climbing in and out of ravines, which seemed to erode further with each rainstorm, I was now getting into country where the valleys were much wider and deeper. Although the people still lived in caves excavated from sheer banks, the general trend of the valley walls was much less steep. On the other hand, the dust layer was much thicker, so the valleys were much deeper. I'd typically come across a valley barring my way across the barren wastes, and it would then take me 60 to 90 minutes to descend into the town at the bottom, and another 90 minutes to get back on top again. Despite that, the climbs were still pretty steep.

Camping up on top was easy, but always dry. If I wanted a campsite where I could have a wash or boil up some unchlorinated water for tea, I was compelled to find a spot in one of the valleys. But, of course, the valley bottoms were the only part of the badlands heavily settled and cultivated. Campsites down in the valleys were hard to find.

The old Boy Scout manual used to advise that most farmers would be happy to let a hiker camp in their fields if he knocked at the door and asked permission first. Elsewhere in the world it was probably good advice. In China such an appeal would have much different consequences. In China, a farmer can't take responsibility for such permissions. Anything out of the ordinary is reported instead to the local leader. This may be a party cadre, or just a hereditary clan elder. The land in question doesn't, after all, actually belong to the farmer who's cultivating it. It's village land, and the hospitality involved is village hospitality. A visiting peddler might be allowed to camp, but a visiting foreigner would certainly have to be invited in and entertained. Never mind that he doesn't necessarily desire it. Never mind that he'll feel uncomfortable accepting food from an impoverished village. The leader feels he has no choice. If the visitor were to camp out, right off the bat it would reflect badly on the village's prosperity and hospitality. The members of the village would lose face. Worse yet, the visitor becomes the village's responsibility. Once he has presented himself, word of his presence will quickly spread. Suppose he's robbed. The village will be blamed, doubly so if they've been so foolish as to let him camp out as he first requested.

Of course, this works both ways. The traveller who simply doesn't feel up to an evening of interrogation and inspection has the perfect excuse for a clandestine bivouac. But when the trail is a sea of mud, the sleet is pelting down and darkness is falling, the foreign traveller can approach any village and count on the same dynamics to save him from a difficult situation. I'd done it with Mr. Lee back in Hunan when I was wet, lost and tired. But I usually went for the clandestine bivouac.

Xi Xu is an example of one that went well. The town is strung along the bottom of a deep river valley running east and west. I reached the top of the south rim late in the afternoon and paused to scan for trails leading up the other side. The most promising led from what appeared to be the town centre, opposite where the dry bed of a tributary stream entered from the south. Considering the hour, I decided I'd best plan to camp in the dry bed of the tributary and cross through town in the morning. If I tried to cross the valley in the late afternoon, I might attract a parade, which would follow me up the far side and stay with me until it was too dark to find a good campsite.

By the time I got down I had only another hour or so of daylight, but there were no houses along the dry tributary and plenty of sandy campsites among rock piles in the streambed. The valley that I'd just descended was so steep that I decided on a bold move to buy a beer to drink with dinner. After selecting and clearing my campsite, I shouldered my pack, forded the main stream and strolled brazenly into town. I found the store and bought my beer, immediately attracting the expected crowd of curious citizens. After a few minutes of interrogation, I excused myself explaining that I was heading south and intending to climb all the way to the rim of the valley, beyond the boundaries of the village, before stopping for the night. I went through the motions of asking a few directions, then set off briskly. A few teenagers followed me, even to the point of fording the stream. But once they were convinced that I was embarking on a 90-minute climb in the bush they reluctantly let me go.

I enjoyed the beer after a long day in harness. I enjoyed the quiet, scenic campsite. But I wasn't entirely alone. Even after dark, two or three parties of men came by out in the dry streambed, each man carrying three or four logs on his back. I couldn't see clearly, but each man's load must have amounted to at least 30kg. There were no forests on the south slope of the valley, so they'd been carrying them a long way. It would have been quite a chore descending the steep trail in the dark. What a way to earn a living.

The next morning I forded the stream for the last time and, as I passed through town, greeted a few of the people I'd met the night before. My duplicity was thus revealed, but I could only hope they'd put it down to the language barrier. Not all my campsites worked out so well, but on this occasion my reconnaissance of the previous evening allowed me to stride confidently away on the correct trail up the north slope of the valley without further embarrassment.

Later that same day I met a man who warned me against walking with my pant legs rolled up to the knee, a custom I'd picked up in the south. I had a pair of shorts, but shorts are so unusual out in the countryside that if I wore them even the most nearsighted farmer could spot me as a foreigner at first sight. So I'd copied the southern rice farmers in wearing long trousers, but rolling them up. On this occasion I was wearing them that way when I took a wrong turn in rugged hill country and ended up on a dead end in this man's front yard. He was sitting in the gateway in front of his cave cleaning a hare that he'd shot that morning. He tried to invite me in for lunch, but I suspected the hare might be the only meat his family would eat that week, so I persistently declined. He gave me the directions I needed, and before I left he tried to tell me something else, but he was an old guy with so few teeth that it was really difficult to make out his words. After going over it several times, I finally figured out that what sounded like the word for "rocks" was actually the word for "snakes." He was warning me that there were lots of poisonous snakes around there, and that I was ill advised to be wandering around on the narrow, grassy trails with my pant legs rolled up. I hadn't thought of that. Cultivated areas are farmed so intensely that the farmers kill off all the snakes and eat them, but they'd thrive in deserted regions like that one. It was good advice.

In fact, the region was becoming so deserted that I crossed ravines where, despite the availability of water, even the bottoms were empty except for a few abandoned mine workings. Coming down from the top, you'd descend through the thick layer of loess soil, then a layer of gravel that would roll under your feet and make the trail dangerous, then across a layer of carbonate rock, and finally you'd come to a layer of shale containing seams of coal. But all the easy coal had been cleaned out years ago, and now the bottoms were deserted except for the odd amateur miner.

The amateurs could be quite a health hazard. They were only after a few chunks of coal to keep them warm through the winter. They attacked the old workings with sledges and crowbars going after one chunk at a time. When they'd extracted one, they'd simply pitch it over the edge of their ledge, intending to come along later with a cart and collect their spoils from the streambed at the bottom. They worked silently, and threw their product over the edge without looking, never expecting anyone to be passing below. When the valleys were narrow, they were a rare but potentially lethal hazard. A bit like the snakes.

Such remote areas, for all their dangers, at least sheltered me from the more mundane risks of Chinese traffic and the Chinese police. Shanxi province does, however, have a main north-south rail and road corridor linking the capital Taiyuan with the metropolis of Xian in the confusingly-spelled Shaanxi province farther west. This corridor follows the valley of the Fen River, and it was this natural barrier that I was now approaching. Once across the Fen, I'd be scaling a final range of mountains before reaching the boundary of ancient China at the Great Wall.

I realized I was nearing civilization when, after weeks of villages in the wilderness, I reached the town of Ma He. In the position shown on the map it didn't amount to much, but a paved highway passed a few kilometres to the west, and when I reached it I realized that most of the town had moved. Along the highway, for the first time in weeks, I had a selection of restaurants and noodle stalls to choose from. Also for the first time in weeks, it started to rain.

I enjoyed my visit to Ma He, best remembered for a hearty hot meal. Along the busy highway I was less of a freak show. Indeed, the towns along the highway might even have been open to foreigners. It wasn't an enquiry that I was in a position to bring up. But when I tried to leave, I had a lot of difficulty finding a trail. The highway had been paved for some years, and the citizens were now in the habit of coming and going by bus. By the time I found someone who could show me the right trail, it had been raining

long enough that the red dust had turned to red mud, and the climb
out of the valley was slippery and difficult.

So difficult, in fact, that a few hours later I had to help push a
tractor that was stuck in the mud. I was only a few kilometres
from the river, but there was no one out in the rain and I was
having difficulty getting directions. The tractor driver, though,
was a captive audience. He wasn't going anywhere until I helped
him push.

It is possible to find a few items of modern farm machinery in
China, but they're very rare. Most fields are much too small to use
that sort of thing effectively. Instead, the Chinese rely on what in
the West would be termed garden tractors. And not just for farm
work. They're about the most common class of vehicle on the
highways, and one of the strange artifacts foreign visitors remember
best about a trip to China. There are three main styles. Each
province has one or two tractor factories and each factory churns
out just one particular style. That's the only design you'll find in
that region. Visit another area a few hundred kilometres away and
another style will be universal. There's very little overlapping
distribution between regional factories. The central planners used
to think it was more efficient that way.

The most popular style is called a *toh luhn che*. It's nothing more
than a diesel engine mounted between two wheels on a single axle
and maneuvered with handlebars. It would be possible to walk such
a contraption down the street like a wheelbarrow, but in fact the
tractor is invariably hitched to a cart, and the driver sits at the
front of the cart and works the extended handlebars from there.
The tractor-cart combination then has four wheels, but the driving
wheels at the front have only the weight of the engine over them.
This sort of machine has poor traction in wet weather.

A second popular design has three wheels at the corners of a triangular frame. The front wheel is again maneuvered with handlebars. The driver sits over the engine mounted just behind. The bed is behind him between the rear wheels. This setup is referred to as a *san luhn che*. As you might expect, the driver's seat can get pretty warm, so these machines are not popular in the steamy south. Another problem is that the engine drives the rear wheels through a differential, which is prone to damage on China's rough tracks. This tricycle design needs only three tires, but it's less stable. On the other hand, with a bit of a load in back it's the better vehicle in wet weather.

Finally, a few factories have begun in recent years to turn out small versions of the conventional Western tractor. They're about the size and shape of a large riding lawnmower. This is the only one of the three styles which hides its workings in a cowling of sheet metal, so it has a certain snob appeal. The large rear wheels pull very well, but it demands four expensive tires to support just the engine and the driver.

All of these tractors serve as trucks, taxis and taxi-trucks on the rural highways. Most Chinese will never have the chance to sit in a car, but almost everyone has ridden in back of one of these.

The tractor I found in the ditch was a *san luhn che*. The track was slick and had such a high crown that the driver had simply been rolling along minding his own business when he found the vehicle slipping to the side and right into the ditch. With two of us we had no trouble getting it out again, and I got some directions as my reward. But it didn't last long. I was soon wandering around again, lost in the drizzle and mist.

In the end I spent the night in a cave cut into a bank at the edge of a terraced field. Almost all the fields were terraced flat in this hilly country, and many of the resulting cut banks had little shelters dug into them where the farmers could park their toddlers or their lunch hamper out of the sun or the rain. The one I chose wasn't very roomy, but it was dry and out of the chill breeze.

Things didn't improve right away the next morning. It had stopped raining, but the mist had thickened into fog. Again there were few travellers out on the roads and numerous forks which reduced me to guessing which branch to choose. Eventually, though, the land began to slope down to the Northwest, and I knew I must be entering the valley of the Fen River. Downhill tracks only get bigger, and I finally came across a coal mine which welcomed me back to civilization and to lower elevations.

I paused awhile to watch a bit of excitement at the mine from a vantage point on the other side of a ravine. Their system involved pushing the coal out of the mine shafts by hand in little carts running on rails, then tipping the load over the edge of the bank to where it could be loaded into trucks at the bottom. The carts were hinged to tip out their loads while standing firmly on the track, but somehow one of the labourers had managed to tip his load over the bank cart and all. The heavy steel cart was stranded with its wheels in the air half way down a 30m bank, and the workers were arguing over what to do. I didn't hang about to watch the denouement, but from where I was standing it looked as if the only possible solution would be to slide the thing all the way down to the loading dock, topple it into a dump truck and drive it back to the top. Perhaps the top was inaccessible by road. I don't know, but the whole episode was generating some animated discussion.

From the mine it was only a few minutes' descent to the town of Yi Tao. This was shown on the map with something a bit larger than the smallest symbol, and so should have been out of bounds for me, but I'd been aiming for it because my map showed that there was a bridge across the river there.

The town itself was a mess. I suppose it was the result of some sort of dispute between the municipal authorities and the industrial bureaucrats who ran the mine. The miners trucked their product right down the unpaved main street using a fleet of *toh luhn ches*. This traffic had torn up the street pretty badly, and you could imagine the authorities arguing over which party was responsible for the maintenance. Meanwhile, successive rainstorms had eroded the street into a major gully. It was passable only along the edges. With a useless gully in front of their doors, the inhabitants had begun throwing their garbage in it. Yi Tao must be hell on a hot day.

I just kept walking. I needed a hot meal, but I pinned my hopes on finding a string of noodle stalls along the highway near the bridge. In the event, I was disappointed. It was a long and impressive bridge over a very drought-reduced river. The toll booths were on the far bank, and there may have been some eateries over there, but there would also be policemen watching for toll dodgers. I crossed the span, then immediately ducked down the abutment and struck north along the river.

I was looking forward to following the river for a couple of days as a change from clambering in and out of ravines all day long. But I'd forgotten what it was like. The flat, featureless farmland quickly palled. The consolation was that the fields had been organized into a rectilinear grid with one axis running almost due north. I had no shortage of tracks as large or as small as I wanted running straight and true for Mongolia. With no need to continually ask directions, I made good progress in the level going. But I was soon wishing for a hill to break the monotony.

Tractors were still shifting loads of coal over some of the larger tracks. I followed one such for a while and discovered yet another kind of modern Chinese entrepreneur. The way was lined with small boys, one stationed at each pothole to collect the coal falling off the carts. Each had his pitch and his little pile of booty, but they were far enough apart that they had no one to talk with all day long. Each had a chance to ask me about three questions as I passed. I enquired whether they were collecting for the coal company, but it seems they were taking the coal home to burn in the family stove. Education was taking second place with that sort of opportunity on offer.

I eventually found an irrigation project with canals running parallel to the river. The banks offered more interesting scenery and more shade than I was getting on the tracks through the fields. Sunny weather had returned, and evolved into a pattern of afternoon thunderstorms. I was a bit safer under the trees.

Late one afternoon, I was following one of the irrigation ditches when I ran into Mr. Wu returning from cutting some forage for his donkey. He invited me to spend the night at his house, and as lightning was flashing in the darkening sky, I was happy to accept. His village was laid out like an army camp with rows of cement housing units, but Mr. Wu alone had a little brick shack on a piece of waste ground apart from all the rest. Of course he knew everyone, and for the evening everyone was his friend, coming to visit and to study me. But I got the impression that Mr. Wu was in some way the odd man out in his village. Certainly his neighbors seemed a bit aghast that I should be staying in the poorest house in the village, but Mr. Wu had befriended me, so I stuck with him.

Over the course of the evening, I learned that Mr. Wu had grown up in the village as the youngest in a family of six children. His father was then 80 and an important man in the clan. He had been able to secure about three-quarters of a hectare of agricultural land for his youngest son's family, but no housing unit. To avoid the problems of sharing housing with an older brother (problems in particular for his wife), Mr. Wu had built himself a very small and, he hoped, temporary house on some unused ground at the edge of the village.

The unused ground was unused because it was a bit of a swamp in wet weather. Mr. Wu had brought in some fill and levelled it, but he still had to cope with the waste water of the whole village standing in a muddy bog next to his house. His little plot accommodates a chicken coop and a stable for his donkey as well as his house, so it's always littered with refuse and animal wastes.

The house itself is a brick box 3.5x7m divided into two 3.5m square rooms. The front door opens into the room on the right, which serves as a sitting room in bad weather. The left hand room is the bedroom, reached through the sitting room. The whole place is built on a little concrete slab, and so has bare cement floors. The sitting room has a screen door, and the transom window over the door is also screened, so it's possible to keep the mosquitoes at bay in summer despite the quagmire. The bedroom too has only one window, but this one is glazed as well as screened. The transom window boasts only a shutter.

The sitting room is furnished with two wardrobes, a chest of drawers with a television set on top, two chairs, and various cardboard boxes for storage. The bedroom is largely taken up by the kang. At one end is the stove for heating it. Otherwise there is space in the bedroom only for a treadle sewing machine.

Except in very cold weather, the family cooks and eats outdoors. Mr. Wu has erected a shed on the right hand end of the building. This houses a coal burning brick stove and two enormous pottery urns for water. Each holds about 500 litres, though they're never both full. The water must be hauled by the bucket load from the village well. Mr. Wu's 10 year-old daughter and eight year-old son handle this chore, each on one end of a pole with the bucket suspended between them. Like the Ngaan family back at the Dong Ting Lakes, the Wus add salt to their water because of its muddy taste.

It's a pretty small setup for a family of four. The night I stayed, Mrs. Wu and her daughter slept with relatives to give me a place on the *kang* with Mr. Wu and his son. I was even more trouble to them because they apparently eat their evening meal about 5 p.m. when the kids come home from school. I'd met Mr. Wu at 6:30 when he'd gone out cutting forage after supper. So when I got there, Mrs. Wu had to re-light the stove and make me a special meal. Fortunately, she had on hand some emergency rations in the form of a big ball of dough, which she could cut up in little chips to boil up as noodles. The thinner ones were okay. She did have some nice homemade pickles, though – basically tomatoes with chili peppers. The morning meal was a bit better organized, with fried bread and millet gruel, fried eggs and more pickles. It must have cleaned out their egg supply. The Wu family didn't seem to eat much meat. They grow their own wheat and have it ground at a local cooperative mill. There was a big sack of flour stored behind the sitting room door. Mr. Wu said a sack lasts the family 10-12 days. I estimated that would amount to almost a kilogram of flour per person per day.

Eating outside the front door left us open to a steady stream of curious villagers. They came in waves. They came in shifts. It felt like the pie-eating contest at a country fair. Finally, even Mr. Wu got tired of hearing the same questions over and over, and we agreed that I'd turn in early while he went off on some errand. Unfortunately, in his absence his wife wasn't able to defend me from a late visitor who showed up after I'd already been asleep for at least half an hour. This guy seemed to be some sort of local cadre, maybe a party member who felt it was his duty to investigate anything so out of the ordinary as a Western visitor. Anyway, he forced his way right into the bedroom and woke me up for another round of the usual questions. Worse, his demeanor was fairly hostile. As usual with such types, I feigned a lack of even the most basic Mandarin, and the interrogation pretty quickly hit a dead end. Mrs. Wu was eventually able to shepherd the guy out and turn off the light.

At breakfast (See photo number 30), Mr. Wu apologized for the intrusion and implied that I was right in guessing that the midnight visitor was a painful but not entirely powerless old cadre. This set me to imagining him trying to inform the police about me, but there wouldn't be a police post for miles, and the village had no telephones. I figured I had plenty of time to take a few photos of the family before making my escape. In fact, the photos took only a minute, but then there was the question of addressing an envelope so that I could send back the prints.

It's interesting how villagers like Mr. Wu lose their literacy. He's obviously a smart and ambitious guy, but he had no envelopes in the house, and only his kids were able to write out his address. They had to consult several neighbors before getting the postal code straight. Many people seem to be able to read fairly well, but out in the country only school kids can write. It's a bit like algebra in Western countries. Everyone has learned it, but if you have a quadratic equation to solve, look for a school kid.

Once back on the bank of the irrigation canal, I decided it would be prudent to make up for my late start with a focused effort to put a few kilometres between me an my last known whereabouts.

It was flat and shady, and I estimate I must have put in close to 50 kilometres that day. The canals had a few branches, but I was able to pinpoint my position from time to time, because some of the villages I could see from the levee had painted their names in large characters on one of the external buildings. I believe that at one time such identification would have been discouraged as a protection against Russian invasion, but with that threat long gone it wasn't clear whether identifying the villages was now official policy or just the work of unleashed graffiti artists. It was certainly helpful to my own little invasion.

Most people have heard about the famous "big character posters" used to vilify enemies during the cultural revolution. The whole idea strikes the Western mind as a uniquely Chinese terror technique. Where did they ever get the idea of communicating this way? Well, from the West, perhaps. Posting up handbills is no longer as popular as it once was, but travelling circuses still do it in rural America. The Wild West "Wanted" poster was a message of this kind. And a few people in America can still remember the Burma Shave signs that entertained travellers in the early days of the motor car. It all sounds a bit quaint in the television era, but in China the television era has just arrived and poster communication is only slowly dying out.

Most Chinese posters aren't posted at all. They're painted right on the brickwork of the wall itself. Twenty years a go the slogans praised the Communist Party and wished long life to Chairman Mao. A few faded remnants of those slogans can still be seen in sheltered locations. But these days the slogans are more practical. The topics seem to be centrally mandated, probably through party channels, because the most popular theme seems to vary from area to area. In one county or province there will be great emphasis on birth control, another area might stress the importance of keeping the children in school, elsewhere the posters might condemn the theft of electricity. The village names painted on the buildings in central Shanxi may be in the same category of centrally-mandated communication.

Chinese the world over continue the tradition of posting up good luck slogans at New Year, a bit like decorating the house for Christmas. In recent years a few organizations have picked up the idea of printing popular holiday slogans on coloured posters. They then distribute these to their employees and customers as a form of advertising. It works well because country folk, as we've seen, have little access to bright and colourful decoration for their homes. Whole neighbourhoods remain festooned with these posters long after the holidays have passed.

I didn't stop for lunch during my day on the irrigation canals, but I did run into a group of workers who gave me a couple of large, ripe tomatoes. I gave these delicacies the best wash I could using chlorinated water from my bottles and ate them gratefully on the move. I was getting pretty tired by late in the afternoon, but I kept pushing because along the canals it was the old problem of no uncultivated land for camping. Finally, late in the afternoon, I found a stream, which my map showed as issuing from a reservoir in the hills to the West. I climbed for one last hour and was rewarded with a quiet, scenic campsite in the hills near the dam. I was exhausted, but I'd left the Fen River valley and was back in wild country.

16

To the Great Wall

My enthusiasm for the view over the reservoir was tempered by the discovery that the lake breeds mosquitoes. I hadn't been using my repellent very often, but I needed both repellent and netting that night. The next morning the reservoir had another unpleasant surprise in store. I found a well-graded and scenic trail along the shore and had followed it about half an hour before a farmer on the hillside overlooking the lake revealed that the trail was a dead end. He was quite explicit that there was no trail over the ridge into the next county. I couldn't believe it and checked with another local I met, but it seemed to be true. The area was very sparsely settled, and the few who did live there seemed never to travel West to the next county. I was forced to retrace my steps to the dam and pick up the only road over the height of land.

The road was actually a paved highway. It was shown on my map and busy with heavy trucks. I'd heard them labouring up the long grade during the night, even from my camp a couple of kilometres away across the valley. Clearly, climbing the road would be no fun. Apart from the noise and the diesel smoke, the trucks descending wouldn't be fully under control, and the whole business might well be supervised by patrolling police. I decided instead to follow a streambed up. The highway followed the valley of the stream, but high up on the slope. The highway wound in and out of the various tributary valleys, while I could walk straight up the watercourse and do the bulk of my climbing in one stiff scramble up nearer the pass over the height to land. There was no danger of getting lost, as I could hear the trucks labouring high overhead and see the grade slicing up the valley wall. There was no vegetation.

In fact, I found a track up the valley bottom and came across a couple of parties of miners. They were exploiting some very small seams of ore and must have been working in competition, because each group had its own crusher and separator. They dug the stuff up, ground it to a powder, mixed it with water and ran the slurry over a revolving drum. The rock powder ran off with the water, but the ore stuck to the drum and was scraped off as a fine black mud. I figured at first that the drum must be magnetic, but it was driven by a small engine. There was no electricity supply that I could see, so it couldn't be an electromagnet. And magnetism would work only with iron ore. I thought iron ore was usually red, and there was no reddish colour to the stream, the tailings or anything else in the valley. That made me think that the drum had some sort of wax or grease coating which would pick up the ore but not the rock. Perhaps something to do with the particle size or crystal shape. Anyway, it was a surprisingly sophisticated setup. I would have liked to learn more, but all the miners were busy. They'd give me a wave and turned straight back to their work. That was the surest sign they were independent entrepreneurs. The separators had probably been lent to them by some big government work unit, but they were independent contract suppliers working out seams too small for the big work units to bother with.

I followed the stream until it eventually petered out and I was forced to climb up to the highway to get over the ridge line. I followed the pavement only a kilometre or so over the summit of the pass, but it was quite an experience. This was obviously coal mining country, and all the trucks I'd heard were loaded, overloaded, with coal. They were big, and the most bizarre fleet imaginable. Many had only one jury-rigged headlight. Often they had no cab at all, just a bench over the engine like an old Western stagecoach. A couple were able to climb only with the driver's helper perched on the front bumper continuously pouring water through the remains of the radiator. Licence plates? Get serious.

In some ways China is a fascinating example of a totalitarian state where the government isn't very effective in imposing its will. Vehicle licensing is a good example. On the one hand there are exhaustive regulations about both driver and vehicle licensing. Drivers are often fined for offenses such as not having had their fire extinguisher recharged recently enough. The provinces issue a uniform style of licence plates showing the name of the province and a number indicating the county within the province where the vehicle is based. Vehicles from the provincial capital get 01. There are different licence plate colours for private vehicles, taxis, trucks and buses. It all seems very organized.

On the other hand, there are a surprising number of vehicles exempted from these controls. The army, the various flavours of police and a variety of other organizations issue their own licence plates without reference to the provincial systems. There is little sense of equality before the law in China, and no doubt these systems originated out of a reluctance among national organizations to submit themselves to provincial control. These days, however, special plates operate as a sort of diplomatic immunity from local traffic regulations. The local police don't dare to discipline drivers of these vehicles, and the drivers quite often take advantage of their immunity. Their high-handed antics are bad for traffic congestion, but even worse for the image of government and the legal system.

At the same time, out in the countryside it's quite common to see unlicensed vehicles on the road. Unlicensed drivers are less obvious, but no doubt common as well. Never mind the fire extinguisher, it's quite easy to find Chinese trucks with no headlights, no windshield, no cab, no bodywork at all. In a police state? Well, as has been observed, this particular police state runs under the rule of men, not the rule of law. Society's order rests not on compliance with the written regulations, but on good working relationships among the officials who administer them. An unlicensed truck can't leave the local area. It runs from the mine to the rail yard, back and forth every day. If it strays over the town line, the driver will be fined before he gets a kilometre. But in a town where you have a good relationship with the mayor, anything is possible.

I suppose the old rattletraps cresting the pass must have had functioning brakes, but I wasn't keen to give them a test. In addition, they had the usual habit of rolling down long hills with their engines off. As soon as I was through the pass, I took the first opportunity to jump off the embankment and slide down to the streambed on the other side.

I was forced to rejoin the highway farther down, but after a few kilometres I was relieved to learn that the coal mine was off to the northeast, while my route continued up a valley to the northwest. I bid the traffic maelstrom good-by and set off on a quiet gravel road up a dry, stony valley.

People were growing a bit of millet, some sweet potatoes and a few beans in the valley bottom, but the most interesting crop was the walnuts. There were quite a few mature walnut trees, some along the road, and I came across a steady supply of fallen nuts. They were hard to open, but very tasty. Much better than the dry and bitter specimens usually found in Western supermarkets. Fresh, it was possible to peel the brown skin off the wrinkly kernel to leave a meat that was white and sweet. Great eating on the move.

I camped by a stream that night and was surprised by a midnight shower. I hadn't seen much rain in weeks and had gotten sloppy about rigging up my fly. Fortunately, it quickly passed. The next day was again dry and sunny and I was able to dry out my gear at noon.

Over the course of the morning the road deteriorated to a track. Bridges over the streams became stepping stones. The occasional truck evolved into the occasional pack donkey. The stone houses in the villages incorporated more and more wood. By lunchtime I had climbed out of the valley and was delighted to learn that the authorities in the next township were developing forestry. I was in a beautiful pine forest.

While still above the first village on the other side of the ridgeline, I took the opportunity to stop for an early lunch in a forest glade where I could dry out my gear. It was an idyllic spot – wildflowers, a tiny stream probably clean enough for brushing my teeth. I had just gotten my gear spread out when I was interrupted by a donkey train packing out logs from the forest. It was the first of several, and of course all the woodsmen wanted to stop, chat and inspect all my strange belongings. It's fortunate they were heading home for lunch and their donkeys wouldn't brook much delay. I cooked up a bowl of noodles and got all my gear dried, but it wasn't the quiet picnic I'd anticipated.

I reached the meadows and villages of the woodcutters during the afternoon, and it was clear that they were making a pretty good living from the forest. They were lucky. Certainly the villages looked cleaner and more comfortable than those I'd seen in the last valley to the Southeast. And they were doing well to have donkeys to haul their wood for them. Certainly in the roadless areas I'd visited before, the woodsmen were always faced with the backbreaking chore of hauling the product out on their own shoulders.

I suppose most of my woodsman acquaintances were napping when I passed, but there were a few old ladies out and about, and they were wearing some unusual headgear. The traditional hat in this part of the country resembled a white chef's hat, except straighter and not so floppy. More like a white stovepipe without the brim. The material seemed to be a sort of linen. It must have been a chore to keep them clean. Rather as the old foot-binding tradition showed that a woman was above going out to the fields to work, so wearing a white hat in these country villages might in some sense symbolize a woman's ability to keep a clean and neat house despite having to cook over a fire.

Beyond that first village I had left the forest behind, and I spent the afternoon climbing a long, infertile valley amid the same sparse garden patches I'd seen in the morning. The ridge tops were apparently devoted to wild brush rather than managed forestry, because I met several parties descending the valley with medicinal herbs they'd collected in the surrounding scrub.

By late afternoon I'd left the last farmstead and was again climbing the steep ridge at the valley's head. The terrain up there was beautiful pastureland with wildflowers and groves of old and stately trees scattered here and there. Cresting the ridge, the scene reminded me of the meadows of rural England as I looked down on the village of Huang Tu Wan at the head of the next valley. A front had come through after last night's rain, bringing icy, crystal clear air. As I surveyed the scene, the breeze cut through my sweaty gear and I knew I was in for an uncomfortable night. I could have searched for a hidden glade to make a wood fire. It would have been a welcome novelty in a country where wood is so scarce. But instead I elected to try my luck cadging shelter for the night in Huang Tu Wan.

It wasn't, of course, very difficult. Nearing the town I fell in with two young men returning from work in a small quarry. As usual, I was the first Westerner they'd ever seen in the flesh and they didn't hesitate to urge me to spend the night in the village. One of them took me first to the house of his mother, where we shared a warm water sponge bath and then a tasty evening meal. Both the bath and the meal, of course, in the presence of half the inhabitants. We then moved for the night to another house nearby which my friend shared with his brother. The three of us cuddled up on the kang. They didn't feel it was cold enough to fire it up, and they were right. We were thoroughly comfortable under a couple of quilts.

The houses in the village were particularly picturesque (See photo number 31). The local fashion was for brick houses with tile roofs, the upper half of the front wall a latticework of unpainted weathered wood glazed with waxed paper. The architecture owed a lot to the caves so popular elsewhere in the province. The back and side walls were completely blank with the extensive paper latticework only in the front wall. But, of course, these houses weren't as snug as caves. Any warm air would rise and seep out between the roof tiles. In the winter these people must spend a great deal of their time huddled under quilts on the hot *kang*.

I was cozy under their quilts, but village sounds kept awakening me during the night. There was a cow tethered outside who wore a bell. Whenever the cow was awake, the bell was awake, and often I was awake. Then, in the middle of the night, came a great crash and clatter in our own house. My hosts explained in the morning that a mouse must have knocked over the washbasin propped against the wall.

The brothers were up before dawn, but they insisted I stay in bed until they had lit the fire, taken the chill off the room and whipped up some breakfast. It's hard to understand how they can quarry stone all day on their Spartan diet. For breakfast we had noodles, pulled by one of the brothers on the spot from freshly made dough and boiled up with some potato pieces, green beans and lots of hot pepper. That was about what we'd eaten the night before *chez* Mama, except that then the noodles had been replaced by millet gruel. No fat, no meat. The houses in the village all had squash, cabbages, mushrooms and various other vegetables strung up to dry. Those must be their staples through the long winter.

It was good enough for me, and after the usual photos and agonizing over the postal code I was anxious to hit the trail in the crisp fall air. I found myself following another dry, stony valley very similar to those of recent days. The same tiny stream and sparse, scraggly crops. Most of the vegetation was thorn bushes. This time, though, that one valley lasted all day, and it wasn't until late afternoon that I found myself climbing out of the valley over the ridgeline. As before, there were pastures at the head of the valley, but instead of groves of stately trees, these pastures were choked with clumps of thorn bush. I'd asked directions at the highest village and been assured there was only one trail up over the pass. Which was true enough if you knew it well. But to the uninitiated the route through the thorny scrub was a maze of cow paths, not one of which stood out as the original through trail. I was lost again, and eventually had to scramble up a steep, thorny slope and follow the ridgeline. By that expedient I found the pass and the trail, but by then it was so late that I was forced immediately to look for a campsite and bivouac for the night.

It was another cold one. I was getting too far north and too late in the season to be camping without a sleeping bag. Wearing all my clothes, and wrapped in my fly and poncho I could just about get to sleep, but I kept waking up with one part or another of me chilled. I was fortunate that it wasn't as cold as it had been the night before. I was up very early and boiling up a hot bowl of instant noodles, but these days I was having trouble eating them. Between sunburn and the dry wind, my lips had peeled and cracked to the point where drinking the hot salty broth was an intensely painful experience.

As I got started and the sun came up, I realized that I'd crossed into a new valley, which was narrow, but much deeper than those I'd been following over the past few days. It ran east-west, so I'd be crossing it directly rather than following it all morning. All through the descent I studied the steep northern slope looking for a trail, but I couldn't see anything promising.

At the village in the bottom I asked directions and was lucky to find a young woman who was just leaving for some fields of sunflowers that she tended high on the north slope. Without her I would never have found the way. The trail was very small, and the ground was so stony that the track was often invisible. When she reached her crop she sent me on with some directions, which I only partially understood, but the rest of my climb proved to involve climbing a rocky outcrop, then following a knife-edged ridge eastward to the point where a tiny trail plunged over the other side. It was clearly a route not often followed.

The other side was less stony, so I could follow the trail over the ground without much difficulty. But with more soil the thorn bushes had taken over and the trail was badly choked. The bushes themselves were tough and springy, and their thorns were needles up to 3cm long. The descent was a slow and painful business.

I finally emerged into clearer country where someone had been keeping goats. Goats have a remarkable ability to clear a trail through gravelly ground. There must be something about the shape of their hooves that naturally tends to push stones aside leaving a bare dirt trail. The goat tracks made much nicer walking until they eventually brought me down to the first village.

There weren't many people around. I asked directions of the only person I saw: a teenage boy herding goats. "Excuse me. Sorry to trouble you. Is this Lan Ma?"

"It is."

"I'm going to Gu Sian. Is this the way?" He shook his head.

"Which road is to Gu Sian?" I asked.

He pointed down a track which appeared to be heading west. I knew from the map that Gu Sian was north, but with only the kid's instructions to go on, I set off down the track. It was a classic mistake. The kid himself had probably never been to Gu Sian, though it was only 20km away. When the kid's father wanted to go to Gu Sian he no doubt headed off westward on the family tractor, because the track the kid had indicated was in fact the way to the highway. These days, no one in Lan Ma walks across the hills to Gu Sian. The kid never imagined that was my intention. My mistake wasn't discovered until hours later when I finally met someone else

I could ask. By then I'd almost reached the town of Bai Wen on the main highway. Fortunately, I didn't have to retrace my steps all the way back to Lan Ma. There was a trail directly across country to Gu Sian, but the guy warned me I was in for seven big climbs and seven big descents before I got there.

Well, he wasn't lying. The stony country was gone and I was back in the dusty badlands I'd left a couple of weeks before southeast of the Li. As before, the views were inspiring. The top of the loess layer was a sort of rolling prairie, but all the settlements were down in the eroded ravines. Previously the trails had twisted and turned to stay on top of the dust layer and avoid the ravines, but around here that wasn't the way. The next few days were pretty strenuous.

Years ago, I'd read in the Boy Scout manual that, "Cold winds blow down desert canyons at night." That was in Canada, and it seemed like pretty useless information at the time, but I'd always remembered it. Now, at last, it came in handy. The ravine bottoms were the only places with water, and it was sometimes possible to find stretches between villages where it was possible to camp out of sight of the trail. When I did, it was important to find a bend, or a jutting shoulder, or to camp in a smaller tributary ravine. Because about half an hour after sundown the cold air would begin flowing down the canyon and the chill breeze would continue until morning. During the summer it would have been refreshing and help to control the mosquitoes, but the season was getting on. With my meagre equipment the breeze was now a problem to be solved each evening.

It was good to be back in the badlands with their expansive scenery. There was very little cultivation up on the tops, just a few fields of sunflowers. I could walk all day and meet hardly a soul. But after a few days of this I found myself one day following a ravine heading northwest that gradually grew larger and deeper. Geologically, it was the same story I'd seen before: a thick layer of loess dust over mudstone and then coal-bearing shale underneath. Following the same stream bed all afternoon took me through the whole series, until I finally came to a couple of amateur coal mines and the stream I'd been following joined a major river midway between the twin industrial cities of Xing Xian and Ngau Jia Ta.

What a mess. In both directions up and down the river I could see the belching stacks of coking plants and cement factories. The riverbed was choked with silt, and the river itself had a slimy look. A busy highway ran along the far bank about 800m from where I stood, and I could hear the steady clamour of horns and the squeak of air brakes.

Ideally I'd like to cross the river in the early morning hours when traffic on the highway would be sparse, but it was too early in the day to camp. The best I could do was try to cut directly across the river and highway and plunge into the barren hills beyond before turning north again. My map showed a tributary stream flowing in on the far bank. It would undoubtedly have cut a ravine, which would shelter some fields and villages, and they'd be served by a trail. The only problem was to choose the proper ravine. The cartography was so indistinct that it wasn't clear if I should search for the tributary up or downstream. I chose up.

Amid the other industrial decrepitude was some sort of disused water control system along the near bank. I was able to follow some old retaining walls as I searched for a place to cross. After a kilometre or so I found what I was looking for. Someone had strung a water pipe across the river, a span of several hundred metres. Rather than burying the pipe in the riverbed, they'd erected towers on each bank and strung a cable across, then hung the pipe span off the cable for support. With nerve, you could walk across on the pipe while holding on to the cable. It clearly wasn't designed for that treatment, but muddy footprints showed that it had been done before and, as far as I could tell by tapping on it, the pipe was now empty. Despite the knapsack, I figured it would hold me. In the last analysis, the crossing wasn't that difficult. It's just that the span was several metres off the ground and, except in midstream, the water wasn't very deep. If the contraption gave way, you wouldn't drown, but you could well break something. I was glad to jump down at the first opportunity.

I followed the west bank as far as the first tributary, then climbed up onto the highway to ask directions. It was a maelstrom of trucks, tractors, pedestrians and dust. Worse, I'd left the riverbed too early. I was still a couple of kilometres south of the valley I was seeking. This was certainly closed territory. I could only put my head down and walk off the distance as quickly as possible, hoping the police didn't happen by.

When I found it, the valley proved to be almost as bad as following the highway. It had been converted into a giant quarry feeding the cement plants. Crushed carbonate rock everywhere: under foot, in the air and in a steady stream of passing trucks and tractor wagons. And the din! I spent a painful hour making my escape. Finally, the road narrowed to a trail along the bottom of a narrow ravine by a clean-looking brook. I was able to find a quiet place to camp and recover from a traumatic afternoon.

The next day, by contrast, I spent in deserted moorland reminiscent of the highlands of Scotland. I had a stroke of luck early. I was wandering up a meandering ravine when I ran into a fellow herding a couple of goats. I was pretty sure of my way, but just for drill, asked directions to the next place shown on my map. To my surprise, he pointed to an almost imperceptible track heading up the wall of the ravine just a few metres from where we stood. I had intended to follow the ravine bottom all the way, but he assured me that the main trail cut directly north over the tops, and if I climbed that little path I'd easily find it.

Well, he wasn't kidding. I spent the rest of the day following the high road to the north. In that time I met only one other party of three men who reassured me that I was on the right road, but I was getting reassurance enough from my compass. The wide, clear but little-used trail headed steadily due north. It made me think of the Roman roads found in Britain, and perhaps there was a certain relation, as I was now approaching the Great Wall. It's easy to believe that this forgotten trail might have been laid out hundreds of years ago, before the days of quarries and cement plants, to re-supply the Great Wall garrisons from Xing Xian.

It was late afternoon before I came to another major valley barring my path. As the trail began gradually to descend, I took a wrong turn on a branch, which appeared to follow a spur down from the heights. I followed it down 15 minutes or so before it petered out in impenetrable thorny scrub. But out on the end of the spur I found an empty shrine assembled by piling rectangular flags of limestone. I sat for a moment before climbing back to the skyline, trying to imagine what was going on. The dead-end trail had apparently been made by goatherds and their flocks coming down off the top to graze among the thorn bushes. A goatherd would have nothing to do all day in this lonely spot, so one of them spent the time piling up slabs of limestone. He could have piled them up to form a shelter, but he chose to build a shrine instead, even though the shrine was too small to shelter him on a rainy day.

Even though he had no idol to consecrate his construction. Did he perhaps feel he was building another kind of shelter for a spiritual rainy day? Or was he just building sand castles at the beach – doodling without a pencil? It's hard to imagine.

I eventually found the correct trail down. Indeed, it was a glorious descent. The dip and strike of the limestone was such that it made a natural set of stairs with risers about 50cm high and treads about 15m wide. The smooth, bare rock let me concentrate on the scenery. The brook formed clear pools that were perfect for a bath after an exhilarating day's walking.

Just at dusk I came to the mouth of the valley and stopped for provisions at a wayside shop. While I was there it began to rain, and the proprietor invited me in for a bowl of noodles. The noodles were good, but I didn't realize what I had let myself in for.

It turned out that there was a school nearby, and once the word got out, we were swamped in a tidal wave of curious young faces. First they pressed at the window, then they began seeping in the door, and flooding in, and packing in, until there wasn't space for any of us to so much as turn around. I tried to continue eating my noodles while amiably answering questions between bites. Then, an organized group of older kids showed up, chased out most of the young ones and took up the interrogation in earnest. It turned out they were the English class.

I was surprised that the storekeeper and his wife put up with all this, even though the children must be their main customers. Later, a bugle call over the school PA system called all the kids back for bed, and I was able to discover that the shopkeeper was actually a teacher, and his wife ran this shop on the side. Their name was Zhou, and once things had settled down they took me over to the school for a more relaxed session in the teachers' room and arranged for me to spend the night. There were two English teachers who were just as anxious as the students to get in some practice, but I didn't mind. For me it was almost a new experience doing the catechism in English for a change.

Mr. Zhou is a secondary school teacher – in what the Chinese call a middle school. This particular institution wasn't surrounded by walls, but housed in three buildings forming three sides of a square about 30m on a side. The central building was three storeys high and contained the classrooms. The boarding students lived in another three-storey building with the school offices on the ground floor. Facing them across the square, the teachers lived in a one-storey row of cave-style housing units. I say cave-style because these dwellings weren't actually excavated from any hillside, but were constructed of brick in the tunnel shape of cave dwellings.

Mr. Zhou, his wife and two children occupy two adjoining units with an interior connecting door. Each chamber is 5m wide, 10m deep and 5m high at the centre of the arch. Each unit has its own door opening into the central square. The rest of that end of both rooms is mostly windows – the lower panes glazed and the rest covered with translucent paper. Other than this, each room is lighted by two fluorescent tubes hanging from the ceiling. But the power is unreliable. One room contains a double bed next to the door, but is largely given over to use as their kitchen. The other contains a couple of armchairs, a treadle sewing machine, a wardrobe, a couple of small tables against the walls and various boxes containing their possessions. The main feature of this room is the *kang*. The teachers share a communal toilet and bathhouse at the end of the row of housing units. These rooms were certainly much larger and better constructed than Mr. Chan's school quarters that I'd visited back in Hunan, but the overall standard of living seemed much the same. Teachers are universally acknowledged to be China's most poorly paid intellectuals.

Outside his front doors Mr. Zhou had erected a small fence of brushwood to define a semi-private front yard for his home. Within this he has his own chicken coop with a couple of chickens and a small pile of firewood he has collected in the hills on his day off. (Chinese schools teach six days a week.) Around behind the school is a pig pen where Mr. Zhou has a share in a pig which he and some other teachers are raising to eat during the winter holiday season.

The inside of Mr. Zhou's housing unit is nicely whitewashed, but it lacks decorations. About all Mr. Zhou can boast is a poster featuring that well-known Chinese hero Benjamin Franklin. It was given to him as a gift and now hangs proudly over the *kang*.

This particular poster is quite popular in China and can be found in many homes all over the country. It's supposed to portray happiness and prosperity. The background shows an idealized version of the mountains at Guilin – karst formations in Southern China widely known for their beauty. Around them are the windswept ancient fir trees sometimes seen on famous Chinese mountains and often miniaturized in the West as potted bonsai. Idealized swirling clouds envelop the scene, and down from the clouds descend two fat babies: a girl in a frilly red frock with a red ribbon in her top knot, and a boy with his manhood fully on display (a common pose for Chinese baby boys in family photographs.) These two are descending mounted on the backs of cranes (the storks of European fairy stories.) The girl carries stacks of Chinese 100 yuan notes, the boy stacks of US$100 bills, complete with the friendly smiling face of Benjamin Franklin.

I was most grateful to the Zhous for taking care of me, as it rained heavily overnight. Still, in the morning we were, by Western lights, mutually impolite to each other. For my part, I wasn't really able to do justice to Mrs. Zhou's breakfast. She fed me noodles with potato pieces. That much of it I enjoyed, but the broth was flavoured with salty preserved tomatoes and a dose of chili pepper. My lips were by that time so cracked and sore that I could hardly stand to eat it. I could insert potato pieces into my mouth without touching the lips, but the noodles were more difficult, and the broth quite hopeless. It was a painful breakfast.

While I struggled with it, Mr. Zhou and his colleagues pawed through my knapsack. They had seen me looking at a map before breakfast, and while I was eating they searched around until they found it and pulled it out again for everyone to have a good long look. They no doubt treat the students that way. It was just a clash of cultures. I held my tongue. A round of photos and I was on my way. These people, at least, had no difficulty finding an envelope and inscribing their address in elegant characters.

A gravel road ran outside the school, and I'd been told to follow that downstream for about a kilometre to where I could cross the deep valley at a dam. The dam proved to be a pretty impressive affair, but another sad commentary on communist engineering. The cement structure must have been 300m or so long and about 100m high at the centre. It was a beautiful creation, but apparently part of yet another failed water scheme. I'd seen many an empty dam on my travels, but a dam that big stands empty in a particularly striking way. If I'd found dry reservoirs only in this area, you could blame the drought, or speculate that they'd been built on the basis of insufficient rainfall data. (Though in China even that's a pretty strange excuse given the pride they take in their centuries-long civilization.) But I'd seen empty dams large and small all through the country. It seems more likely that there was some sort of communist-style campaign to build irrigation works, and the engineers felt compelled to build them even in locations they knew were unsuitable. I suppose these white elephants weren't very expensive in cash terms, but they must have tied up a lot of communal labour for a year or two. What a waste.

Once across the dam I was back in scenic and empty country similar to the beautiful walking of the day before. I was on a proper road this time, but there wasn't anyone much about. The road had kilometre stones, and in one stretch I did 25km up hill and down dale without seeing a single vehicle of any kind. From each hilltop there were great views to the west. I was looking down over gradually descending country to the course of my old friend the Yellow River, with the high loess plateau of Shaanxi province on the far horizon. It was beautiful.

Well, it was beautiful in a bleak and windswept sort of way. I was lucky to have good weather. There was no cover apart from the steep eroded ravines. For miles there was hardly a tree. One result was that the little hamlets lacked the medicine shops that had been so common farther south. It reinforced my suspicion that medicine shops thrive when the owners can collect all their traditional herbs for free on the surrounding hillsides. Here they'd have slim pickings. Perhaps also the system of barefoot doctors never got as firmly established in northern Shanxi as it did nearer Mao's birthplace. There weren't as many spare clinics and unemployed medics to found medicine shops when it fell apart.

As luck would have it, after spending all day in solitude I found myself at dusk approaching what the map promised to be a fair sized town. I'd learned by this time not to enter a major centre too late in the day for fear of attracting a parade of curious followers who'd follow until dark and make it difficult to camp. I cast around for a campsite before reaching the populated area and settled at last on a worked-out coal seam. The road was following a stream in the bottom of a ravine, and on both sides were coal seams that had been exploited and then abandoned leaving small shaley caves. I spotted one on the far bank which was partially screened from the road and scrambled across. It wasn't large – about 1.6m high at the entrance and a couple of metres wide. It may have gone fairly deep into the hillside, but I couldn't check because it was flooded after the first few metres. But the sill of crushed shale at the mouth made a smooth and reasonably comfortable campsite that was sheltered from the wind, from radiative cooling during the night, and from the eyes of passers by. I had become an expert at living on the lam.

In the morning I traversed the town at first light. It was just a wide place on a major east-west highway, but disfigured by the usual coking works, a cement plant and a couple of factories that built giant Ali Baba earthenware jars. The highway obviously carried a lot of coal truck traffic during the day, but I avoided the worst of it at that hour and was even able to find a shop just opening for business where I could replenish my supplies.

You may recall that we crossed the Yellow River weeks ago, just after our release from detention in Luoyang. How did it get back into the story at this late date? In fact, the Yellow is one of the world's major rivers, 5,000 kilometres long. Its course runs basically west to east, but in north central China it makes a loop to the north and back south again for several hundred kilometres. During its run south it forms the western boundary of Shanxi province (dividing it from Shaanxi farther west). As I made my way north I had all along been gradually edging west and obliquely approaching· this boundary. Now I could see the deep river valley off to the west, eroded down through the loess and deeper through quite a bit of bedrock as well. As I headed north I was continually crossing tributaries which, this close to joining the Yellow, had eroded very deeply into the loess layer. The ravines I was crossing were getting so deep that climbing down was taking the better part of an hour of switchbacks and stairs, and climbing up was even worse. I'd do six or seven of these climbs in a day, so basically I was almost always struggling either up or down. They were exhausting days.

Ice cream freezers around here were nothing more than a dream from the past. In their absence the little wayside shops hadn't much in the line of snack food, and I rarely had any opportunity for a snack along my way. But one day I came across a lady in one of the little ravine villages selling what she described as *woh te*. She was carrying a metal basin covered with a cloth which she pulled back to reveal a large slab of relatively firm bean curd. On the other end of her carrying pole was a bucket of water containing a couple of small metal plates about the size of Western saucers. To serve a portion, she'd cut a chunk off the block of bean curd and serve it in a plate covered in a clear sauce. One bite identified the sauce as raw garlic mashed up in vegetable oil. It made a most unusual refresher. I had seconds. They were only 80 fen a serving.

Otherwise, I was getting pears and walnuts to eat, given to me in each case by people I'd met by asking directions. It was one of those situations where the local products were delicious but you couldn't buy them in the local shops because everyone had his own private supply. A nice exception was one afternoon when I greeted a couple of little girls in passing, and a few minutes later found them running after me. They'd been playing around some bushes with berries growing and had collected a few handfuls especially for me. I suppose I was risking pretty serious disease eating unwashed fruit from the hands of country kids, but the occasion seemed to demand it. The berries were some sort of current or choke cherry – sour, but refreshing after a day in the harness.

As I got within a day or so of the Great Wall, I can honestly say that even after almost three months on the road I was still looking forward to every day's adventures. I was in no sense anxious to get it over with, but I was starting to feel some pressure. I was afraid particularly of getting picked up by the police within sight of the goal. What a disappointment that would be after coming so close to walking across China. Then there was the weather. After a clear night, I'd awake to find frost on the inside of the tarp wrapped around me. I couldn't continue much longer without a sleeping bag. Finally, my map supply was really running dry. My next province was Inner Mongolia, and I hadn't been able to find any map at all for sale. I'd be reduced to navigating with a 1:1.5million map of all North China.

China is rather pathetically keen on state secrets. The bookstores carry a whole category of publications that are classified as "internal" – they're for sale to Chinese only, not to foreigners. Most maps, unfortunately, are in this category. A few years ago, it was difficult to buy a map any more detailed than a map of the whole country. These days any bookshop, and many newsvendors in the cities, will sell you a pocket road atlas showing the major highways in all the provinces and rough street maps of the cities. Most major cities also have some sort of detailed street map generally available. This has broken the ice. Booksellers are familiar with the internal document system and will normally refuse to sell a provincial map to a foreigner, but it's a bit like the closed area system. It would never occur to ordinary citizens that provincial maps might be secret. They'll normally do their best to shop around and help you buy one. It often takes a fair bit of shopping though, because, as with everything in China, distribution is a bit erratic and things are often out of stock.

Invaluable to the visitor in their own right, maps are also a real conversation piece in the countryside. When they're for sale, it's invariably only in the cities. Most rural people have never seen a map that shows their local area in detail. Almost anyone who can read will eagerly pore over your map reading off the names of all the nearby villages and pointing off up various valleys indicating the general direction to each place named.

You might occasionally run into someone who asks how you, a foreigner, were able to get your hands on such an interesting map. I usually lied that I'd bought it in a bookstore in Hong Kong. You should never, of course, reveal the name of anyone who helped you buy one in China. It's also a situation where jokes about borrowing it from the CIA library might not go down well.

My Shanxi map showed a line of U-shaped symbols, unmentioned in the legend, which I took to represent the Great Wall cutting across the extreme north of the province. As I approached their location, three difficulties converged. I was approaching the Yellow River, and my map showed a major highway along the near bank. The only crossings shown were bridges in major towns – important bridges, which in China might well be guarded by police sentries. Across the river was Inner Mongolia, for which I had no map. What to do? At the very least I was going to have to follow the highway a few kilometres up or downstream in search of a ferry.

I had plenty of time to consider my approach, and eventually decided to make an early camp in the hills above the town of Liu Jia Ta and try to hit the highway at dawn before the police started their patrols. That had the added advantage of giving me ample opportunity to find a cave to sleep in, as sleeping in the open was getting to be a very chilly proposition.

I got moving at 4:45 on the big day, about an hour before first light. I fumbled my way down to a gravel road where, even in the dark, I was able to stride along fast enough to keep warm. The town had exactly one bulb burning at that hour, so I can't tell you much about it. It had a big factory, though. I could tell because it made a steady roaring noise like... Wait a minute. That's the river. As the sky began to lighten I suddenly realized that it was no factory. I'd been listening to the roar of the Yellow River – the same fierce current I'd heard when I crossed it near Luoyang weeks before. It was on my right, so I'd missed the highway junction in the dark and was heading south. I retraced my steps, and by the time I came to the junction I could see that the gravel road I was following was much wider than the one I'd been on originally. But in the pitch dark they'd just merged together and taken me south.

The wall was there too. Though along that stretch it was difficult to see why they'd needed a wall at all. The river ran in a giant gorge with sheer shaley cliffs on both sides. The current was a maelstrom of rapids and whirlpools. Crossing it at all would be a good trick for any Mongolian invader, much less trying to scale the cliffs against a defending force.

The Great Wall was originally assembled in the 3rd century BC by connecting some older, more limited fortifications. After a long period of warfare, one feudal king had just defeated all his rivals and declared himself emperor. His own kingdom was the most westerly of the lot, with its capital near the present-day Xian, so his was one of the principalities most exposed to Mongolian incursions. Even while fighting among themselves, he and the rulers of the two other northern states had built defensive parapets along their northern borders designed to slow down horse-borne invaders. After assuming control, the emperor took steps to link up these defensive works into a continuous wall. This stretch along here was presumably the strongest and best defended, as this is the stretch nearest Xian. I don't suppose the original looked much like the reconstruction now visited by tourists to Beijing, but even on the basis of what remains today, it must have been an impressive structure.

Indeed, the wall along that stretch seems to have consisted of a series of watchtowers like the one shown in photo number 32, one on each promontory along the east bank. There may have been some sort of wall structure connecting them, but it was long gone. The stone had been pirated, perhaps for building houses, and the land returned to cultivation. The towers themselves had been reduced to piles of adobe. Big, though – at least 10m tall and maybe 3m in diameter. It was surprising there was so many of them still standing. With the stone facing stolen, they must dissolve pretty steadily in the rain. I knew from experience that it wasn't a very rainy part of the country, but even so you'd suppose that they must once have been much bigger.

The impassable gorge put paid to any hopes of quickly finding a ferry. In any case, I was advised that the best trail north was on the east bank. So I was faced with a couple of hours on the dusty and dangerous highway.

Along the way were a couple of tower ruins, and it seemed likely that if I were to explore the fields I might be able to find indications of any interconnecting wall or ditch structure. I was torn between the desire to take a couple of hours to thoroughly explore the ruins and the need to get off the highway before morning traffic, particularly official traffic, had a chance to arrive from the nearest city. In the end, I decided that the ruins were probably best appreciated from a distance. In the course of stripping off the stone facing, the vandals would certainly have had time and equipment to destroy or carry off anything else of interest, I could already see, even from a distance, that the farmers had dug shelter caves in the base of the adobe towers for their afternoon naps. Closer scrutiny would probably reveal a litter of cigarette butts and perhaps the odd broken bottle. It would only spoil the effect. So I stuck to the road and took in the panorama of ruins, gorge and sky instead, imagining the life of the conscripted soldiers who manned this outpost of the empire twenty centuries ago. Even hurrying along, the view evolved only slowly in these vast open spaces. I had ample time for contemplation.

My early start didn't do any harm, but I still felt myself lucky to get through my stint on the highway successfully. The highway veered east away from the river at the town of Gwan He Kou, so my map assured me. In the event, the town proved to be at the bottom of a deep tributary gorge, while the highway stayed up on the rim. A trail wound back and forth down the steep ravine wall, and the town taxi consisted of a man with a donkey. The patron climbed on foot, but the donkey would carry his gear up to the bus stop on the highway. I met them on my way down.

The town itself was built all in stone. The gorge was shale and mudstone, very easy to quarry and build with. It was probably the farmers up above who'd stripped the Great Wall for building stone. It was probably the ancestors of these townies who'd built it. I crossed the tributary stream on an impressive arched stone bridge and set off up the main gorge of the Yellow River on the narrow edge of an irrigation canal cut into the side of a cliff. It was slow going, as it was a long drop into the river if you missed your footing.

The trail quickly improved, and I was delighted to find myself in more scenic, solitary walking, now beyond the pale of ancient China in the barbarian lands beyond the Great Wall. In most places there was a bit of meadow at the base of the cliffs. In the morning I had continuous shade. And from time to time I was able to find springs of what was likely to be reasonably clean water seeping directly from the wall of the gorge. The river was a kilometre or so wide and the cliffs were a couple of hundred metres tall, so it was spectacular walking. The river roared steadily by my side. No boats, though. The current was far too swift and, at this season, too shallow as well.

I hadn't gone very far when I saw on the rim far above me the remains of an extensive stone fort. It must have been the main garrison at the point where the Great Wall first reached the river after its long run over the mountains from the Pacific. That fort had once been the northwest corner of the empire. It was hard to see much of it from below, but even from that vantage point it was obvious that it had once been large and elaborate. I would have liked to explore it but, built to defend the gorge, it had no obvious way up.

My trail up the riverbank must surely have been a traditional route. But there was little sign of it, probably because the river floods every year and washes away any traces. There were the remains of a few old farms along the river, but they were now abandoned. The Chinese aren't fond of isolated farmsteads. They depend in life on the aid of clansmen and the spirits of their ancestors. As I walked the mud banks along the river, I saw only a few footprints made since the last high water. I'd been through sparsely populated areas, but here was a stretch where I was truly alone. If I broke an ankle, no one would come along to help. I took it easy and spent some time cogitating on the Great Wall and on China.

In the late afternoon I unexpectedly came upon a shiny new bridge across the river. I had no reason to be surprised, of course, as I was now navigating without a map. Still, I'd been expecting days of solitude. The bridge was finished, but the long ramps down the cliffs were still under construction, so I may well have been its first user apart from the construction crews.

I asked several workers for advice, but I got little joy. They spoke some kind of Mongolian dialect, and in any case weren't from the local area. In the end I decided to cross, only because the river was said to swing to the west farther upstream and on the far bank I'd be able to cut off the bend. With the road still being blasted, I climbed the cliff on the west bank with the aid of a risky little goat track. It was a bit exposed, but the view was great.

17

In from the Cold

It was already late afternoon by the time I reached the cliff top. From there, my first night in Inner Mongolia didn't go as well as I might have hoped.

It began when I at last ran into someone from the local area – the first I'd seen since Gwan He Kou early that morning. He was an old man herding goats. Conversation was difficult, but I understood him to say that he brought his goats out to this bleak cliff top at 6 a.m., sat with them all day and returned home at about 8 p.m. He set me on my way, and as I wandered off I wondered to myself what he could do out here all that time. The view out over the gorge was vast and inspiring, but not inspirational enough to inspire 14 hours of cogitating every day for a lifetime. I suppose that great minds would relish the quiet and solitude and take the opportunity to think great thoughts, but the old goatherd didn't look like much of an Einstein to me. It must be quite a life.

There wasn't much cultivation on the Mongolian bank of the river. It was probably a consequence of a lack of water. The grasslands were broken by little limestone ledges poking out here and there. You could perhaps quarry them for building stone, but the population was so sparse that there wouldn't be much of a demand. It seemed that feeding grass to goats was about as high tech as it gets in that neck of the woods.

But not long after leaving the old man I came to the remains of a brick works. Production had ceased, and the bricks used to line the beehive underground kiln were gradually being salvaged for building purposes elsewhere. About all that was left of the site was a one-room adobe hut. That immediately attracted my attention, as with the cooler weather and my lack of equipment I was always in need of sheltered places to spend the night. The trail at that point was nothing more than a path, almost untravelled. It was a bit early, but I decided to boil up some noodles sheltered by the remains of the kiln and stake out the hut as a place to spend the night.

All seemed well as I prepared a leisurely supper and enjoyed the view. At dusk I still hadn't seen a soul, so I moved into the decrepit hut and spread out my gear for a sheltered night. I had just about settled in and was drifting off to sleep when the old goatherd turned up. He didn't live there, it was just that he'd been watching me out of curiosity, and seeing that I was settling down for the night he'd come over to invite me to visit his village. It was a nice gesture. I appreciated it. I would have taken him up if I hadn't already been in bed and on the verge of dropping off. As it was, I sat up and conversed with him for a while, but ended up by gratefully declining his invitation.

Sadly, that wasn't the end of the story. I can imagine him returning home and recounting to his family the strange tale of the foreigner camping at the old brickworks. Somewhat later I was awakened by someone politely clearing his throat in the doorway. It was the old man, back with what was probably his son, daughter-in-law and two children. The younger man spoke much better Mandarin and, after waking me from a sound sleep, was able to take me through much of the catechism before I finally convinced him that, much as I appreciated his offers of hospitality, I was quite comfortable where I was and didn't want to trouble him.

The third bunch brought a flashlight...

I eventually got to sleep, but not until most everyone in the nearest village had seen the foreigner and heard the usual questions answered. It was only the second time that one of my campsites had been discovered. On the other occasion I'd taken the trouble to pack up quickly and shift my camp as soon as the original discoverer had gone to rouse his friends. I knew now that on that previous occasion I'd made the right choice. Live and learn. I just hope the Mongolians weren't too offended by my continuing refusal to accept their hospitality.

Having snubbed the villagers once, I certainly didn't want to impose on them for breakfast. The country thereabouts looked as poor as any I'd seen. I packed up early and hit the trail. With no map and no landmarks, I was really just mushing across the grasslands following the needle of my compass. There were very few farms or villages anywhere to be seen, probably for lack of water. As I headed north I had to take every opportunity to fill my bottles.

At one point I came across a beautiful sand dune. It was a little outpost of the Gobi desert borne on the wind and deposited in the lee of a ravine. I was vaguely aware that somewhere to the north, China has carried out one of the world's most successful desert stabilization programs. They've planted a belt of evergreens a kilometre or so wide and hundreds or even thousands of kilometres long, which breaks the wind like a snow fence and prevents the desert sand from encroaching on the grasslands to the Southeast. I'd almost forgotten about it until I saw the sand dune, and indeed I'd only read about it in the context of a disease that had been attacking the pine trees and threatening the success of the scheme. Thus reminded, I was looking forward to seeing this engineering marvel, but I never did. Before reaching it I rejoined the river after its bend and descended again into the gorge. Down there I must have passed through the tree belt without ever knowing it.

I hadn't really much choice. At a scale of 1:1.5 million, my map showed me the course of the Yellow River, the main cities and not much more. I could wander around in the grasslands following my compass, but if I strayed back into a land of hills and impassable ravines, I'd be doomed without nearby towns to ask for. I couldn't ask a goatherd the way to a city a week distant. I was able to learn, however, that a trail followed the bottom of the Yellow River gorge all the way north to the city of Tog Toh. From there, my map showed a tributary which I should be able to follow northeast to Hohhot, the capital of Inner Mongolia. That would have to be the end of my trip. North of Hohhot I'd be approaching the national frontier where most people would be aware that I wasn't allowed. If they found me near the border I shouldn't be surprised to find myself serving a jail term. I settled on Hohhot as my destination.

In the navy they talk about "homebound revs". Mysteriously, the engineer somehow always seems able to crank a few extra rpm out of the ship's engines when it's homeward bound. Now that I'd reached the last fold of the last map, I expected to feel a similar sensation – an anxiety to finish up and get back to Hong Kong and humdrum routine. Surprisingly, it didn't work that way, perhaps because the Yellow River gorge provided some of the most scenic walking of the whole trip. It was getting cold at night, but after 3 months in harness I was still savouring every day.

In the days of horses the trail up the gorge must have been a major transportation artery. These days everyone travels by bus and they've let it deteriorate. The surface was rough and stony, washed out in places by the floods. But many of the tributary streams were bridged by substantial old stone bridges, and as I got farther north I came across crews rebuilding some of them, though these days they had to pack in the cement on their backs.

On the other hand, there were places where the trail cut across gravel bars in the bends of the river, and there the annual floods obliterated all trace of the route from year to year. I sometimes had a few footprints to follow, but for the most part it was just a question of following the river until the trail appeared again. In the bottom of a gorge you couldn't go far wrong.

Or so I thought, until one sunny noon hour when I realized that I'd been dicing with death for days and never known it. I had been following a mud bar along the river's edge and was just cutting across a little trickle of a tributary when the apparently firm silt beneath my feet gave way and I found myself rapidly sinking above the knees. It was quicksand.

I'd never seen quicksand before. I'd read about it, including something about how your partner was supposed to pull you out by extending a branch or throwing you a rope. No joy there. I shrugged off my pack. I couldn't really throw it to safety, but I sort of heaved it backward and it landed on the firmer margin of the mud bar I'd just left. That made it the only firm handhold in sight. Without really thinking about it, I reflexively twisted and threw myself backward, grabbed the pack and used it as a handhold to pull myself out of the silt.

I'd never felt the bottom. If I'd gone in any deeper I might have had considerable difficulty getting myself out again. If the surface had been a bit firmer I might have gotten too far from the shore before realizing I was in trouble. Thinking about it left me a bit shaken, considering especially how many mud bars I'd crossed during the last few days completely unaware of the danger. I was now covered with mud and inclined to go for a wade in the river, except for the thought that there might be more trouble waiting out there beneath the rolling brown waters. I waited and did my washing in a rockier place farther on.

Along the banks of the river I visited my last peasant home. It came about because late one afternoon I came upon one of the bridge repair crews just as they were washing up to head home. After a chat we set out together for a long walk that developed into a rabbit hunt. As I was to discover, the workers don't get much meat in their rations, so when they spotted a rabbit they were dead keen to catch it for the pot. It looked like a mug's game to me. Their only weapons were their shovels and all the stones lying about. But they spread out and with great enthusiasm tried to encircle the creature and run it down. It would be a pretty decrepit rabbit who couldn't outrun a pack of humans in flip-flop sandals over rough stones, and of course it got away. But the workers gave a pretty good try. Obviously they played this game often, perhaps with this same rabbit. Ah, well. We were a group of about a dozen. One rabbit wouldn't have provided much meat to go around.

After almost an hour's walk, the gang of us at last trooped into the courtyard of an old man who lived by himself down in the gorge. He had a four-room stone house, a set of outbuildings including a stable and a pigsty, the whole setup enclosed in a stone wall to form a courtyard. The workers had been detailed from a nearby village to put in some work upgrading the track through the gorge, and it had been arranged that they would board for the duration with the old man. It was the ancient *corvée* system, still alive and well.

When we arrived, dinner was already on the table. It consisted of steamed buns and potatoes, which had been boiled up with a little bit of pork fat and some spices to make a sort of gravy. In fact, it was tasty enough, and it certainly filled you up. But it wasn't exactly a balanced diet. With only starch to look forward to, I could understand why they were so keen to catch that rabbit.

There were only a couple in the gang who could really converse comfortably in Mandarin, so I'd spent most of my time on the walk home chatting with them. But after dinner the old man decided that my visit called for some special hospitality, and he invited me into the room he'd reserved for himself where he broke out a bottle of rice liquor and a couple of heads of garlic. Although we could converse only in sign language, we hit it off pretty well and spent the evening drinking liquor and eating cloves of raw garlic. I believe snacking on raw garlic is a popular custom among the Slavs, but that was the first time I'd seen it in China. It certainly left a funny taste in your mouth the next morning.

For breakfast, the crew got millet gruel, but the old man broke into his stash of instant noodles in my honour. It was very nice of him, although the gruel would have been easier on my cracked lips. After breakfast we posed for a few snaps, and I was on my way. The crew headed back downriver to their work site and the old man was again left alone with his animals.

Over the next few days the story of the gorge trail began to fall into place. I encountered first a new power station, then a new rail bridge, then a highway bridge. Around these points of access the gorge track had been upgraded, and crews were busy quarrying the walls of the gorge for building stone. Apparently the whole industry had once been concentrated in the hands of one or two state work units who mined only at a few selected places. Now the business had opened up, and villages all up and down the river were exploiting whichever stone deposits they could reach. When production was limited to a few selected spots, the rest of the gorge track had been allowed to fall into disrepair, but now, with the river un-navigable, villages wanting to get into the stone business were obliged to repair the road to get their product out. Too bad for me, as the gorge gradually degenerated into a long series of noisy and dusty quarries. Fortunately, production was slow enough that there wasn't much product being hauled out along the road except over a very few limited stretches. Despite all the activity, I met relatively few people. Everyone was working up on the cliffs, and as I passed all they could do was wave.

I would have enjoyed having a look at the power station, but unfortunately there was no way I could get across to the other bank. There was no dam. It was a flow-through design that simply tapped a portion of the rushing current to turn some generators. It looked very new. It would have been interesting to see how they kept the tremendous silt load from clogging up the works. If they had tried to build a dam it would have silted up in no time.

A few days of rock dust and falling boulders and I was ready to bid good-by to the Yellow River at the first opportunity. I was looking for a quiet rural route into the capital Hohhot, but my lousy map made asking directions difficult. I had no names of small towns near the river that I could ask about. Inquire about going to Hohhot, and everyone would immediately suggest I take the bus. Finally I found a couple of people who were willing to agree that a small river flowed from Hohhot down to join the Yellow just south of the city of Tog Toh. In the event, the river proved to be almost dry in the fall and divided into several braided channels, but it was ideal in that it cut across the windy, open grassland and had small levees with walking trails along the banks. I was walking blind, but after a couple of days with a strong wind at my back I came rather suddenly to the outskirts of the provincial capital.

I'd visited several of the capital cities of China's provinces, but it immediately struck me that Hohhot must be one of the smallest. In the course of two hours I passed from open fields by the banks of the stagnant stream to the noise and traffic of the city. After being stared at for months, in the course of fifteen minutes I passed into a world frequented by Western tourists where no one paid me any special attention. For a couple of days I'd been dreaming of checking in at a tourist hotel, having a hot shower and enjoying a buffet breakfast Western style. I had been worrying, in fact, about whether or not such a hotel would accept someone gaunt, sunburned and dressed in rags. Maybe if I stood right up close to the counter...

But when I finally climbed up from the stream bank onto the city streets, the first thought that struck me was a rather different one. I suddenly realized that in finding a hotel I had a whole new resource at my disposal. There, on the corner, was a man in police uniform. I smiled and wandered over.

Appendix

So You'd Like to Try It

I hope you've come away from this tale convinced that China is one of the world's great undiscovered walking destinations. It has beautiful scenery, a network of well-graded walking paths and friendly inhabitants who have never in their lives seen a foreign face and are prepared to make you welcome. At the same time, the country folk remain so poor that for most of them your few yuan spent for beer and noodles make a real contribution to their local economy. If you enjoy walking, these are all good reasons why you should give it a try.

Of course there are obstacles. For most people it's a long way to go. The walking may be cheap, but the plane ticket to get there is not. The maps are not much good. The language isn't something you can pick up as you go along. But many of the other obstacles are probably not as difficult as you would at first imagine. Let me suggest a few simplifying expedients.

You're not likely to have three and a half months' leisure to walk across the country as I did. Most people can set off for just a couple of weeks during their annual vacation. In this situation it's probably best to plan on confining your trip to the southern provinces of Guangdong and Fujian. There are three reasons for this. In the first place, they're easy to get to from Hong Kong, and Hong Kong remains the most convenient gateway to China. Secondly, it has been officially announced that all areas of these two provinces are open to foreigners. That means you have no need to avoid the police, and there's no danger that you'll spend a couple of days of your holiday at the police station under investigation. Since you're legal, if you want to get out of the rain with a night in a hotel you're free to try. (Though for other reasons most Chinese hotels refuse to take foreigners.) Finally, marginally useful maps of Guangdong province are available in Hong Kong. Anyone coming from abroad should be able to find months of enthralling walking in Guangdong and Fujian provinces alone. Going farther inland involves a major leap in difficulty. Save it for a second trip.

If you're starting in Hong Kong, you'll have no problem getting there, but finding an affordable place to stay can be a challenge. Most of the cheap places limit themselves to people who can speak some sort of Chinese. If you don't, invest in a membership in the Youth Hostels Association before you leave your home country. There are several youth hostels in Hong Kong. The most popular with China travellers is the one at Mount Davis. Apart from being cheap, this is an excellent place to speak with people who have just come from China and have all the latest information. The Hong Kong hostels are often booked up, especially on weekends, but the Youth Hostels Association has a fairly complicated international reservations system. Use it and save yourself anxiety after a long flight.

If you're not a Youth Hostel member and don't speak Chinese, the conventional accommodation is the famous Chungking Mansions at the corner of Nathan and Peking roads in the Tsimshatsui district. Always an experience.

The Chinese say they encourage tourism, but they haven't gone so far as to ease their visa requirements. They still demand visas of almost all visitors. With the right letters of introduction it's possible to get a multiple entry visa valid for several months, but the standard visa is good for just a single visit of 30 days. Toward the end of the 30-day period the police in the major cities are quite cooperative about extending this (once only) to give a total stay of 60 days. But it requires a trip to the city. The local police in the country areas can't do the extension for you.

China has embassies and consulates all around the world which issue these visas. In principle, that should allow the well-organized traveller to apply by mail from the comfort of his own home. In practice, the overseas visa offices tend to enforce all sorts of obscure regulations that call for extra documentation. If they find out that you've ever been a journalist, for example, or that you've spent a lot of time in Taiwan, they may begin asking lots of silly questions. The way around this is to apply in Hong Kong where the visa office provides same-day service and rarely causes any trouble over standard tourist visas.

Right on the corner of Gloucester and Fleming Roads in the heart of town there's a small door in the wall of a massive monolith marked with an inconspicuous brass plate "Visa Office of People's Republic of China." Bring them your passport and a photo, fill out a form and you can pick up your visa the next day. The form asks you your destination and the purpose of your trip. Don't challenge them with anything unconventional. Just put "tourism" and list some common destinations around Guangdong province. Guangzhou and the Seven Star Crags will do. The usual visa is good for one entry, but you can ask for two entries for a bit more money. On each entry you're allowed to stay 30 days – enough walking for most enthusiasts.

While waiting for your visa, buy and study some maps. There are a variety of Guangdong maps available in Hong Kong bookstores, and you'll probably want copies of most of them. Some are only in Chinese, others in English, others in both. None will impress you in terms of either scale or cartography. About all you can hope for is that by referring to several simultaneously you'll be able to work out an interesting route. Don't be tempted by maps of Shenzhen and the Pearl River Delta. At first they look attractive, because these maps offer greater detail than maps of the entire province. Unfortunately, Shenzhen and the Pearl Delta are the highly developed industrial areas of Guangdong – the areas you'll probably want to stay away from.

In Hong Kong you can always find somebody to help you over the language barrier, but once you start reading maps you'll have to face using Chinese. Stop for a moment and consider. When is the earliest you could consider taking a trip like this? Next summer? The year after that? Why not take a few night courses in the interim and learn some Chinese? Yes, it's a difficult language, primarily because so few of its words are derived from the same roots as any language you know. But a winter of night classes two or three nights a week is enough to make an enormous difference. For the record, the language in Guangdong province is Cantonese. The language in Fujian is called Hokkien. The national language is known in the West as Mandarin. You'll meet many people in the countryside who don't speak any of these well. Study whichever course is available in your area. They're all about as alike as French, Spanish and Italian. Learn the basics of one and you can fake it a bit in the others.

Hong Kong is also the place to buy some Chinese money. You can try buying it before you leave home, but your local bank will probably disappoint you. Hong Kong is full of specialist exchange booths where you shove some Hong Kong dollars under the glass and they shove you back a wad of yuan. The best are on the side streets near the Macau ferry terminal on Hong Kong island. The problem is that they work only in Hong Kong dollars. No travellers cheques, no other currencies. There are also full-service money changers that handle all currencies, but check their rates carefully. The banks have good rates but make an exorbitant service charge for changing money. If you can't buy yuan before leaving home, probably the best bet is to buy Hong Kong dollars instead. In Hong Kong, change those for mainland currency at the exchange booths. In theory you can now change money in the banks in China, but don't count on it. There will be paperwork and passport drill, and they'll probably deal only in Hong Kong and U.S. dollars. The banks in China still have their uses, however, because the Hong Kong exchange booths deal only in 50 yuan notes and larger. These are a bit hard to cash in the countryside, so you'll want to visit the banks to break them into 10s.

Finally, visa in hand, you'll want to buy a ticket into China. There are all sorts of ferries and bus services over the border, but most of them operate entirely in Chinese. One exception is Citybus which operates a couple of trips each morning to a place called Dongguan an hour or so north of the border. Dongguan itself is part of the industrial zone, but it's a reasonable jumping off point. Citybus has an office in the basement of the China Hong Kong Ferry Terminal at the corner of Canton Rd. and Kowloon Park Drive in the Tsimshatsui district of Kowloon. They speak English and will sell you tickets in advance once you have your visa.

Another easy way to get into China is to walk over the border. Not from Hong Kong, but from Macau. Most people don't need a visa for Macau, and there's a ferry about every half hour from Hong Kong. It's also an interesting place in its own right. From downtown Macau it's an easy walk to the border gate. On the other side you're still in an industrialized region, but if you head northwest rather than north toward Guangzhou, you can walk out into the countryside in a day. You can't readily do this from Hong Kong, as there's a closed zone along the border that requires a special pass.

Getting right out into the remote Chinese countryside means that you'll have to attack the journey in three phases. In most parts of the country almost every village will have some sort of bus or minibus at least once a day to a city with a railway station. From there you can reach the provincial capital, and the provincial capitals are linked by a network of domestic airlines to Hong Kong and the other ports of entry. Travelling out this way is pretty straightforward. Travelling in is more of a problem. The problems arise from difficulties in obtaining information, and from the tribulations involved in buying tickets.

Cities with airports always have a downtown airline office for buying plane tickets. Some of these are better organized than others. You'll have to show your passport, but you'll get your tickets without too much difficulty. There may even be a place to sit while you're waiting. It's standard procedure to run a special bus from the ticket office for each flight.

Catching the train is less simple. The problem is overcrowding. The basic system is to go to the railway station, look around until you find the ticket office, then carefully pick a line and get in it. The care is required because each window sells tickets only for certain destinations or certain trains. You can easily spend half an hour in an unruly line, get to the window, find out you're in the wrong line and have to start again. The windows will be labelled either North, South, East and West or will have specific train numbers posted above them. There will be a big board on the wall overhead, showing which trains go where. Once you get to the right window there won't be any choice. Pass the lady a pencil and a slip of paper with your destination written in Chinese. She'll write down the price and you pass back the money. You then ask someone to read the resulting ticket and tell you when you're leaving. Not what time; what day.

Unfortunately, these packed ticketing halls are China's crime black spots. Assume that somewhere in the process at least one person will try to pick your pocket. Clutch your money inside a pocket. Leave anything else of value at your hotel. If you carry so much as a packet of tissues in your hip pocket you may well find that the pocket has been slashed with a razor blade, as mine was.

There may be two easier ways. In some of the major cities there are train ticket agencies, which save you the fraught trip to the station. It sounds good, but it might cost a bit more, for three reasons. First, they'll charge you a fee. Then, they may try to sell you a first class ticket. Finally, they're not usually computerized, so each office has only a certain number of tickets for each train. The ticket you want may be hard to get, and you'll have to spend a few more nights in the hotel.

The other route is through the scalpers. You'll find them working the lines at the ticket office. If you can strike the right one, he will provide a good service, but you'll probably have a good deal of difficulty without a Chinese friend to fight in your corner. False tickets are a particular problem. Even the Chinese get burned.

In many ways the bus services work best of all. If you're heading out into the countryside you could be the first Western customer they've ever served, and they'll probably treat you very well. The problem is information. The bus you want will usually leave from somewhere near the train station, but the station area will be swarming with taxi touts with a vested interest in convincing you that the bus you want doesn't exist, or doesn't run again until tomorrow morning. If you show your map to enough bystanders and patiently repeat the word "bus" in English, someone will eventually point you toward the right terminus. Of course, it may actually be true that it doesn't run again until tomorrow, but at least by then you know where to get a taxi.

Here is a list of everything I carried during my three-and-half month walk across China.

The Gear

Knapsack	Stove
Sheet sleeping bag	Gasoline bottle
Tent fly	Cup
2 tent poles and caps	Chopsticks
Tent fly	Knife

Mosquito net
6m of twine

12 paper napkins
Spoon
Pot

Long underwear shirt
Sweat pants
3 pairs of hiking socks
Heavy sweater
Hat
Sweatshirt
T-shirt
2 pairs of underwear briefs

10 envelopes of coffee mix
50g tea
4 packets of shortbread cookies
200g raisins
150g meusli
2 packets of instant noodles
2 bottles of water
1 bottle of soda

10ml toothpaste
Disposable lighter
Matches
4 aspirin
Mosquito repellent
Toothbrush
Razor
3 spare razor blades
Spare eyeglasses
15 Band-Aids
Sunscreen

Camera
Flash attachment
6 rolls of film
2 spare batteries
50 water purification tablets
Compass

Various maps
Train schedule
Passport
Hong Kong ID card
Hong Kong $4000

Wearing

Running shoes
Athletic socks
Briefs

Notebook
2 pens
Pocket tape recorder
Spare tapes
Ticket home
Dictionary
Door key

T-shirt
Cotton drill trousers
Nylon windbreaker with hood
Watch
Money belt

Notice how little is really necessary. Despite the glorious walking, this is heavily populated country with shops and homes all along the way. If you stick to Guangdong and Fujian, the climate is subtropical. You can carry even less than I've listed here.

With this amount of gear you don't need a large knapsack. Mine was a simple 50x30x20cm affair with an internal X frame and three external pockets. Though small, this is not a daypack. In particular it has a well-designed and padded belt. Two of the external pockets were large enough to each hold a 1.25 liter bottle of soda. Its brown colour helped to keep my bivouacs inconspicuous.

The sheet sleeping bag was a length of polyester fabric folded over and sewn into a sack along the lines of the sheet sleeping bag normally required by Youth Hostels for their visitors. Again, a dark colour is less conspicuous. The lightweight fabric is less for warmth than to keep you from rolling around and to keep the ants out. I normally slept on the poncho with the tent fly for a blanket. In case of rain, I would cut some sticks to use as tent stakes and rig the tent fly as a shelter. The fly was a standard North Face general purpose fly designed to cover a 2m pup tent. I didn't carry the tent, just its poles. To prevent the poles wearing holes in the fly I put a 35mm film container over the top of each pole to spread the load on the fabric. The mosquito net is an item readily purchased in

Southeast Asia, but perhaps less available elsewhere. This particular model was a pyramidal one 30cm in diameter at the base and 54cm high. It's sold as a mosquito net for a baby's crib. It was originally white, but I dyed it a tan colour to make it less conspicuous. With mosquitoes about, I hung it from trees or bushes over my sleeping spot using the twine. When not required to fend off the mosquitoes, it made a modestly effective insulating pad under the sheet sleeping bag.

Because the sheet sleeping bag isn't very warm, I slept in the long underwear shirt and sweat pants. I kept these for sleeping and never walked in them, though they were available as a reserve against hypothermia in case of emergency. The heavy sweater, hat and sweatshirt were essential in the cold-weather part of the trip, but during a summer walk in the southern provinces they would be unnecessary. In any case, all three are easy and cheap to buy in China. If you need a sun hat, a locally made straw hat costs next to nothing and doesn't draw attention as any sort of Western hat would.

If you wear corrective lenses or take any sort of special medications, you should of course bring extras with you. The same goes for sunscreen, mosquito repellent and whatever you prefer for treating your blisters. Standard aspirin, lighters, toothpaste and so on are available at most of the small local shops you'll see every day. Razors and blades are available, but may not deliver the comfort you're used to at home. You'll be shaving in cold water, remember.

As in most countries, a tourist in China is required to carry his passport around with him and present it to the authorities on demand. Fortunately, most of the authorities don't know that. I carried my passport in a money belt sealed in a plastic bag and was very rarely obliged to produce it. This is not to say that I wasn't asked for identification. The Chinese themselves all carry identity cards. They expect you to have one too, and they'll be very curious to see it. Anyone who's a Communist Party member or considers himself a state cadre might ask you for identification without any actual legal right to do so. You can feign incomprehension and often get away with it, but don't challenge his right to ask. The PRC is under the rule of men, not the rule of law. Standing up for your rights is a recipe for trouble.

The reason you don't want them poring over your passport is that it will take hours, and once they've started it will be very difficult to extricate yourself and get back on the road. They've heard of passports, but they don't have them themselves and they'll be intensely interested in yours. Of course, they won't be able to read anything except your China visa, so they'll ask you to explain everything else. Page-by-page. I avoided this by carrying my Hong Kong ID card. I deflected requests to see my passport by claiming that Hong Kong is part of China and I was only obliged to carry an ID card very similar to the one they carry themselves. Coming from anywhere else you probably wouldn't be able to get away with such a blatant lie.

Most people wouldn't bother to carry the notebook and pens, tape recorder and spare tapes. The need for the dictionary is less clear-cut. Most of the maps you can buy will be in Chinese characters. If you know a bit of Chinese you can use the dictionary to look up the names of the places on your route, and that should help in asking the way. Chinese is written in ideographs. As a result, it has no alphabetical order. Without some basic training, looking up a character in the dictionary is no simple matter. Even then, the dictionary will give only the Mandarin pronunciation. The local people will know the name of a place only in the local dialect. The dictionary pronunciation of the characters on the map may leave them mystified. Even if you can read Chinese, you're often further ahead to show a local person the map in the first place and let him tell you the name of the place you're heading for. Of course many people can't read a map. Many older people, women in particular, can't read at all. But with some practice you get adept at picking out the more literate citizens.

Tickets and reservations in general are often hard to get in China. When roaming around the north far from Hong Kong, I took the precaution of pre-purchasing an air ticket and reservation home and carrying it around with me. Closer to Hong Kong you'll prefer bus or train tickets, and they can't be purchased in advance in this way.

I carried an Optimus 8R, a single burner stove that burns ordinary gasoline. Gasoline and kerosene are available even in the countryside, but don't expect to find camping gas. Walking in a country where the watercourses are heavily polluted and the villages have no running water, nothing is ever clean. I carried a packet of napkins sealed in a plastic bag as the only clean oasis in my environment apart from my Band-Aids. Occasionally they also had to serve as toilet paper. In some parts of the country small packets of tissues are sold in the shops, but not everywhere.

Many Hong Kong tourists distrust the cleanliness of the chopsticks in China's restaurants and carry a bale of disposable chopsticks in their luggage. This is involves a lot of carrying, though I suppose they could double as tent stakes. I invariably used the restaurant chopsticks provided, though I re-washed them first in a cup of hot tea. This is standard procedure in Chinese restaurants and gives no offense. If you're not adept with chopsticks you can use your spoon, but a spoon is useless with noodle dishes. If you bring a fork you'll really have dish-washing problems. Far better to practice your chopstick technique before you come. A few weeks will do the trick.

I carried a heavy Swiss army knife. I found that I used the scissors frequently. The awl blade was good for lancing blisters, and the saw blade for abrading callouses on my feet. I occasionally used the tweezers on thorns. All in all, the weight was worth it, just.

A big advantage of China as a venue for walking is that you're not obliged to carry any food. You pass shops every day, which stock at the least beer, instant noodles and a couple of varieties of not-very-nice biscuits. I brought with me from Hong Kong coffee mix, shortbreads, meusli and raisins as treats to be rationed out in moments of difficulty or celebration. If you have a mercurial disposition you might appreciate more. If you really hate carrying, you don't need any. Almost all Chinese shops sell jars of fruit, which make nice juicy treats if you don't have to carry them far.

On the other hand, clean water is a constant problem. I carried cheap plastic bottles for my water. This was sometimes inconvenient, as people would offer me boiled water which was still hot and would melt the plastic. Afterwards, the cap would no longer seal properly. Bring one bottle that will stand up to boiling water.

Common batteries (AA, AAA and D) are sometimes available in China, but the quality isn't great. If they leak they'll ruin your camera or flash. I took the precaution of bringing in spares, heavy though they are. Definitely bring in film and water purification tablets you can trust. I carried a Minox 35mm camera because it would fit into my pocket, always at the ready. The Minox 16mm would be lighter, but it looks so unusual that you might actually be accused of spying. The Chinese have some delusions of grandeur in that regard. Certainly bring a camera that's not too susceptible to dust and dirt. Forget about your camcorder. There's no reliable way to renew the batteries.

I'm a married man, but I left my wedding ring at home. Not because I was in search of sexual adventure, but because wearing gold attracts too much attention. As it was, people occasionally offered to buy my Casio plastic watch and even my shoes. The people in the countryside are starting to earn a bit of cash in the new free market but their shops don't sell such things. Imagine a Saudi sheik in full regalia pulling his Ferrari into your local service station. That's something like the image you invoke walking into a rural Chinese village. Don't push it. I made a point of carrying only a modest wad of Chinese bills in my pocket. Most of my cash, and all my foreign currency, was always out of sight in a money belt.

And with that I hope I've said enough to convince you to give it a try. I sincerely believe that I've given you all you need to get started. Your experience will certainly be different from mine, but if you enjoy walking you can buy that expensive airline ticket confident that you're embarking on a holiday you'll remember for the rest of your life.

Further Reading

The last decades of the twentieth century have seen a substantial migration of what the Chinese refer to as intellectuals leaving China for the West. A few of these emigrants have subsequently published accounts of their life under communism, some of them to popular acclaim. Inevitably, though, these autobiographical tales foçus on the mistreatment of intellectuals during the cultural revolution. The portrait they paint of life in the countryside is invariably an unwilling outsider's view, and invariably an unfavorable one. I hope that the tale of my own adventures as a willing outsider will help redress this imbalance to at least a small extent.

Fortunately, the same opening up that has allowed emigration has also facilitated the work of visiting scholars, and some of their publications can be of great help to the Western reader attempting better to understand life in the Chinese countryside. Many of these publications are unabashedly academic in tone and make pretty dry reading. There are, though, a few which anyone interested in China can enjoy reading for recreation.

The classic in this genre is William Hinton's *Fanshen – A Documentary of Revolution in a Chinese Village* published by Random House in 1966. It shows communist rule from a perspective not shared by some of the more famous authors on the topic. It's good background, but today many of Hinton's observations are distinctly out of date. Prof. Huang Shu-min's *The Spiral Road – Change in a Chinese Village Through the Eyes of a Communist Party Leader* addresses in detail some of the changes implemented in the 1980s and the Communist Party's efforts to keep control. It's available from Westview Press. But Prof. Huang's account will convince you that to really understand life in the countryside you'll have to dig deeper, below the level of party control. For this perspective I recommend Prof. Mobo Gao's *Gao Village – A Portrait of Rural Life in Modern China*. Gao village is Prof. Gao's own home village, and his account really gets to the grass roots and beyond. It was published by Hong Kong University Press in 1999, and is well worth a read before attempting your own research in the Chinese countryside.

Index

About the Author

A Canadian by birth, Bill Purves has led a double life. For 25 years he has worked as an engineer and manager. He has also maintained a 35-year career as a competitive runner. Since 1983 he has been perfecting both his management and his running skills from his home in Hong Kong. He is the author of two other books about China: *Barefoot in the Boardroom* (Allen & Unwin) about China's working class and *Three Chinas* (Dundurn Press) about its intellectuals.

Hong Kong Pathfinder

by Martin Williams

ISBN 962-8783-21-1, 7th edition

Hong Kong Bestseller! Hong Kong is known as a thriving business centre with tightly packed high-rise buildings and a frenetic stressful pace. Yet Hong Kong has a greener, more tranquil side: forty percent of the land area is country park, and even the most remote parts are seldom more than a couple of hours from the confines of the city. Martin Williams leads you on 23 day-trips, to rugged hills, forested valleys, reservoirs and waterfalls, temples and villages, abandoned forts and delightful islands. This pocket-sized, newly revised edition features 24 maps and 16 pages of colour photographs.

"A boon for neophyte ramblers in Hong Kong and a handy reference for old hiking hands." — *Discovery*

"A thoughtful and meticulously researched guide." — *Action Asia*

Walking to the Mountain

A pilgrimage to Tibet's holy Mount Kailash
by Wendy Teasdill

ISBN 962-7160-27-X

This is the story of a journey made on foot across Tibet to Mt. Kailash, the "Jewel of the Snows," that has been attracting pilgrims of all religions for thousands of years. Wendy Teasdill hitch-hiked from Lhasa and walked the last four hundred miles because the summer rains had swollen the rivers so much that vehicles could not cross them. She walked alone through the plains of the Brahmaputra, between the Himalaya and the trans-Himalaya, living on hard-tack biscuits, noodles and nettles. She survived to tell the tale of the people, landscapes, dangers, delights and insights that she encountered along the way.

"Teasdill provides a vivid personal account of how she was drawn to Mount Kailash. With the resolution characteristic of a pilgrim she walked and forded rivers. Inspired by the beauty of the landscape and her admiration for the Tibetan people she met, she reached her goal." — The Dalai Lama

Quality Books

From Asia 2000

Fiction

Dance with White Clouds	Goh Poh Seng
Lipstick and Other Stories	Alex Kuo
Chinese Opera	Alex Kuo
The Last Puppet Master	Stephen Rogers
Sergeant Dickinson	Jerome Gold
The Ghost Locust	Heather Stroud
Shanghai	Christopher New
A Change of Flag	Christopher New
The Chinese Box	Christopher New
Last Seen in Shanghai	Howard Turk
Cheung Chau Dog Fanciers' Society	Alan B Pierce
Riding a Tiger, The Self-Criticism of Arnold Fisher	Robert Abel
Childhood's Journey	Wu Tien-tze
Getting to Lamma	Jan Alexander
The Mongolian Connection	Scott Christiansen
Connections — Stories of East Asia	David T. K. Wongi
Temutma	Rebecca Bradley & Stewart Sloan

Poetry

Round — Poems and Photographs of Asia	Barbara Baker & Madeleine Slavick
Traveling With a Bitter Melon	Leung Ping-kwan
Coming Ashore Far From Home	Peter Stambler
Salt	Mani Rao
The Last Beach	Mani Rao
Water Wood Pure Splendour	Agnes Lam
Woman to Woman	Agnes Lam
New Ends, Old Beginnings	Louise Ho
An Amorphous Melody — A Symphony in Verse	Kavita

Order from Asia 2000 Ltd

Fifth Floor, 31A Wyndham Street, Central, Hong Kong
Telephone: (852) 2530-1409; Fax: (852) 2526-1107
E-mail: sales@asia2000.com.hk; Website: http://www.asia2000.com.hk